Desperately Seeking Asylum

Desperately Seeking Asylum

Testimonies of Trauma, Courage, and Love

Helen T. Boursier

ROWMAN & LITTLEFIELD
Lanham • Boulder • New York • London

Published by Rowman & Littlefield
An imprint of The Rowman & Littlefield Publishing Group, Inc.
4501 Forbes Boulevard, Suite 200, Lanham, Maryland 20706
www.rowman.com

6 Tinworth Street, London SE11 5AL, United Kingdom

British Library Cataloguing in Publication Information Available

Library of Congress Cataloging-in-Publication Data

Names: Boursier, Helen T., 1960– author.
Title: Desperately seeking asylum : testimonies of trauma, courage, and love / Helen T.
    Boursier.
Description: Lanham : Rowman & Littlefield [2019] | Includes bibliographical references
    and index.
Identifiers: LCCN 2019020426 (print) | LCCN 2019980218 (ebook) | ISBN
    9781538128336 (cloth) | ISBN 9781538128343 (ebook)
Subjects: LCSH: Refugees—United States—Social conditions—Anecdotes. | Refugees—
    Abuse of—United States—Anecdotes. | Refugees—Central America—Social conditions—
    Anecdotes. | United States—Emigration and immigration—Government policy. |
    Mexican-American Border Region—Anecdotes. | Refugees—Legal status, laws, etc.—
    United States.
Classification: LCC HV640.5.C46 B68 2019 (print) | LCC HV640.5.C46 (ebook) | DDC
    305.9069140973—dc23
LC record available at https://lccn.loc.gov/2019020426
LC ebook record available at https://lccn.loc.gov/2019980218

Dedicated to the families and children who are desperately seeking asylum.
Thank you for sharing your testimonies of trauma, courage, and love.
May this book honor you.

Contents

Acronyms

ABA	American Bar Association
ACLU	American Civil Liberties Union
BIA	Board of Immigration Appeals
CAT	Convention against Torture
CBP	Customs and Border Protection (formerly Customs and Border Patrol)
CHRCL	Center for Human Rights and Constitutional Law
DHS	Department of Homeland Security
DOJ	Department of Justice
EOIR	Executive Office for Immigration Review
ICE	Immigration and Customs Enforcement
IIRIRA	Illegal Immigration Reform and Immigrant Responsibility Act of 1996
INA	Immigration and Nationality Act
IWC	Interfaith Welcome Coalition of San Antonio
NAFTA	North American Free Trade Agreement
ORR	Office of Refugee Resettlement, U.S. Department of Health and Human Services
UAC	Unaccompanied Alien Children
UCC	United Church of Christ
UMC	United Methodist Church
UN	United Nations
UNHCR	United Nations High Commissioner for Refugees
USCIRF	United States Commission on International Religious Freedom
USCIS	United States Citizenship and Immigration Services

Acknowledgments

I offer my deepest appreciation and respect to the families and children who shared their personal experiences of trauma, courage, and love. I am grateful for everything they taught me and also that they trusted me to be a portal to share their stories as their public testimony. I also thank the friends and colleagues mentioned in this book. They generously shared their witness and allowed me to write about them. I appreciate Roberto Salmón, Frank Dietz, and Jerry Stacy, who took the time to critically read the manuscript and make suggestions for changes and additions. I offer special thanks to Hope Frye, who has been a phenomenal collaborator. She shared her expertise of forty years as an immigration attorney and provided invaluable insights on how U.S. immigration policies and practices impact refugees seeking asylum, particularly unaccompanied minors who are detained. I extend my love and gratitude to Mike, who has been my husband for forty years. This book wouldn't be possible without his unfailing love and support.

Some of the content was adapted from my earlier book, *The Ethics of Hospitality: An Interfaith Response to U.S. Immigration Policies* (2019), and from "The Great Exchange: An Interfaith Praxis of Absolute Hospitality for Immigrants Seeking Asylum," in *The Meaning of My Neighbor's Faith: Interreligious Reflections on Immigration*, edited by Alexander Y. Hwang and Laura E. Alexander (2019); both are used by permission. Artwork created by refugees seeking asylum also is used by permission.

Introduction

Setting the Context for the Conversation

The United Nations (U.N.) calls migration/displacement the global crisis of the twenty-first century, but immigration concerns at the U.S.-Mexico border aren't a new phenomenon. They actually date back to when the United States invaded Mexico during the Mexican-American War (1846–1848). *Desperately Seeking Asylum* explains why refugees are now seeking asylum at our southern border, how the United States is culpable for their suffering, and how we can offer a more just and compassionate response. Although much of what I share here applies more broadly, my focus is on refugee families and unaccompanied children who are seeking asylum in the United States from the violence in their homelands, primarily Guatemala, El Salvador, and Honduras. Their stories are the ones I personally know and the background I have researched.[1]

This book emerged from my experience as a volunteer chaplain with refugee families seeking asylum. In 2014 I began visiting detained families at a for-profit immigrant family detention center located seventy miles from my home, and in 2015 and 2016 I facilitated art as spiritual care with the mothers and children at that same center. I've also hosted refugee families in my home, shuttled families from the detention center to the bus station, stuffed backpacks to help the families on their journey, and brought my portable art studio to the bus station in downtown San Antonio to do art with children as they waited with their mothers and fathers for their bus to depart. I've spent countless hours interacting with literally thousands of families seeking asylum. We've talked, laughed, cried, and prayed together, both inside and outside of detention. I consider these experiences to be miracle, grace, and privilege, and it has been my abundant joy to be in solidarity with these beautiful families seeking safe haven in the United States. My diverse interactions with the families inform my public witness and advocacy, from attending a variety of rallies, vigils, and witness events for refugees to advocating for these families seeking asylum through my preaching, teaching, and writing.

1

The witness that unfolds before you is their story, but it is also *our* story. During my deep background research into why these families and children are escaping from their homelands, I came to realize that there's no one person, administration, or agency to blame. The U.S. culpability for the violence they're fleeing is deep and wide, including past and present political and economic policies and practices. I weave the testimonies of the families and the volunteers who assist them with the interlocking historical, philosophical, sociological, political, and economic elements. I also specify how the United States violates international humanitarian standards and expectations for receiving refugees seeking asylum, and how "we the people" are part of this complex problem at our southern border. *Desperately Seeking Asylum* brings together diverse people and sources to explain the daunting mess that we've made of immigration policies and practices in the United States as they relate specifically to refugees seeking asylum.

TECHNICAL DIFFERENCES BETWEEN "REFUGEE" AND "ASYLEE" STATUS

The vast majority of the families and children (and of course many single adults as well) who are knocking at our southern border are seeking asylum. They're not "regular migrants." The traditional distinction between "migrants" and "refugees" is the element of voluntariness. Migrants choose to relocate to another nation; refugees have been forced into the decision due to external circumstances beyond their control. Within the general category of refugees, the United States differentiates between "refugee" and "asylee" (that is, asylum seeker) as technical terms that define two pathways for nonresidents to make their application to live in the United States. A refugee claim has been made "off campus," either in one's homeland or another nation outside of the United States. An asylum claim is initiated on U.S. soil once the claimant has arrived. I use the terms "refugee" and "asylee" interchangeably throughout this text, even though, in my context, the families technically are seeking asylum status, as they begin the application process upon arrival to the United States. Clearly, a family fleeing a death threat does not have the luxury to wait while wading through government bureaucracy for a decision, yay or nay, on "refugee" status. The families and children leave their homelands under life-threatening emergency to plead their case in person to request asylum. Despite the government distinction differentiating the point of origin when the application is placed, both categories (refugee and asylee) describe these mothers and fathers and boys and girls: they are refugees and they are seeking asylum.

MEET THE PEOPLE SEEKING ASYLUM

Currently, the majority of the people attempting to cross the Mexico-U.S. border to seek asylum are from Guatemala, El Salvador, and Honduras. They're fleeing violence and death threats. Tucked together just below Mexico, together these three small countries are approximately the size of the state of Oregon. Each country has its distinguishing characteristics, but commonalties link the three nations together as the region known as the Northern Triangle. It is located between the world's biggest cocaine source (the Andes) and the cartel in Mexico that traffics this narcotic to the largest market, the United States. Violence surrounds this booming drug industry. The area sees increased violence from organized crime and internal displacement, both caused by the power struggle with the criminal cartels amidst the so-called war on drugs and the added challenges of getting the product from the producers in Colombia to the consumers in the United States. Fear of death is a given. It's particularly targeted at the most vulnerable: women and children. It is a fact, not fiction, that the families are escaping a nightmare. Death threats, violence, and often the murder of a close family member push the families to seek asylum. A Roman Catholic sister who assists a priest during his weekly visits to a for-profit family detention center said, "When I'm at the chapel with the families, I see the terror on their faces at the thought of being sent back. They lift desperate prayers of desperate people."

The United States is their safe destination because they consider it a "sister nation" where many have family already legally residing, including spouses, mothers and fathers, brothers and sisters, children and grandchildren, and aunts, uncles, and cousins. Their family members often sponsor their journey, post the bond for their release from immigrant family detention, and become their legal family connection to the United States. These asylum seekers consider their reunification with family members long past due. For example, at a bus station in downtown San Antonio, I was greeting families recently released from detention as they stood in line to get their tickets, and one woman said she was going to be with her mother in Maryland. This woman was twenty-three years old and hadn't seen her mother in twenty years. She was standing in line with her own daughter, who was three years old, the exact age the woman was when she last saw her mother.

The cycle of suffering and loss is staggering. Consider the mother who was parted from her child twenty years ago, a mother who suffered in the United States while she was separated from her child all those years, and the suffering and vulnerability of the three-year-old daughter left behind, now a grown woman and seeking asylum herself. I'm humbled by the strength of the familial connection, not only this particular mother and daughter, but the innate force that pushes and pulls for the survival of the family.

In Central America, the familiar term for family fidelity is *cargo*. In Latin American culture it signifies the "burden" one has to pass along a favor. It's a responsibility that cannot and will not be ignored. It's assumed that a favor will be done for you, but one day it will be your turn to pass the favor on. Essentially, *cargo* defines a cultural loyalty born out of deep familial love, loyalty that mothers and fathers view as a blessing and as a future obligation. Every step of their asylum journey, they are mindful of the *cargo* they received to help make the journey possible, and they also appreciate that one day it will be their turn to return the *cargo* for another family member who needs help on the long walk to safety.

They make the risky journey with the possibility of and hope for a safe future. These families and children exemplify the essential requirement of hope: they believe that there is a *possibility* their asylum can be achieved. A mother or father needs only a glimmer of possibility to cling to hope. When asylum seekers believe safety is even remotely possible, they will claim that hope as their strength for the journey. Hope encourages, prompts, propels, and emotionally, spiritually, and even physically uplifts the refugees to find the courage, the energy, the stamina, and the tenacious wherewithal to walk toward that future.

They also have a positive expectation about the outcome regardless of what obstacles unexpectedly are placed before them. Their hope moves them beyond mere wishful thinking to practical action. Hope moves them beyond wanting asylum to believing it's actually possible. They believe in life over death. So, in hope, they make the pilgrimage to safety in the United States. Ultimately, these families and unaccompanied children believe they will be *safe* here. One mother said, "I decided to make the trip to ask for asylum because the United States is the only country able to help me. The evil persons will not look for me here. They will not oppress my children. We can live in peace." Families seek asylum in the United States partly because of the image our nation has cultivated, symbolized by the Statue of Liberty and personified by the words of Emma Lazarus welcoming the "huddled masses yearning to breathe free." Another asylum seeker said, "I trust this place, the United States, because the laws here protect everyone. Here we have a hope for a future. I want my daughter to have a dignified life. In the United States there is protection for the good heart. Here the leaders fight for the people."

If the families survive the risky overland journey, they become entangled in the daunting "due process" of the U.S. immigration matrix with its twists and turns of unjust policies and practices, which deny and defy international legal and humanitarian expectations. This nation of immigrants consistently creates innovative and "legal" ways to slam the door shut on the mothers and fathers and boys and girls who are desperately seeking asylum. My hope and prayer is that their testimonies of trauma, courage, and love will transform your understanding of the people who are knocking at the door on our southern border and illuminate why we should open the gate and offer a compassionate humanitarian welcome for these refugees seeking asylum.

Helen T. Boursier
March 1, 2019
New Braunfels, Texas

I

TESTIMONIES OF TRAUMA, COURAGE, AND LOVE

MEET THE PEOPLE SEEKING ASYLUM

1

Desperately Seeking Asylum

Why the Families Flee Their Homelands

It doesn't take much imagination to appreciate that permanently relocating from one nation to another isn't something anyone does on a whim. It takes a strong motivator to say goodbye to family, friends, possessions, and everything familiar to take small children on a grueling overland journey fraught with life-threatening dangers to then enter another country and request asylum. Something or someone pushed each refugee to the point of saying "Ya! Me voy!" (Enough! I go!) The families know the risks before they begin the journey. In fact, friends and family often beg them *not* to go. Despite the warnings, dangers, and misgivings, as one mother said, "It is better to die fighting than to do nothing and just let death happen." It's a choice for life and a plea for safety.

LIFE SEEKS LIFE

Their testimonies resonate with what German theologian and former World War II prisoner of war Jürgen Moltmann asserts: "Life thirsts for life; life becomes a living force through other life."[1] These refugees seek life, just as any one of us also seeks life. A retiree from Massachusetts who attended a witness event for migrants in Arizona talked about how all the people around her fight to live once they have a diagnosis of cancer. Despite all the costs, the medical procedures, and the pain and inconvenience, they still do everything they can to live longer. She asked, "Why do we deny migrants who are trying so hard simply to live? We struggle against cancer, so we must appreciate life. Why do we keep others from this same basic desire to live?" The families feel this same appreciation, and desire, for life. They're not looking for, or expecting, a yellow brick road to happily ever after. The asylum seekers have what Moltmann would call a "thirst and hunger for life." Not a fancy life—bare life.

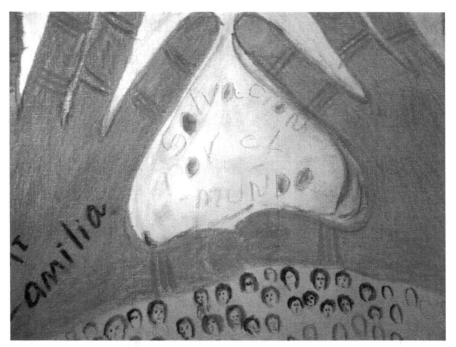

Figure 1.1. A detained mother's prayer through art, produced as part of an "art as spiritual care" session for detainees inside the Karnes County Residential Center in Karnes City, Texas. The session took place on June 5, 2015, after another mother attempted suicide upon learning she was to be deported.

A father in Honduras had a death threat hanging over him because he witnessed a murder; he fled to the United States with his young son because a family member owns a landscaping business on the East Coast and agreed to give this refugee seeking asylum a job. The father would rather live in his own country, but the death threat forced him to seek asylum in the United States. A volunteer with migrants explained, "It's not a 'get rich quick' scheme. It's a 'work hard to support your family' scheme." He added, "This is a 'run for your life' plan. It's not a 'spin the wheel for dollars' agenda." When violence forces Central Americans to flee, they maintain absolute trust in God every step of their journey. As one mother simply said, "Because God loves us, we are here."

WITNESS OF THE FAMILIES

Reality is shocking in Guatemala, El Salvador, and Honduras. Fear due to direct threat to life is the number one reason migrants give for fleeing their homelands. The consistent words in their stories center on every type of violence, victimization, police and government corruption, and hopelessness. They face death and destruction daily in their homelands.

The Vocabulary of Suffering

Families in the Northern Triangle live with an unconscionable level of daily fear. The families seek asylum once that "regular fear" becomes a targeted direct threat to life for themselves and/or their children. The personal details of their stories differ, but the language of suffering is consistent from one testimony to another as the families share their experiences of the terror that became their catalyst for migration. Marcelo Suárez-Orozco calls it the "vocabulary of sorrow," these words of suffering, trauma, and intense emotional, spiritual, psychological, and physical pain.[2] The most prevalent terms for suffering used by the families and children at our southern border include:

- *mareros* or *pandillas* (gangs)
- *desaparecidos* (disappeared)
- *tortuados* (torture victims)
- *huérfanos* (orphans)
- *delincuencia* (delinquency)
- *amenazaron* (threatened)
- *asesinos* (murderers)
- *gente disachable* (disposable people)
- *golpeado* (beaten)
- *la renta* (rent, extortion money)
- *violación* (rape)

Each word brings a powerful mental image to the families because the meaning of each of these technical terms goes beyond the surface definition. For example, *delincuencia* does not translate one to one to what "delinquency" describes in the United States. Here it means the pranks that teenagers pull, like toilet-papering a house, spray-painting graffiti underneath a bridge or on an abandoned building, vandalizing the rival school's mascot, or skipping class. The U.S. version is annoying, and certainly there is necessary accountability, such as property damage that needs to be repaired. The consequences in the Northern Triangle to *delincuencia* are much more intense. The word describes the overall culture of illegal actions, from petty theft to assault, rape, and murder. Similarly, *la renta* does not equate to simply paying for an apartment or an appliance. No, *la renta* is the technical term for the extortion money the gangs force families to pay in exchange for safe passage between home and school or work. The price typically increases as the gangs raise the stakes from safe passage to threats of sexual violence, impressment into a gang, or literally the choice between life and death.

A quick way to get a sense of the reality behind the suffering is to surf Google Images for *los mareros* (the gangs). You will see a rash of ugly photographs of fully tattooed, angry-looking men who prey upon these families who now are seeking asylum. The pictures differ from one country to another, but the promise of intimidation and threat to life remain clearly evident in each image. It's this threat to life that pushes the families to flee.

The Language of Hope

The mothers and fathers also use technical words to express the deeper sense of their hopes, dreams, and reasons for seeking asylum. Foremost is *seguridad* (security) or *proteccion* (protection), which they use to mean safety and protection from harm. They also use *vida pacifica* (peaceful life) as their ultimate hope and aspiration in being granted *asilo* (asylum) in the United States. They do not have grandiose plans. They simply want to have a *vida mejor* (better life) for their children. It's easy for an affluent member of a receiving nation, like the United States, to hear "better life" and automatically go to the default assumption that these families are economic migrants who want better-quality food, clothing, housing, education, and jobs. However, they refer to baseline qualities attributed to bare life. "Security" is not about building up equity in a nice home or stashing away funds for a long retirement. "Better life"

Figure 1.2.   A second mother's artwork from the June 5, 2015, "art as spiritual care" session inside Karnes.

expresses their hope for their children to be able to walk to and from school without being physically and/or sexually molested. They want to be able to walk to and from work themselves without the threat of violence, personal victimization, extortion, and/or death shadowing every step of the way.

GANG ACTIVITY AND "UNORGANIZED CRIME"

Refugees use the word "gang" more times throughout their testimonies than all of the other key words combined, and justifiably so because strong gang presence is the biggest contributor to the violence in all three countries of the Northern Triangle. The gangs create neighborhood insecurity where the families live and work and where the children attend school. It's natural that gangs prey on the young, for the gang members are young themselves, ranging in age from twelve to twenty-four, with some older adults in leadership. Children are drawn into the violent gang vortex, as the youngest members often are coerced or forcibly recruited from the neighborhood where the cliques rule. A U.S. citizen who runs a children's home in Honduras explained how little boys get sucked into the system at a very young age as "runners" who literally run drugs into a rival neighborhood. She said by the time they are teens, they're already fully indoctrinated into a gang. A mother explained that she's seeking asylum to protect her son and daughter from a gang. She said, "If my son does not join their gang, they will kill us both. They also threatened my daughter because she did not go with the son of the gang leader." They've seen too many others around them suffer violent deaths. It's not fake fear. The fear is justified. The terror is real.

As the families have attested, the gangs use threats of violence and sexual assault as their preferred methods for neighborhood control. Local gangs focus on harassing, threatening, oppressing, extorting, violating, and killing the local citizens who have the misfortune to reside within gang turf. For example, a mother whose son is ten said they came to the United States because the gangs were pressuring her son to join. She explained that her son and his friends used to play in a nearby park, but a number of boys their age were found dead in the creek at this park at different times. This mother felt like she had to get out before the gangs killed her son.

Gang rivalries and revenge killings are commonplace, wreaking havoc throughout these three small nations. An increasingly prevalent atrocity is the gang rape and/ or torture of women, leaving harsh visible marks on their bodies. Sometimes their young bodies are dismembered and defaced after death. Boys aren't exempt from mutilation and violent death. A volunteer with the families shared, "A mother explained how she had been harassed, as all of the mothers are, for money and to put her son in a gang. She refused to give in. They took her son and dismembered him and then they left him at her front door. She had a picture of her son's dismembered body on her cell phone as a point of proof for her case for asylum." The virtual impunity of the perpetrators exacerbates the urgency to make a hasty exodus. The number of perpetrators of violent crimes who are prosecuted is negligible, and the number of convictions of violent crimes is dismally low in comparison to the rampant violence.

Although homicide rates are staggering, families are not fleeing because of random acts of death and destruction to other people. When the trigger is pointed in their direction, they feel they have little choice but to leave their homeland under cover of darkness and seek safety elsewhere. One mother explained, "I have much fear of returning to my country. They kill without pity. I cannot do anything there to protect my children. There is so much gun fighting. If they like you, they do not kill you. But otherwise, they kill you. I left because the evil man wants to kill me." Another mother said, "We decided to leave, my son and my niece, because they assassinated my husband." A third mother explained the culture of violence that impacts the vulnerable who are preyed upon by the gangs:

> There are so many bad people in my town. They deprive us of basic things we need to buy for our children, like food. They burn our cars. They burn our businesses. They make our children afraid to go to school, afraid to play outside, and afraid to walk home from school. These bad people do not respect us. They do not respect our children. Worse, they do evil things to our children. Our children are scared, fearful, and afraid. They cry. We are here for a better future for my family, for my children, and for me. We came here to be safe.

By "better future," she means a safe place to live without fear.

THE MALE-DOMINATED CULTURE OF MACHISMO AND MISOGYNY

Machismo and misogyny seem to undergird the broken societal system, contributing to the overall dysfunction and violence of the region. The deep-rooted machismo structure feeds into the violence the families suffer, inside and outside of the home. Of course boys and men are also victims of sexual violence. However, particularly in the culture of machismo, women and girls are far more likely to be the victims. Machismo or *machista* (from Spanish and Portuguese *macho*, for "male") defines being "manly." It fosters an inflated sense of masculine pride that includes exaggerated actions reflecting what it supposedly means to be masculine. The terms encompass the desirable traits of courage and fearlessness, but also dysfunctional behaviors like heavy drinking, seducing women, and behaving in a domineering and abusive way toward spouse and children. Although many systemic issues have been imported into the region, machismo is one that comes from within Central American culture.

Explaining the machismo-driven suffering inflicted by her husband/father of her daughter, who belongs to a gang, a woman said he beat her many times. She lost her first child because of his blows. He almost killed her the last time, so she realized that she had to flee for her life. She said, "There's so much violence. I had to leave or be killed." Another mother said the man who raped her seven years ago recently began harassing her with phone calls and random visits to her home. He demanded "his" daughter. He threatened murder if she didn't surrender her six-year-old daughter to him. The mother said that he claimed ownership of this innocent child only because "he wanted to use her for his ill purposes." She explained, "He would use her, and then he would kill us both."

Family dysfunction interacts with the machismo mentality. An American who runs an orphanage in Honduras spoke of a family that was so dysfunctional that the children stayed out on the streets all day because there were so many problems inside their home. She said, "They're not in school, so they hang out on the street all day. It's very easy to get sucked into a gang and all the violence that goes with it. Once a child sleeps overnight on the street, opts not to go home, they have hit the point of no return." She spoke of one girl who stayed on the streets because her home life was so messed up. A young man became her "protector" and then he raped her. At that point, the girl's family said now the two were "married." Then they invited the man who had raped her into their home to live. Drugs also exacerbate the machismo structure. One refugee explained the violence she had received at the hands of the father of her child:

> *You Have Only One Life to Live*
> The father of my daughter
>   beat me
> He beat my daughter.
> Too many times.
> Too many!
> Enough!
>   I left my house!
>   It no longer has a hold on me.
>   He no longer will beat us.
> My daughter and I will be safe.
>   *
>
> He is a narcotics trafficker.
> He threatened my family.
>   He threatened me.
>   He abused me.
>   He drugged me.
> He beat me whenever he felt like it.
> I have had much fear
>   for a long, long, long time.
>   *
>
> Because of him
>   I cannot return to Honduras.
> I left December 17th.
> I arrived January 2nd.
>   *
>
> I knew the trip would be risky.

> But
> You have only one life to live
>   and also your children.
> I want my daughter to live
>   so we came to ask for asylum.
>
> Mother, January 20, 2016
> *Ya! Me voy!* (Enough! I go!)[3]

Before a mother makes the decision to flee her homeland to seek asylum in another country, first she must find the courage to break the psychological, emotional, cultural, and spiritual shackles that have bound her to the horrors of the only life she knows. Explaining Latin American culture, Octavio Paz notes, "Women are imprisoned in the image masculine society has imposed on them; therefore, if they attempt a free choice it must be a kind of jail break."[4] A refugee from Honduras described her own break to safety. After explaining that she was raped many times by her stepfather when she was a little girl, and more recently by two other men (one month apart), she said, "Enough! I do not want to continue living in a country where there is so much violence against women. It's for this reason that I came to the U.S. to seek asylum." The *Wall Street Journal* confirmed the increased violence against women in its 2018 article "Latin America Turns Deadly for Women."[5] Another mother told me that, after being abused and mistreated by her husband for many years, she made the decision to migrate. She said, "I cannot stand to be mistreated anymore. I escaped to the U.S. because I thought by coming here, he cannot follow." She simply wants to live a safe life with her children.

When the women finally leave their homes, it's after they've suffered way too much abuse for way too long. One mother explained that her suffering began with a text message to her cell phone. The initial demand for extortion money gradually increased until the stakes became higher. She said, "The day arrived when I was no longer able to pay their extortion fees. They followed me. They trapped me in an alley with no way out. Their words made my heart stop. My soul suffered." She added, "I gave up. I decided to leave my country. Although Guatemala is very beautiful, that had to end for me. To keep my family alive, we had to leave." She planned her trip quickly: twenty-four hours later she was traveling north with her daughter.

U.S. CONTRIBUTIONS TO INSTABILITY AND VIOLENCE IN THE NORTHERN TRIANGLE

The United States contributes to the collateral damage through our purchase of narcotics, supply of illegal arms, and deportation of gangs, all of which add to the suffering in the Northern Triangle. U.S. corporations in Central America disrupt the economy and exacerbate poverty. *The Guardian* recounted the internal economic connections that date much of the poverty, violence, murder, and injustice in the

Northern Triangle back to the Spanish (i.e., European) conquest and the subsequent and ongoing control and oppression by the elite echelon of these three small nations. *The Guardian* reported, "Experts on the region argue . . . that when politicians or activists have come forward on behalf of its dispossessed, the U.S. has consistently intervened on the side of the powerful and wealthy to help crush them, or looked the other way when they have been slaughtered."[6]

The U.S. has been supporting the powerful who oppress the poor for a long time. Archbishop Oscar Romero, who was murdered by a death squad while he was saying Mass in San Salvador in 1980 and who was elevated to sainthood by the Roman Catholic Church in 2018, wrote a letter to President Jimmy Carter on February 17, 1980. Romero begged the United States to stop funding arms and stop sending military equipment to El Salvador because "your government's contribution will undoubtedly sharpen the injustice and the repression inflicted on the people, whose struggle has often been for respect for their most basic human rights." Romero shared the letter as part of his homily to his congregation before forwarding it, and he noted in his journal that he sent the letter because the military aid "would mean great harm to our people because it would be destined to snuff out many lives."[7] Yet, the United States continued to support the ruling elite.

The Guardian nailed the issue in an opinion piece on the connections between U.S. actions and Central American families desperately seeking asylum. Michael Deibert summarized that "it is rather irresponsible for the United States to take such an active role in creating the conditions that make people want to flee the countries that make up the Central American isthmus and then profess shock when they do so."[8] *We* are one of the reasons *they* are coming *here*.

Corporate America Fosters Economic Instability in Central America

U.S. big business adds to the economic instability that contributes to the overall insecurity and violence the families are fleeing. Independent farmers and small business owners have been squeezed out by the corporate America road, which pushed its way through Central America via the North American Free Trade Agreement (NAFTA). Just as big-box stores shut down mom-and-pop stores in the United States, corporate America's big-business practices also have wiped out many of the independent entrepreneurs in Central America.[9] *They* are unemployed and impoverished thanks to *our* consumerism and commercial greed. *We* are part of *their* problem, and *we* need to become part of the solution.

The unstable economy, unemployment, and massive poverty also factor into the instability that feeds the violence. For example, Honduras has a legal, but clearly unjust, policy and practice that allows businesses to lay off all of their workers after eighty-eight days so that they fall below the ninety-day mark at which the employees would receive official work benefits. A father from Honduras who worked at a U.S.-owned banana company that routinely closes the plant every eighty-eight days and then reopens it two days later explained, "You may, or may not, get rehired. It's one thing when we're laid off when we're young and it might mean we can't buy sodas or go to the movies, but it's entirely different once we have families and the obligations which go with it." His hired/fired/hired/fired employment status destroyed any stability that he could provide for his family and also put them at constant risk from the neighborhood gangs who were extorting him for payment, which he couldn't meet during the interim times of forced unemployment.

Drugs, Guns, and Gangs

The Northern Triangle is a major transfer point for cocaine, much of it headed northbound to the United States. Approximately 80 percent of all suspected drug flights departing from South America first land in Honduras.[10] Altogether, an estimated 90 percent of the cocaine trafficked to the United States in 2016 was transported through the Mexico/Central America corridor, equating to approximately three to four metric tons per month. The vast majority of cocaine arrives via maritime conveyance. Traffickers use motorboats and commercial ships to transport their illegal drugs along the coastline. They also use buses and tractor-trailers to smuggle shipments along the Pan-American Highway. The drugs are headed northbound to consumers located in the United States.

Washington needs to take responsibility for solving the issues that we, as a nation of illegal drug consumers, create. U.S. citizens also need to accept responsibility for our culpability in the drug problem, which is contributing to the violence the families are fleeing. I don't personally buy or consume illegal drugs, and, perhaps naively, I don't think I know anyone who imports, sells, or uses illegal drugs. Nevertheless, I live in a nation that consumes massive quantities of illegal drugs, which means that it's my problem because it's our problem. We have a drug issue that is wreaking havoc on the lives of Central American families, and we have a collective responsibility to name it, own it, and work to remedy this massive problem. These systemic factors join to create interconnected global injustice, which falls hardest on the most vulnerable citizens.

Paying for Drugs with Illegal Arms

Perhaps even more troublesome than the connectional drug component is that illegal guns are the most common payment for narcotics, arming the criminal gangs and contributing to the skyrocketing homicide rates. The documentation is staggering and dismal for the huge amount of illegal arms that originate from the United States. Although it's not possible to track the exact number of firearms exported and illegally trafficked to Mexico during any given year, we can document the number of guns seized that can be traced to the United States. For instance, a 2009 government report indicated that approximately 87 percent of the firearms seized by Mexican authorities during the previous five years originated in the United States. Furthermore, of these seized firearms, around 68 percent were manufactured in the United States, and almost 20 percent were manufactured in other developing countries, imported to the United States, and then trafficked to Mexico. About half of the confiscated guns were rifles and shotguns.[11]

We like to point the blame elsewhere, but guns and drugs generate accountability and culpability concerns on both sides of the border. The United States imports the illegal drugs and pays for them by exporting illegal firearms, which exacerbates the culture of violence in the Northern Triangle. A Mexico citizen affirmed, "We're crossing over with the drugs, but the U.S. is where the drugs are consumed. It's a problem on both sides." He added that the issue with transporting illegal arms also works both ways. He said, "Mexico sends the drugs and the U.S. sends back the guns. In the U.S., any person can buy a gun when they're twenty-one years old. In Mexico, that's not so. Only the criminals have the guns." Of course, the criminals use these guns to continue their violent oppression against honest citizens who simply want to live peaceful, safe lives.

Exporting Gangs

U.S. foreign and immigration policies directly and dramatically impact crime in the Northern Triangle, which kicked into high gear after the United States began deporting serious criminals to their homelands after the passage of the Illegal Immigration Reform and Immigrant Responsibility Act (IIRIRA) of 1996. More than two decades later, these gangs are deeply entrenched in the violence that preys upon innocent families. The 18th Street gang (also known as M-18 and Barrio 18) and its main rival, Mara Salvatrucha (MS-13), are the two major gangs operating in Central America with ties to the United States. The 18th Street gang was formed in the 1960s in Los Angeles by Mexican youth who were not accepted into existing Hispanic gangs. MS-13 was created during the 1980s by Salvadorans in Los Angeles who had fled the country's civil conflict. Both gangs later expanded their operations to Central America. The violence they're capable of is staggering, but the gangs should not be used to foster fear policies and practices against refugees requesting asylum. The families who are preyed upon are innocent victims.

New deportations from the United States restock the gangs. Guatemala, El Salvador, and Honduras have received the highest numbers of U.S. deportees (after Mexico) for the past several fiscal years. According to a 2017 report, Immigration and Customs Enforcement (ICE) removed 33,570 Guatemalans, 22,381 Hondurans, and 18,838 Salvadorans that year (compared to 128,765 Mexicans).[12] Researchers generally downplay there being a direct link between the criminal street gangs, like Mara Salvatrucha and 18th Street, and the transnational drug logistics chain. These "local" gangs are not the main movers and shakers. Rather, they are more like "facilitators" of drug trafficking. Nevertheless, without some group facilitating the drugs through the region, they wouldn't make it to market in the United States, so clearly the role is critical to the overall flow of drugs, guns, and gangs.[13] A Catholic sister who regularly volunteers with refugee families in San Antonio lamented, "I wish we'd stop calling it 'gang violence.' It really is organized crime. They rule territories and they put their own people in office. The families have no protection from the police or the government because of this organized crime, which is present from the top down."

FRAGILE (WEAK) GOVERNMENT

Global migration has decreased in terms of people escaping repressive or authoritarian states, but it has increased in terms of people leaving fragile states that can't or won't provide basic support for their citizens. Families and children from the Northern Triangle are fleeing their homelands because the fragile or weak governments make it impossible for them to live safe lives. A volunteer described speaking with a migrant and his small son from Honduras at a soup kitchen in Nogales, Sonora, Mexico. The father took out his cell phone and showed "a photo of his slain brother lying on a street in a pool of blood. With a dispassionate face he click[ed] through the photos on his cell phone."[14] He knew he faced the same fate as his brother, so he took his little boy and fled. At a shelter for migrants in Nogales, the father was planning to cross into the desert with his young son. They're ideal candidates for asylum in the United States, but the only way the father can plead his case for asylum is to arrive alive on U.S. soil. Since they likely would be rejected outright if they attempted to enter through the overly clamped-down "legal" point of access, they will take their chances and make the risky walk through the Sonoran Desert in southern Arizona. The mothers and fathers, sons and daughters, might not be fleeing direct state persecution (though some are), but they are fleeing state incompetence. It's not safe to remain, and so they flee.

Government and Police Corruption

Government and police corruption and inefficiency contribute to insecurity in the Northern Triangle. Complaints to the local police frequently go unanswered. A mother explained that she'd filed a complaint against her husband for domestic violence after he beat her and their daughter. When he was released on parole, he promptly went to claim his daughter. The mother said, "He wants to use and abuse her. He made threats to kill me and to kill my daughter. I notified the police, but the police never do anything. Time passed and nothing happened. No help. It was then that I thought to come to the United States to request asylum to keep my daughter safe." The testimonies of the families resonate with what's been documented in academic literature: crime runs wild, and impunity is virtually guaranteed because of the ineptitude and/or corruption of local and national governmental authorities. The families choose the "lesser evil" and risk the overland journey to the United States.

A mother of a young family seeking asylum in the Unites States whose husband was detained at a separate detention facility explained that everything changed for her after her brother and daughter were killed. She said, "In our country there is no security. There are many problems. Insecurity. Delinquency. Each day is worse." She explained that since her brother and her daughter were murdered, she felt like she'd lost a part of her life. She said, "Each day my heart suffers. I do not want my son to suffer the same fate: death." They came to the United States to reunite with family members who had already migrated. She said, "We were forced to leave the country that we love. If we remained, we would die. So we made the journey here so that we could live." She and her husband will have to navigate the asylum system separately, praying that they will be reunited with their family safely together in the United States. Another mother testified:

The Laws Do Not Help People
Fear was behind my decision
      to leave my country
      to protect my son
      to protect myself.
   *

He assaulted me.
He caused me much medical.
He threatened to kill me.
He threatened to kill my son.
   *

The laws do not help the people.
The laws do not protect us.
      We had to leave.
I knew the walk would be difficult
      but
I had more fear to remain in my country.
   *

We departed January 7th.
We arrived January 15th.
   *

Fear was behind my decision.
      We are here for protection.
      We are here for safety.
      We are here for asylum.

         Mother, January 20, 2016
         Ya! Me voy! (Enough! I go!)[15]

The violence against women and girls is particularly prevalent, terrifying, and unrelenting.

FEMICIDE AND FEMINICIDE

As mentioned previously, an increasingly prevalent atrocity is the gang rape and/or torture of women in some manner that leaves harsh visible marks on their bodies.

Sometimes their young bodies are dismembered and defaced after death. The cultural acceptance of such violence against females, confirmed by the virtual impunity of the perpetrators, exacerbates the urgency for women and girls to make a hasty exodus when death threats are directed at them, so they can escape feminicide. "Feminicide" is a technical term expanded from "femicide," which means the murder of women and girls because of their gender. Feminicide connects the same violent acts of femicide to encompass state culpability. Hence, "feminicide" is a political term because it not only condemns the perpetrators (those who hire the killings and commit the actual acts), but also holds the state and judicial structures responsible for brutality against women, including those who tolerate the violence and anything that inhibits women's safety.

For example, Guatemalan law's broad definition of violence against women specifies physical bodily damage and also impeding a woman's economic well-being as serious crimes. After the Guatemalan congress approved the Law against Femicide and Other Forms of Violence against Women (Decree 222008) on April 9, 2008, for the first time ever women could "press criminal charges against partners for domestic violence or the prohibition of family planning methods."[16] Unfortunately, establishing the law has not equated to slowing down femicide, as there has been an *increase* in femicide cases. Impunity has been the primary culprit. There are very few prosecutions, and convictions are virtually nil.

The refugee women don't name femicide explicitly in their conversations, interviews, or writings, but fear of femicide is vivid and clear in what they say in their testimonies. For instance, a mother explained that the father of her child abandoned her when she learned she was pregnant but then came to see his daughter when she was seven years old. Now he calls every day, demanding that the mother give him his daughter. He threatened to kill the mother if she didn't comply. She said, "He will put her to his ill use with the gangs. For this reason, I arose in fear to immigrate to the U.S. to prevent my daughter's death. He would use her, and then he would kill us both." Another mother explained, "The gangs use the young. They violate them. They use violence. Later, they kill the girl and her family. My daughter is my motive for being here." When femicide runs rampant, as it does in the Northern Triangle, "feminicide" is the technical term to force attention on the necessity for the bigger system to take responsibility for reshaping a safe place for women and girls to live—not only in their local communities, but also in the state, nation, and world.

2

Fleeing for Their Lives

The Dangerous Overland Journey

Horrible circumstances compel people to make difficult decisions. A pediatrician who volunteers with unaccompanied children who are seeking asylum said, "Children don't migrate. They flee!" The same could be said for the mothers and fathers who are picking up their children and running for their lives. The decision to migrate is a radical, risky, yet necessary choice. Their desperation overwhelms what deficient information they may have received with regard to the scare tactics of U.S. policies, detention under deplorable conditions, and separations from children and spouse upon arrival to the United States. These families and children are exercising the internationally acknowledged right to escape for their lives, and they expect the receiving nation to help them. They might not know the language of the United Nations High Commissioner for Refugees (UNHCR), the Convention, or the principle of nonrefoulement (explained in chapter 4), but they do sense that the United States has a moral responsibility to offer them protection when they cross the international border to request asylum.

MIGRATION AS THE NORMATIVE
HUMAN AND RELIGIOUS EXPERIENCE

We act shocked and appalled that so many displaced people are coming to the United States, but these families are caught up in the normative human condition. "Migration" is a more appropriate term than "immigration" because people have been migrating for thousands of years. Even a cursory survey of the history of humanity, of civilization, confirms that people have been sojourning from one place to the next since the beginning of recorded history. Migration is a normal process of humanity. It's also normative in the sacred narratives of world religions.[1] The witness of migration in the sacred ancestors of world religions is so prevalent that philosopher of religion Thomas Tweed theorizes that religious people "cross and dwell." He argues that while it is faith that often induces people to dwell, faith also necessitates when one must cross to a new place to dwell. For the religious person, it is "not only about being in place but also about moving across."[2] These refugees crossing through Mexico to dwell in safety in the United States are survivors, but they're treated like criminals.

PODER DESDE—POWER FROM WITHIN

Gender injustice targets the mothers and girls in their homeland, but gender also includes innate strengths for "survival and resistance," what Monica Maher calls "*poder desde* or 'power from within.'"[3] The Spanish word *poder* is a noun meaning "power" or "to be able." It is also used as an auxiliary verb that connects being able to be or do with something else in the present or future. Hence, its definition contains the construct for possible action, empowerment, and personal choice to gain control over one's life. The inner strength of *poder desde* provides the fortitude for these mothers from the Northern Triangle to make the decisive choice to immigrate for safety's sake. As one mother said, "It is better to die fighting than to die doomed by the gangs." They opt to risk everything to save their children from exploitation, sexual violence, and death, while escaping from the femicide prevalent in their homelands.

The risks of the overland journey to America are public knowledge. The mothers aren't naïve about the dangers, as one mother indicated when she said, "Knowing what could happen, we left everything behind, undertaking a very dangerous and difficult trip filled with pain and risk." Another mother said, "So much evil covers the land where I was born. I seek a safer place for my daughter, where she can live without fear and without death threats." The asylees would prefer to remain in their homelands, surrounded by family and friends, but targeted violence makes safety/life impossible. Many of the families come to the United States because they have relatives there who are willing and able to help them. A volunteer pointed out, "They don't have family in Mexico, or anyone there who will help them, but they do have family here." They come here, where almost all of the families from the Northern Triangle have someone who is ready, willing, and able to help them.

PAINFUL GOODBYES

Strong family ties make saying goodbye to home and country a painful first step that lingers throughout the journey. A mother said, "I do not want to leave. I love my

Figure 2.1. **A mother shares her reasons for making the journey through Mexico to request asylum in the United States.**

country, but I cannot live in it. Our lives run with danger." Another mother said, "I left my mother and father. Already it is very difficult without them in my life or in my son's life. We both miss them so very much." Another said, "We made the difficult decision to leave our country and all our family. I couldn't stop crying on my long trip from Honduras, for I missed my family. I mourned for them in my heart." The sojourners often say goodbye to spouses because there's not enough money, so one must remain behind.

Many mothers and fathers also make heart-wrenching choices of which children to bring and which to leave behind. A mother explained, "I left Honduras on Sunday at 10 a.m. with my oldest son and my niece. I left two daughters in Honduras. It was difficult to leave them, but they understand that I must protect their brother's life." Another mother said, "My two youngest daughters came with me, but my oldest daughter stayed home." A mother wrote a symbolic (unmailed) letter to the spouse she'd left in her homeland: "Hello my love. I miss you. I would love in this moment to be by your side. I love you. I send you many kisses. Our daughter also sends her love. Our baby. We miss you."

The children also suffer from the separation. A seven-year-old said that he misses his sister, but "I don't miss seeing my father beat my mother." Another child shared similar thoughts:

Things I Miss from Home
I miss
>> my pets
>> my friends
>> my neighbors
>> my sister.
I do not miss
>> the people who are bad
>> the people that hurt my mother.

Seven-year-old boy, March 10, 2015
Memories from Home[4]

A fifteen-year-old boy said the hardest part of his trip was saying goodbye to his family, including brothers and sisters who had remained in El Salvador. He added, "I also had to say goodbye to Maggy. She is a very special girl that God permitted me to know." He explained, "The most difficult part of the trip was feeling sad, lonely, and all the disappointment." He hoped they would be able to return to his homeland, because he didn't want to live separated from his family or his special girl.

COYOTES—HUMAN SMUGGLERS

It used to be that migrants could walk unaided through Mexico from the rest of Central America, but it's much harder now, so many migrants opt to hire a *coyote*. Named after the animal, *coyote* is a technical term in Spanish for the human traffickers the families hire to guide them through Mexico and across the border to the United States. Like their animal namesake, the guides are wily, making it their profession to "sneak" people into the United States. A volunteer in Arizona clarified, "*Coyotes* look at you as a product," adding, "There's not one cartel for the *coyotes* and another cartel for drugs. There's just one cartel in Mexico that runs everything." For the families who hire the services of a *coyote* and join an organized group, the route they take depends upon the *coyote* they hire, the connections the *coyote* has, and the amount of money each traveler is willing and able to spend. Some hire the services of a *coyote* to take them all the way through Mexico, and others pay the fee only to cross the border to enter the United States.

During one of my days volunteering at the Greyhound bus station in downtown San Antonio, where the families are dropped off by ICE after they pass their credible fear interviews (see chapter 7), I asked the adults individually if they had used a *coyote* and why or why not. On this particular day, every parent said no. One mother had taken the bus the entire way, so she didn't need one. The other adults said they didn't have the money to pay a *coyote*, so they opted to make the journey solo through Mexico with their young children. I asked how they knew which way to go—did they simply head north and walk? A mother laughed and explained that she asked people along the journey which direction to go. She made the trip from Guatemala with her seven-year-old son, and they traveled alone the entire way.

Another day at the bus station, I asked several families how much it cost to cross the river. Human trafficking through Mexico is a big moneymaker. Their responses included:

- $3,500 per person from Mexico City to cross the Mexico-U.S. border
- 17,000 quetzals (approximately $2,200 U.S.) for mother and child to travel from Guatemala to the United States, payable in parts
- $5,000 for a mother and child to travel from Honduras to the United States

A mother of two teenagers said she'd been very lucky that they'd traveled by bus. The entire trip took only eight days. Her sister, a legal resident in the United States, sent the bus money and also $1,000 to pay the "guide" to take them across the river, where they were picked up by the border patrol the next day. The cost of a *coyote* from Mexico to Tucson or Phoenix ranges from $3,000 to $10,000. A volunteer in Arizona explained, "You pay once you arrive and they will give you three chances for the same fee." Customs and Border Protection (CBP) often deports the families from Mexico back to a different port of entry (POE) so they cannot find the same *coyote* and make another attempt to enter the United States.

For those who hire a "guide" for the duration of their journey, the *coyote* controls the route, including modes of transportation and whatever forced overnight accommodations might be included along the way. As one volunteer said, "The *coyote* doesn't give out much information in advance. You are completely at their mercy." Some are honorable, but many are not. The fact that human trafficking is illegal on both sides of the border means there's no legal apparatus in place in Mexico or the United States to protect the vulnerable victims. The families are literally at the mercy of the *coyote*. One mother wrote this about her experience:

> *The Children Suffered*
> We left my house August third at 5 a.m.
>   It was on a Monday.
> Some in the group were Quiche.
> I traveled with my son
>   and two of my friends.
>   *
> We passed through Carmelita and Vera Cruz.
> At one point on the walk we crawled under a bus.
>   It was difficult to breathe.
>   It was so hot.
> The children suffered.
>   *
> We arrived at a small town.
>   We stayed four days.
>   They did not feed us.
> The children suffered.
>   *

We left in the back of a truck trailer.
      It was 7 a.m.
      without food
      without water.
We were in the trailer
      one day and one night
      without food
      without water.
      *

We arrived at Reynosa at 9 p.m.
      We stayed two days.
Then we crossed the river.
      Immigration picked us up at 2 p.m.
      *

They took us to the *hielera.*
Then the *perrera.*
Then family detention.
We are here to request asylum.

                          Mother, September 9, 2015
                          My Journey[5]

It's difficult to record what has been called an "invisible crisis" when only the stories of the survivors generally can be documented. The actual route a migrant takes is a key variable that contributes to the length of time, modes of transportation, and any sense of safety along the way. There are risks traveling through the countries in the Northern Triangle because of the sociocide explained in chapter 1, but life-threatening dangers intensify exponentially after the families cross from Guatemala into Mexico. In fact, Mexico has been called a "death-trap" for immigrants.[6] In the 2017 Fragile States Index, Mexico tied for the biggest decline in stability (out of 178 nations) from the previous year.[7]

It is 1,778 kilometers (1,105 miles) from the Guatemala-Mexico border to the United States, traveling the most direct route along the coast through Mexico and then turning slightly inland toward McAllen, Texas. Google Maps indicates it takes twenty-four hours to make the journey by car. For perspective, the California coastline is 840 miles, and the width of Texas on Interstate 10 is 877 miles. The migrants traveling through Mexico rarely ride in cars, and they seldom follow the most direct route. Instead, they make much of the journey on foot, through the mountainous region, slowly journeying amidst the social violence that has made Mexico one of the most dangerous territories in Latin America. In addition to "normal" travel risks for an overland journey, including hunger, thirst, dehydration, sprained ankles, broken limbs, drowning, and even being attacked by a wild animal, the families must survive threats of assault, kidnapping, rape, and/or being held captive until they pay more money to their *coyote.* Knowing these dangers are present on the trip through Mexico, still they make the journey because it's less horrible than where they came from. Whatever the route, Mexico is not a safe country to cross. For example, a mother shared these details about her traumatic journey:

> *A Very Difficult Trip*
> I am 24.
> My daughter is 6.
> We are from El Salvador.
> We took the hardest route.
> The trip started with 15 people.
> Not everyone made it.
> *
>
> We had to cross a river
>   to get to Mexico.
> There was fear in my heart.
> I imagined the boat would overturn.
> Then thanks to God we made it.
> All went well.
>   We arrived in Mexico.
> *
>
> We stayed two nights at a ranch.
>   Filled with fleas.
> We had two days with no food.
> My daughter asked me for food.
>   I had none to give her.
> I cried so much.
> *
>
> I advise people to think
>   long and hard
>   *before*
>   making this journey.
> It is a very difficult trip.
>   Hard.
>   Full of suffering.
> The easiest part is finding immigration.
>
>   Mother, March 15, 2016
>   *My Journey*[8]

TRAVELING IN GROUPS FOR SAFETY'S SAKE

The *Caminata Migrante*, also known as "the Exodus," which began in San Pedro Sula, Honduras, in October 2018 and arrived in Tijuana, Mexico, on Thanksgiving weekend 2018, made migrant caravans headline news, but migrants routinely have traveled through Mexico in groups for safety's sake. This large-scale *caminata* simply made very visible what's been normative in Central America for years. Sometimes a caravan is organized by the "guide" the families pay to lead them through Mexico. Other times families gradually connect with other travelers as they make their slow journey north. Migrants who cannot maintain the pace are left behind to die. Others are trafficked for labor or sexual exploitation. The rest travel in groups because there's safety in numbers.

International cooperation to ensure safe passage of the families is virtually nonexistent, and troubles can begin as soon as immigrants cross the border into Mexico. For example, between January 17 and February 14, 2014, military personnel and agents from the National Migration Institute launched what they called a "rescue" as they detained 1,438 undocumented foreigners, the majority of them Guatemalans, during an operation in southern Mexico. The possibility of being "rescued" by Mexican authorities is just one of the traumatic challenges that threaten migrating families. Pueblo Sin Fronteras, a binational human rights organization that coordinates two migrant shelters in Sonora, Mexico, in an area known as the most violent and exposed along the border zone, wrote a public statement after members of this all-volunteer group traveled to southern Mexico to accompany the Exodus to Tijuana. It specified:

> [W]e have asked Mexican institutions to comply with the laws that govern the issuance of humanitarian visas and the recognition of refugee status, because the system that currently exists for these processes in Mexico is full of irregularities and human rights violations. These include the incarceration of asylum seekers, the confinement of asylum applicants to violent and impoverished regions and cities, arbitrary and illegal delays, and a lack of infrastructure for addressing refugees' most urgent humanitarian needs.[9]

In addition to these hurdles to navigate during migration through Mexico, women and girls have an added vulnerability to sexual violence and femicide. Unfortunately, the machismo mentality flourishes in Mexico, with a culture of violence against women exactly like what the mothers hoped to leave behind in the Northern Triangle. A lot of the women get birth control shots in anticipation of being raped. Doctors Without Borders indicates that one-third of the women it surveyed in 2017 were sexually abused (that includes rape) and 10.7 percent were raped.[10] However, the testimonies the mothers share with volunteer clergy at refugee respite locations in San Antonio and southern Arizona suggest that the statistic is much higher. For example, the spiritual care coordinator at a shelter in San Antonio estimated that 80–85 percent of women and girls were raped during the overland journey. Rape is so common that the medical exam for women upon arrival to the United States includes a pregnancy test.

The *coyotes* lock their customers in safe houses while they extort more money to ensure safe passage to the United States. They also threaten to abandon the families, or turn the women and girls over to sex traffickers if a woman refuses a *coyote*'s sexual advances. It might be part of the pre-trip agreement for a female migrant to provide sexual "favors" in exchange for safe passage. Mothers who don't make such an agreement beforehand discover it's an ongoing struggle to protect themselves from being raped or molested on the journey. A mother commented that she was fortunate to have her teenage son with her because "he provided important protection for me during the journey."

Deprivation also includes the expected suffering from exposure, physical exhaustion, hunger, thirst, and physical pain from three weeks of walking in rugged terrain. Suffering is compounded by whatever meager arrangements the *coyote* makes for overnight lodging (if any), food and water, and transportation. For example, one mother wrote, "We stayed eight days in a house, locked up. They gave us breakfast and lunch. There were twenty people, including children. We suffered much. We had no money. My son cried. He did not want to be there. Then we left in a truck." Another asylum seeker shared how a young woman, who was traveling solo in the group, was separated from everyone at the first "safe house" to which the *coyote* brought the band of travelers. The migrant explained, "The rest of us could hear her screams during the night. She did not rejoin the group the next day. We never saw her again."

The traveling families have to remain on their guard about being exploited, tricked, or betrayed. A teenager who traveled with his mother explained, "Many people along the road offered their wares for sale. Some were from the underside of humanity. They want to hurt and delay you from your purpose." Kidnapping and extortion also are common. The families rarely travel with a phone, but they tuck scraps of paper in their pockets with the contact information of their destination family. They also memorize the phone numbers of relatives in their country of origin and their family connection in the United States. It's all too frequent for a migrating family to be kept in a safe house while the *coyote* extorts the sending or receiving family to pay more money to ensure the safe arrival of their loved ones.

The trauma the travelers experience can be visible, invisible, or both. A hospitality volunteer at the bus station in downtown San Antonio asked a mother who was newly released from family detention why she was still wearing the "resident issue" T-shirt she had been given at the for-profit facility. The mother showed her the tattered shirt that had been torn from her body when she was raped during the journey. The families literally have only the clothing on their backs, so she had presented herself for asylum at the border station wearing her rape-tattered shirt. The detention center, like any prison, releases its former inmates with whatever they had upon incarceration. In the mother's case, they returned her torn shirt but also let her keep a uniform T-shirt. When another mother at the bus station responded "*Sí*" (yes) to the hospitality volunteer who asked whether she was pregnant, her teenage son gently said to his mother, "No, Mother. Remember, you're not pregnant." She'd been raped on the journey, and her traumatic memory made her believe she was pregnant.

THE ARDUOUS, LIFE-THREATENING OVERLAND JOURNEY

The testimonies of the families reveal the life-threatening challenges along the journey. The mother of a young child wrote about the difficulty of traveling "through foreign places alone, knowing no one to depend on." She added, "Walking with a baby is very difficult." Several described the fear they felt when the families were packed inside a truck trailer. A young teen who'd come from Honduras with two sisters and their mother—because the gangs killed their father and then wanted to "hurt my sisters and me"—described the night the group spent in a truck trailer "without air" as being particularly difficult for her. She explained, "We passed through electric fences that were very dangerous, and we experienced much cold and hunger. We crossed a river with much fear." An unaccompanied teenager from Honduras who hadn't seen his mother in six years, since he was eight years old, was determined to reunite with her in Kansas. A volunteer in Nogales, Mexico, relayed, "He was strong, resolved, and determined when I spoke with him." The volunteers warned him of the desert in summer and the miles he would have to walk before he arrived at the nearest town. The volunteer added, "He shrugged and gave a shy smile." He planned to connect with several other young men and continue his journey with them.[11]

Modes of Transportation and Average Travel Time

The average travel time through Mexico is about twenty days, with the biggest variable being walking versus alternative modes of transportation. The vehicular options include passenger cars and trucks, plus buses, rafts, and motorboats to cross the river between Guatemala and Mexico, and between Mexico and the United States. One mother's quick summary of her trip included, "We traveled day and night—to all hours. We traveled by bus, truck, rafts, motorboats, and on foot. When I tried to sleep, a man tried to abuse my person." A few have been able to ride a bus for most of their journey, which then takes only six to eight days.

Most specified that they did a lot of walking to save money. As one mother said, "We did not have money for the trip, so we took the more difficult route and walked most of the way through Mexico." Another simply said, "The bus is expensive. So we walked." She told her daughter never to let go of her skirt for the duration of the journey, and she added that having her seventeen-year-old son along was helpful for her family's safety. A teenage daughter explained her family's experiences in this way: "We traveled in buses and then we walked. The journey through the mountains was the most difficult. They did not always feed us. It rained every day. It was horrible." A young mother said that a fellow traveler in her group who was in her early twenties disappeared when they stopped at a safe house. She said, "We never saw her again. We know what must've happened to her."

Trains and Tractor-Trailer Transport through Mexico

Some families ride packed in the back of tractor-trailers for twenty or more hours straight, and some risk *la Bestia*, or "the Beast," which is the name popularly given to the freight trains that migrants have boarded to travel north through Mexico since the 1980s. When the train makes its various stops along the northbound journey, sometimes people from a church are there to help the migrants. Other times, the gangs jump onto the train when it slows down at a station. A mother explained that they would lock arms to protect their daughters from the gang members who tried to pull their daughters off the trains. A teenager described his family's decision not to jump on *la Bestia*, a decision that ultimately saved their lives:

> We were walking so many days that my family was saying they could not walk anymore because their feet hurt so much. I had to carry all the knapsacks because already my mother was pregnant. Along the way, we met people who would help us; they gave us food and clothing. One person even gave me a pair of shoes because already mine were so worn from walking. We walked and walked with this group of people. They became like family. When we came to the trains, we decided not to get on the train. We were the lucky ones because it turned out that many of them were killed and their bodies were mutilated. I don't know what else to say. They were like family to us.

Another high-risk factor is *coyotes* making the migrant families ride packed inside a fifty-two-foot box trailer hauled behind an eighteen-wheeler as part of the travel itinerary. If, and how long, a migrant travels enclosed in a tractor-trailer varies. Although it might seem unlikely that they could know this, the families always have specified the exact number of hours they were locked inside the truck. Essentially, they know what time they are locked inside and what time they finally arrive at the destination and are released, so it is easy to do the math. The duration is a key point of their testimony because their suffering was so horrific. For example, a Salvadoran woman wrote, "They put sixty people inside, adults and children. I don't know what cities we passed through. We spent thirty hours in the trailer. No food. They brought us water only two times. Very little. There was only a tiny bit left for my daughter. My daughter cried desperately. No food. No water. The heat inside the trailer made it difficult to breathe. We saw nothing. We arrived at a house in Reynosa." If the families can survive thirty hours crammed inside the back of a truck, the overall journey is much quicker. For this mother-daughter, the journey through Mexico took only six days. After three days in Reynosa, they were taken to the river, where they took a boat across to the United States. The mother concluded her story by saying, "I was very brave."

Riding in the back of a box trailer is a dangerous travel mode on both sides of the border. For example, on July 23, 2017, a deadly human trafficking incident left ten people dead and thirty-one hospitalized after they'd been trapped in an abandoned tractor-trailer in a Walmart parking lot in San Antonio, Texas.[12] A city council representative from San Antonio received a "heads-up" phone call in the middle of the night from a police officer about the fatalities, which had occurred in his district. The councilman responded by going to the scene, arriving just as eight bodies were being put into bags (two of the injured died at the hospital, bringing the total fatalities to ten). He reflected later, "When you see in front of you the consequences of all our debates, none of it matters because there are eight souls in body bags. Regardless of what you feel of this, you know it's a broken system when more people will still get in the back of a truck, even though ten people just died in the back of this truck. The reality is that they're coming and they'll continue to come. We might as well come up with a comprehensive approach to make this work." He added, "We should be glad that people want to come to the U.S., that this is a country with resources and opportunities. We should be concerned when this is no longer a country that people want to come to. That's a concern: when people don't want to come here."[13]

POINT OF ENTRY TO THE UNITED STATES

The newest challenge for migrants is to be allowed legal admittance to the United States. A Catholic sister who assists migrants in various capacities explained, "The whole dynamic of what goes on at the border now impacts migrants and their ability to enter the U.S. through a legal point of access. Now CBP is standing in the middle of the international bridge and not allowing people to cross." The Mexican government also makes passage through its country more challenging. She added, "If the families are traveling from other Central American countries and they don't have a transit visa to pass through Mexico, then the Mexican officials take them away and lock them up. Meanwhile, [those who do reach the U.S. border] have to stand on the Mexico side of the bridge while they wait to be allowed to cross the legal point of access entry to the U.S." The families want to seek asylum, and to do so through the legal point of access, but they are squeezed between changing laws and procedures in Mexico and in the United States.

The sister elaborated on the dangers of being in limbo: "The gangs control the border. The families have to pay $1,500 to $3,000 to cross the river. The families are so vulnerable on the Mexico side of the border. Every moment they wait on the Mexico side of the border for the U.S. to allow them permission to cross the bridge at a legal point of access, their lives are in danger." She added, "The families want to ask for asylum. They have to be on U.S. soil to ask for asylum, so we [the United States] are doing everything we can so they can't cross, unless they cross the river and 'sneak' in illegally." Desperation often pushes the families to the river so they can gain a sense of safety by being off of Mexican soil and onto U.S. soil. She noted, "Of course, then they have the crime of 'illegal entry.'"

Crossing the Arizona Desert

Sojourners who cross the Arizona-Mexico border at an "illegal" point of entry have the desert to deal with. The massiveness of the southern Arizona desert is difficult to fathom. A first-time visitor said, "As we drove past the huge expanse of desert, I found myself wondering, 'How in God's name do the migrants ever cross this?'" During an immersion seminar in southern Arizona this volunteer attended, a local explained, "The desert is massive, and it's easy to get turned around. Today we have a blue sky, a little bit of haze, green from the rains. We have this beautiful scene, and we can't see or hear the people who are walking through the desert, not knowing where they're going to get something to drink or where they're going to sleep."

The guide explained that blazing heat is the obvious hindrance during the long, hot summer. The life-threatening factors change when winter arrives. She asked, "What's it like to cross in the winter? It's freezing at night and it also rains. The temperature can swing thirty degrees. Hypothermia is a real risk. You can also drown out here. It's the rainy season and flash flooding is possible." She added, "Remember we saw a jet fly over? There's a bombing range further out. It has structures that the migrants might misconstrue, but they're bombing targets. There also could be unexploded bombs on the ground, so the migrants are literally walking through a minefield."

The increased anti-migrant rhetoric in Washington, D.C., is enacted by border agents, civilians, and nongovernmental agencies in the southern Arizona desert. Another Arizona volunteer reported, "The blistering heat and the freezing cold of the desert are no longer CBP's only 'deterrents to migration.' Add rubber bullets and tear gas. Add too those people whose mission now is to drain every Humane Borders water tank." This gloomy report concluded with an encouragement: "Stay strong and positive. Focus on what is possible and that is massive. You prove that every trip."[14]

The biggest challenge for sojourners walking through southern Arizona is the length of time they must spend in the desert before they emerge to safety. An Arizona volunteer explained, "There've been a lot of changes just since 2006. It used to take two and a half days to walk through the desert, but now it takes four to six days due to the increased border enforcement." The longer a sojourner must stay in the desert, the more at risk they are to death by dehydration, hypothermia, snake or scorpion bites, or terrain-related injuries. An unaccompanied teenager said her "guide" got lost in the desert, and they walked in circles. If they hadn't been picked up by the border patrol, she said they probably would have died in the desert. Because she's an unaccompanied minor seeking asylum, she was transferred to an Office of Refugee Resettlement (ORR) facility in Texas.

Migrants may know the risks to some extent, but they cannot grasp the depth of the pain, suffering, and deprivation until they're actually in the desert and making the long walk. The ones who die without identification are called *desconocidos* (unknown). The families will never know exactly what happened to them. They simply disappeared on the migrant journey through the desert. For those who don't make it through the Sonoran Desert region in southern Arizona, surviving family can use an open search engine to locate migrant remains. It's referred to as the "Red Dot Map." The Arizona OpenGIS Initiative for Deceased Migrants started in 2001 and is managed jointly by the Pima County Office of the Medical Examiner and by Humane Borders, Inc. One of the initiative's goals is for anyone to be able to search for dead migrants based on what they know about them—their name, gender, year of death, the county in which they died, etc.[15] Each red dot on this Arizona map indicates the official spot where human remains have been discovered. Human remains left in

Figure 2.2. A cross made by artist Alvaro Enciso, a Colombian migrant who lives in Tucson, marks the site where the body of Miguel Vasquez Lara was found in May 2001.

the desert are a silent witness, a way for migrants who did not survive to share their stories of pain and suffering.

SUSTAINED BY FAITH

Throughout their traumatic journey, sojourners are sustained by faith, visions, fear, and the *poder desde* to push on toward the borderlands. A father who received hospitality with his young son at the Catholic Charities of the Rio Grande Valley migrant aid station located at Sacred Heart Catholic Church in McAllen, Texas, said, "I found God on my journey." After a momentary hesitation he added, "Or maybe God found me." A mother specified that in the middle of "fear beyond all fear during our twenty days of suffering," it was only through the strength of God that she was able to continue. Another mother said when they "passed by places where we sensed fear and trembling" that it was only the "voice of God in my soul that told me not to fear." Another mother I spoke with said that the trip was much more difficult than she had expected, and that she learned that in this life there are risks. During her journey, she came to understand that God is not constrained by the international boundaries of any given country. She said, "With God, there are no borders."

THE EASIEST PART IS FINDING IMMIGRATION

The families might cross the border at an "illegal" point of entry under the guidance of a *coyote*, but they want to turn themselves in to U.S. Immigration. When the families cross the border, they don't run. After describing the rigors of their journey, they consistently report, "The easiest part of the trip was finding Immigration." As soon as the families cross the river, they approach the first U.S. government official they see and ask for asylum. They want to find Immigration; that's their ultimate hope, goal, and point of coming to the United States. They are refugees seeking asylum. They believe the public image of the United States, and they trust that it is an honorable nation that will welcome the oppressed and protect the vulnerable. They expect to live with their families who are already here. They also expect to be granted asylum. An advocate from California who provided legal assistance for migrants when the whopper-sized caravan arrived in Tijuana on Thanksgiving weekend 2018 (see chapter 11) wrote a summary report that includes a synthesis of the expectations of the travelers:

> Several asylum seekers that I met in the camp expressed to me the idea that the U.S. was going to help them once people here (including Trump) became aware of their situation. People were painting American flags. They said that they were painting these flags as a gesture of kindness towards the U.S. I can tell they came here looking for the mythical land of the free and home of the brave but given the way our country has been responding, I fear that they are going to realize the place they are looking for does not exist. I hope that our country will find the strength to have compassion and that the faith these people have in us won't be misplaced. I think this is a moment in history when we have the opportunity to ask ourselves who we are as a country and what our values are; I think we should be grateful for that opportunity and I hope we find the courage to do the right thing.[16]

Instead of hospitality and welcome, the families and children are stunned at the harsh treatment they receive from U.S. Immigration, CBP, and the for-profit detention facilities, which taken together comprise their "Welcome to the USA" experience.

3

The Harsh Reality

"Welcome" to the United States

When refugees seeking asylum make their initial request for asylum, border officials quickly lock them up inside CBP facilities. Adults and children disappear inside these federally funded U.S. government detention chambers of injustice. We, as a nation, justify incarcerating families and children in appalling facilities by lumping them together with the gangs who commit violent crimes, conveniently disregarding that these families and unaccompanied minors are the innocent victims and not the perpetrators. We label these mothers and fathers and boys and girls "illegal aliens" who are nothing but "rapists, murderers, and thieves," to justify that they are therefore criminals who need, and deserve, to be locked up.

One of the biggest concerns is the lack of transparency about what goes on inside these government-run and taxpayer-funded detention facilities. Very few from the outside are allowed inside, and insiders are required to maintain full secrecy or their employment will be terminated. For instance, a social worker who'd agreed to speak at an education event about children who are detained was told, "If you speak at the event, don't come to work the next day." Likewise, on December 15, 2016, soon after I presented a paper at an academic conference, ICE rescinded my security clearance as a volunteer chaplain at a family detention center and canceled the all-volunteer art ministry that I'd facilitated with refugee women and children while they were detained. I was given the justification that I had "used the families" for my thesis. In reality, ICE objected to my full disclosure of how the families are received upon arrival to the United States. I had heard so many horror stories from the families that my obligation to my oath of office, so to speak, as an ordained minister called my conscience to witness on behalf of these families who have been treated so abominably. A colleague later said that I was "fired" from my volunteer pastoral care ministry because of insubordination.

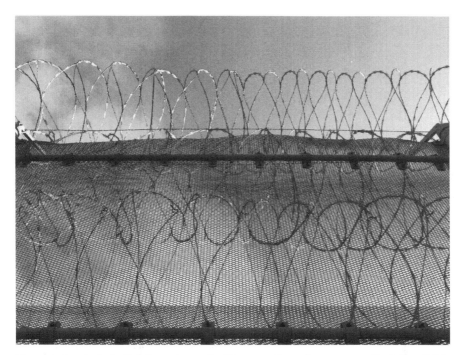

Figure 3.1.   A chain-link fence topped with concertina wire serves as the inhospitable border along portions of the American side of the U.S.-Mexico wall near Tijuana, Mexico.

An immigration and civil rights attorney asked, "Where's the oversight? Who is checking up from an independent basis to ensure compliance to basic human rights standards?" *We* are part of this gross injustice: we voted for it; we fund it; and we disbelieve, ignore, or disregard the cries of the families pleading for safety. It's happening. It's real. These facilities exist, and families seeking asylum are suffering gross injustice inside state-funded, state-authorized detention facilities.

LOCKED UP IN CBP FACILITIES WHILE PLEADING FOR ASYLUM

The facilities CBP uses to incarcerate the families upon arrival almost defy description. The families label each with a single word to describe their experience: *hielera* (cooler) for a holding cell and *perrera* (dog kennel) for migrant housing. The families may be moved from one *hielera* to another and then to the *perrera*, or they may be held in one *hielera* before being moved to the *perrera* and then to family detention. Deportation is possible at any point depending on how their plea for asylum is received by the border officials.

A volunteer with refugee families said, "I keep a photo of the *hielera* and the *perrera* on my phone. You can describe it to people, but it is totally different and more impactful to see the pictures of where these women and children are kept when they first enter the U.S." Similarly, I always provide printed photographs of both facilities when I speak or preach about immigration and/or family detention. As I was putting things away after speaking at a church in San Antonio, a seven-year-old pointed to a picture of the *perrera* and asked, "What's that? It looks like trash." A mother who had been detained in the *perrera* had described it exactly so when she said, "I felt like I had fallen into the garbage dump." Both CBP facilities are meant to be temporary, but their harshness traumatizes the mothers and their children, adding another layer of horror to their already painful and distressing experiences.

Despite consistent complaints about the temperature inside these processing facilities, which have cinderblock interior walls and concrete floors, the temperature remains well below the comfort zone for the families. These families don't have air-conditioning in their homelands and are not used to the cool temperature of an air-conditioned facility. There aren't any windows to allow sunlight inside. The electric lights remain on twenty-four seven. A priest in McAllen, Texas, whose church hosted families after they were reunited following the Trump administration's family separation travesty (see chapter 5) during the early summer of 2018, said:

> We received families when they were reunited with their children. They had been separate for two or three months. At night, when we turned the lights off for the children to sleep, they came to tell us thank you. It was the first time they'd been able to sleep with the lights off for months. In the morning, I went to turn the lights on, and half of the beds were empty. I thought, "Oh no, where did they go?" They were snuggled up in the same bed with their parents.

The parents frequently lament how much their children suffered not just from the glaring lights, but also from the cold, food, and isolation at the CBP border processing facilities.

HIELERA—THE COOLER OR REFRIGERATOR

The *hielera* serves as the holding cell where the families are brought when they first arrive to the United States, whether they cross "legally" at one of the official border points to request asylum or "illegally" at some point along the Mexico-U.S. border. The *hielera* has a single toilet, which is located at the end of the narrow room behind a privacy wall that is three-quarter height, similar to how the interior structure might be divided in a public rest stop facility along the interstate highway in Texas. The *hielera* typically has benches around the interior perimeter of the room, and some include another section of benches down the center aisle. The mothers and fathers describe being packed into these containment rooms, either crammed on the benches or lying body-to-body on the cold, hard floor.

Stories about their arrival experiences are replete with suffering, anger, dismay, fear, and anxiety, as their "welcome" to the United States adds another layer of trauma to their already overflowing testimonies of suffering. A mother described the *hielera* as "a horrible place because it is very cold and the treatment of people is very bad." A few said they were given "something very strange" to cover themselves with (a space blanket), and all have lamented that "the food is very bad." The length of time one family spends in the *hielera* varies from twenty-four hours to five full days. One mother explained, "We were there three days, sleeping on the floor. My daughter cried for the three days we were in the *hielera*. They gave us a sandwich for food, and juice to drink. No water. It was very cold." Another mother reported, "I begged for water for my daughter, but the officials wouldn't give her any." Another said, "The temperature was extremely cold. Children were crying all the time. Human heat was not enough to warm the babies." A father said he and his sixteen-year-old daughter were detained in the *hielera* for five days and five nights. He explained their experience:

> *Five Horrible Days in the Hielera*
> It was very sad.
> We suffered so much.
> The *hielera* was horrible.
> > So very cold.
> > No blankets.
> > We didn't bathe.
> > We didn't even brush our teeth.
> It's a horrible place.
> > Horrible.
> Everyone was crowded
> > small, cramped, tight
> > very cold
> It's a horrible place.
> We suffered much in the *hielera*.

> Father, October 25, 2018
> *Our Arrival to the USA*[1]

Their descriptions, and the images available by searching Google Images with the key words "U.S. Border Patrol facilities," are reminiscent of survivor Elie Wiesel's description of his family's ride in a train headed to a Nazi concentration camp. They were crammed into a cattle car with eighty Jews: "We were left with a few loaves of bread and some buckets of water . . . lying down was out of the question, and we were only able to sit if we took turns." For Wiesel, "the heat became unbearable."[2] For the migrant families, it's the freezing cold they find unbearable. The families also experience emotional abuse. A comment lament from adult after adult is, "The people there spoke to us in rude and commanding ways." The militarization at the border in the name of national security makes sure to keep these vulnerable asylum seekers in submission through cruel and punitive physical, emotional, and psychological mistreatment.

The families expect that, upon arrival to the United States, they will be reunited with the family members awaiting them, the ones who likely helped fund the trip and who plan to host them once they arrive. Families expect welcome, not more suffering and more injustice. The inhumane "herding cattle" treatment includes harshness on multiple levels. The father of a four-year-old explained the indignities of their arrival experience:

> *The Hielera Was Horrible*
> The *hielera* was horrible.
> Cold.
> We ate frozen sandwiches.
> We drank Aqua Pura.
> Five days.
> We did not bathe.
> Cold.
> Sleeping on the floor.
> Crowded.
> Cramped.
> It was very, very cold.
> My daughter cried and cried.
> There was nothing I could do.
>   I am her father.
>   I was helpless to protect her.
> She suffered in the *hielera*.
> The *hielera* is a horrible place.
> Then they sent us to the *perrera*.
>
> Father, October 25, 2018
> *Our Arrival to the USA*[3]

The guards know the cold temperature is intolerable for the families, yet they continue to keep the air-conditioning set well below their comfort zone. The border facilities, particularly in Texas, New Mexico, and Arizona, are located in a very hot climate. Unless it's December or January, the temperature along most of the southern border is 90 to 100 degrees Fahrenheit—even higher June through September. The semitropical climate is hot and humid, but the guards exacerbate the migrants' suffering by setting the air-conditioning way too low. It keeps the families huddled together on the floor and along the benches as they desperately attempt to gather warmth from one another. The mothers and fathers complain, but the guards respond, "It is what it is."

In addition to the usual complaints about the biting cold and horrible food, a mother also reported, "The guards were very mean." One guard kicked her in the face to awaken her one morning. She said another guard yelled at her, "Go back. We don't want you; you are thieves stealing our jobs." Another mother said, "While we were there, men threw bread in at us three times a day as if we were dogs." The guards also refused to give this mother feminine products when she repeatedly requested them. A father relayed, "I thought I was going to die in there. It was too cold. I couldn't keep my child warm." When this father arrived at a hospitality house in San Antonio, he dropped to his knees and prayed and wept. He was so relieved and grateful to receive compassion, kindness, and genuine hospitality.

The testimonies of the families quickly start to sound the same because they're receiving the same horrible treatment.[4] Children, whether with a parent or unaccompanied, suffer the same harsh and subhuman experience. Like the adults, they're sent from the refrigerator to the dog kennel, what the families refer to as the *perrera*, where asylum seekers are further dehumanized.

PERRERA—THE DOG KENNEL

The distasteful yet descriptive name *perrera* aptly describes the refugee housing, which looks like a dog kennel. The *perrera* is fully enclosed—walls and ceiling—with chain-link fencing. The amenities include port-a-pots located within each chamber of the fenced areas. Before the Trump administration issued a "zero tolerance" immigration policy, the mothers already said the *perrera* was the cruelest and most agonizing part of the immigration journey because they were separated from their children. Their stories have varied slightly regarding the ages of the children who are pulled apart from their mothers and placed in separate confinement cages within the dog kennel compound, but age eleven or twelve is the most consistent line of demarcation. The younger children remain with the mothers. The older ones are separated by age and gender. They don't have any communication or interaction with their mothers for the duration of the *perrera* experience.

A mother said, "After the *hielera*, they took us to a place called the *perrera*, a name of very bad taste indeed. There was better food, but at bedtime my heart hurt because they separated me from my daughter. Those two days we were there was agony." Improvements over the *hielera* that the mothers highlight include better food and accommodations for sleeping, with thin pads to lie on "and a paper that was like aluminum foil for a blanket." Some have been allowed to make a phone call to their family and some have been allowed to take a shower. One father specified, "They did not let me bathe. Five days passed without bathing. It was very terrible for me all that happened there."

When family separation made headline news in the early summer of 2018 and snippets of this facility were shown in the national media, many people refuted the existence of a "dog kennel" facility. People said it was "fake news." I even had a CBP official I sat beside on an airplane refute the reality, saying, "I thought those pictures were proven to be fake." The "fake" part was that the photos of the *perrera* were from the Obama administration timeframe, which some felt got the current administration off the hook. Refugee advocates, on the other hand, said, "That's just the point: this injustice has been going on for a long time and not 'just' recently." Another similarity between the Obama administration and the Trump administration is that, long before Trump's official family separation policy was launched, the CBP was separating mothers and fathers and boys and girls within this massive facility, known as Ursula. It's located at 3700 West Ursula Avenue in McAllen, Texas.

Ursula is one of President Barack Obama's contributions to family detention. It was quickly built in response to the influx of family migration in 2014 to expand the capacity to house women and children for longer timeframes. The U.S. Commission on International Religious Freedom (USCIRF) reports that the Ursula facility can hold up to 1,000 people in caged "pods," which can hold 250 people each. Fully enclosed in chain-link fencing, each pod includes benches, mats, televisions, and porta-pots. The lights stay on twenty-four hours a day.[5] Ursula is located two blocks from Los Encinos Park, but the families never see daylight and the children never play in the park. A participant who attended a public witness event outside of this *perrera* facility reflected:

> I'm not sure what I expected. It looked on the outside like an old warehouse building. There was virtually no outside activity. The outside gives no indication of what's going on inside unless someone told you. They clearly shield everything from public view; even the employee parking lot was screened off. There were no windows anywhere. And we know that inside, the lights are on all the time, yet there is no sunlight allowed inside. I've seen the outside of prisons, like the ones you see along the highway, and you see more on the outside of a prison than what you could see of this facility.

After the families have endured the inhumane treatment at these CBP border facilities, if they're not deported, often the next step is a for-profit detention facility.

PRIVATIZED IMMIGRANT FAMILY DETENTION— ALSO KNOWN AS "BABY JAIL"

Family detention emerged when the influx of refugee families seeking asylum intersected with changing policies and practices for catching and releasing migrants. The million-dollar business to incarcerate or "detain" refugee families has a twofold origin: (1) the rising violence in the Northern Triangle, which is forcing more people to flee to the United States for safe asylum; and (2) the militarization of the U.S. border and the subsequent shift in U.S. immigration policy to enforcement. Instead of catching and then releasing the families to continue on to relatives awaiting their arrival in cities across America, we lock up mothers and fathers and children who happen to be noncitizens. Their "crime" is that they weren't born on this side of the international demarcation in the sandy soil located between Mexico and the United States.

The technical language uses "detention" to describe locking up immigrants, including refugees seeking asylum. While migrants and refugees are being "detained" to determine whether they will be allowed legal status or be deported, most of the facilities where they are held are jails. Many of the facilities are privately owned and operated. It's a whopping big business that taxpayers fund.

Figure 3.2. Two toddlers play together in the recreation room inside the immigrant family detention center in Karnes City, Texas. Advocates have nicknamed such centers "baby jail."

Holding facilities shifted to privatized for-profit detention when ICE set a goal in 2003 to remove all deportable persons by 2012. Beforehand, because there weren't enough existing facilities to house all of the undocumented immigrants, they were issued orders to appear in court for a deportation hearing and allowed to go free until the day of trial. The groundwork for increased detainment was put in place during the Clinton administration when the forty-second president of the United States launched his "immigration reform" and private prison companies jumped onto the lobbying bandwagon. The detention center system initially was created to provide temporary housing for those who didn't show up for their deportation hearings. They were locked up, or "detained," until their due process justified deportation. Again, the word "detention" is a misnomer, because it means migrants are locked up in prisons alongside convicted criminals who have actually done something wrong. Family detention evolved to include mothers and fathers traveling with children ranging in age from infancy through teens. Fathers and children who are age eighteen or older and traveling with their families are separated and incarcerated in adult-only facilities.

The public often likes to give President Barack Obama a pass regarding the appalling treatment of families who are seeking asylum. The reality is that the Obama administration established the most widespread family incarceration in the United States since the Japanese internment camps circa World War II. At the cost of inhospitable and unjust treatment of refugees seeking asylum, the detention facilities aligned with the Obama administration policy to use incarceration as a deterrent for other families. The focus is on incarceration until deportation, *not* assistance for refugees seeking legitimate asylum in the United States. A USCIRF report reaffirms, "The use of detention as a deterrent is counter to both international refugee law and the administrative purposes of immigration detention." The report also chastises the government with its findings that "asylum seekers continue to be detained under inappropriate penal conditions before their credible fear interviews, and in some cases, even after being found to have a credible fear. Of particular concern is ICE's use of criminal prisons and jails and private immigration detention facilities designed like criminal prisons to hold increasing numbers of asylum seekers."[6]

Despite these observations and objections, the immigration detention industrial complex continues to expand. ICE recently asked private companies to submit preliminary proposals to build a detention center for adult detainees, male and female, between San Antonio and Laredo, where there are already seven detention centers. The expanded adult-only facilities impact the families who travel as a traditional family unit: mother, father, and children, including children who no longer are minors. The families are split up at the border, with the mother remaining with the minor children, who are detained at a family detention center. The father and any older siblings are incarcerated separately in adult-only facilities.

After Central American refugees began making headline news across the United States in July 2014, under the Obama administration, the Department of Homeland Security (DHS), the government agency that implements and oversees immigration enforcement, set up about 1,200 family detention beds and cribs in two locations: Artesia, New Mexico, and Karnes City, Texas. Artesia was projected as a place of respite for the families, but it was a disaster from the beginning. The American Civil Liberties Union (ACLU) filed a class action lawsuit in December 2014 that delineated a list of violations the vulnerable detainees experienced, including being cut off from communication, legal assistance, and any possibility of a fair outcome to the legal "due process" in their request for asylum. The written and video reports filed by lawyers who visited the center made a farce of what the Obama administration had promised would be a compassionate response, which was to include "respect for the law" regarding the many young Central Americans coming to the United States for humanitarian assistance. Instead, the families were locked up in a remote facility, and nearly three hundred families were quickly and silently deported.[7] As activists and lawsuits were working to close Artesia, two for-profit family detention centers were quickly adapted from preexisting structures in two rural communities in Texas to house mothers and children. Karnes City is located approximately sixty miles southeast of downtown San Antonio, and Dilley is located approximately seventy-five miles to the southwest. Local advocates refer to the facilities in these two towns simply as Karnes and Dilley.

Karnes and Dilley

Karnes County Residential Center originally was a lockup for undocumented adult male migrants until it converted to family detention for mothers and children in July 2014. The first families arrived by the busload the next month. In January 2016 it nearly doubled from its initial 532 beds to house 1,000 women and children. Like more than half of the immigrant detention facilities in the United States, it's operated by a for-profit, private prison company, the GEO Group, which houses some 80,000 people worldwide. (GEO is not an acronym; the company chooses to spell its name in all capital letters.) The facility is overseen by DHS with ICE staff assigned on-site.

Meanwhile, another for-profit family detention facility, South Texas Family Residential Center, opened in December 2014 in Dilley, Texas, with the capacity to lock up 2,400 mothers and children. CoreCivic, the private prison company formerly known as CCS and the largest prison company in the United States, created this massive detention facility in south Texas from what had been a camp used for oil field workers. After opening Dilley, ICE then transitioned out the temporary family detention facility at the Federal Law Enforcement Training Center in remote Artesia, New Mexico. The long-standing Berks County Residential Center located outside of Philadelphia in Leesport, Pennsylvania, continues to be operational.

The USCIRF report specifies particular concerns regarding how the mothers and children are detained at Dilley and Karnes:

> [D]espite the positive application of adult civil detention standards at Dilley and Karnes, USCIRF's position is that both present an institutional and jail-like setting inappropriate for children and counter to the U.S. government's own standards for child detention as defined in a 1997 legal settlement known as the *Flores* Agreement. Both are secure facilities that look like prison or jail complexes, with hardened perimeters secured with fencing, razor wire, and/or barbed wire/concertina coils, and multiple locked external doors. Internally, the women's and children's freedom of movement is restricted by locked doors and prohibitions on accessing some areas, as well as set schedules. Headcounts are another measure of internal security.
>
> In USCIRF's view, these conditions create a prison-like environment contrary to the *Flores* Agreement, which requires ICE and DHS to hold children in their custody in the least restrictive setting, in non-secure facilities licensed to care for dependent, not delinquent, minors. The conditions at Dilley and Karnes differ significantly from those observed at the Berks County Residential Center, a nursing home facility that was transitioned into an ICE family detention center. The Berks facility does not have a hardened perimeter fence, and residents are permitted to walk the grounds outside of the facility and to go on field trips.[8]

Despite these critical observations from a bipartisan entity that includes presidential appointees, family detention marches on. It took another shift during July 2018 in the middle of the family separation mess that the Trump administration created (see chapter 5) when fathers and sons were locked up as a family unit at Karnes, and mothers and children (boys and girls) were locked up at Dilley. So far, fathers traveling with daughters have been allowed to skip family detention and go directly to their family members awaiting them in the United States.

I've been volunteering with refugee families since 2014, and I was used to seeing all the mothers and children in detention and then at the bus station after they were released from the for-profit facilities. Adding fathers and sons was a later invention of sorts. They once were released from the border, but when Karnes shifted to fathers and sons during the summer of 2018, they were locked up just like the mothers and children, so they became part of the stream of migrants traveling through the Greyhound bus station once they passed their credible fear interviews. I was unexpectedly overwhelmed with emotion at all the fathers and sons at the bus station when they entered this aspect of the immigration matrix. When I said something to the coordinator for the bus station ministry, she responded, "It's surprising and overwhelming because you don't think that these men would be unable to protect themselves and their children." Many of the sons were in their mid-teens. They probably will become adults before their cases make it to court.

The government initiated a pilot program during September 2018 whereby the fathers at Karnes were given the option to release their kids to facilities overseen by the Office of Refugee Resettlement (ORR). The children would become "unaccompanied minors." They would then go through the same process as when they had been separated under Trump's family separation policy (otherwise the children would stay in family detention for the duration of the process). There was a two-fold injustice caveat: First, that children who remained with their fathers in family detention for the duration of the asylum process would grossly exceed the *Flores* limitations for detainment of children (see chapter 4). Second, fathers who released their children to ORR would no longer be detained in the family-friendly facility at Karnes. Instead, the dads would shift over to the regular prison-like facility for the duration of their asylum-seeking process. Of course, these important details probably weren't explained when the fathers were presented with these two options. The pilot program lasted only a few months. Karnes transitioned to a facility for female migrants during the spring of 2019, with the expectation that it would once again be used to detain mothers and children.

OFFICE OF REFUGEE RESETTLEMENT: LOCKING UP CHILDREN

When unaccompanied children arrive to the United States seeking asylum, they're callously labeled Unaccompanied Alien Children (UAC) and placed under the oversight of the ORR. They are detained in facilities during the "due process" meant to unite them with a suitable sponsor, usually a close relative who is waiting to receive them. During fiscal year 2017, more than 134,000 migrant children, from babies to teenagers, were held by the government in for-profit detention centers located across the United States.[9] An advocate for children said, "The detention of children is a crime against our moral fiber. I don't care if you came here legally or not. Leave out all the language about being poor, undocumented, asylum, and illegal. Leave all that out. They are children. They are babies." This advocate emphasized, "No child should ever be detained." Children certainly don't belong in dog kennels, coolers, or massive ORR detention centers. Apprehensions of families and unaccompanied minors at the border increased by roughly 100,000 in 2018.[10] In other words, the number of children detained is going up, not down.

Harsh Treatment of Children

Unaccompanied minors who cross the southern U.S. border every year are subjected to the same dehumanizing treatment as adults. They're locked in the coolers and dog kennels, and then they're taken to for-profit shelters that are overseen by ORR. A pediatrician told the story of going to a processing place for unaccompanied minors. He explained, "I saw them stripped down with all of their belongings—clothing, shoes, and teddy bears. The agent put everything into individual plastic bags, which were then tossed onto a pile in the corner. The mountain of plastic bags grew and grew as several hundred children were 'processed.' Some of the children had phone numbers written on their bodies in permanent ink, a number to family in the U.S. It was a number that could possibly save their lives." The pediatrician said that it might seem like a stretch to go all the way back to Auschwitz, but he believes that concentration camps and detention centers clearly share some strong similarities.

The stories children share about their CBP border experiences are equally harsh. One child said, "It was painful how hungry we were." An eleven-year-old girl shared her experience at the *hielera* known as Ursula, located in McAllen, Texas: "Every time I fell asleep on the concrete floor, the police would come in and kick me. Then I'd fall asleep again and then the police would walk back over and kick me again." Then she asked, "Why did the police do this to me again and again?"

The largest and fastest-growing ORR facility for locking up children was located at the Tornillo Port of Entry in Tornillo, Texas, southwest of El Paso. Known as "Tent City," it opened June 14, 2018. Originally it held about four hundred boys who had been detained after crossing the southwest border unaccompanied or who had been separated from adults during Trump's family separation policy. A reporter who visited the facility said, "It looks just like you see on the news. It's an emergency shelter like you'd use for response to a disaster." The reporter added, "Of course, these children are neither a disaster nor an emergency." Soon after the shooting on October 27, 2018, at Jewish Tree of Life Synagogue, which resulted in eleven fatalities and six injuries, a first-time visitor to Tornillo said, "I went to the concentration camp for children in the desert. I bet Hitler did the same thing. The outside is painted all white with nice signs, and there's even a sculpture out front. It's hard to imagine that they're killing Jews in their synagogue and we're killing children in a white tent city in the desert." Tornillo was intended as a short-term facility, with its initial closure date set to be July 13, 2018. Instead, the facility became designated for teenagers and continued to expand, with the capacity to include up to 3,800 beds, until its closure in January 2019.

It's important to note that a child in detention can't leave. Just like adults who are locked up, they're in custody. They don't have any freedom. A volunteer advocate for children who are detained asked, "Why are they being detained? Why are there children who have aunts, uncles, parents, or older siblings who want to be sponsors and who are willing to take responsibility for the child and yet these kids are still locked up? Why? They are not criminals!" She responded with a sense of angst and disgust, "They are being detained because they are being detained!"

TAXPAYERS FOOT THE BILL

Children and families are disappearing in these state-authorized facilities, which profit from their suffering, while taxpayers foot the bill. How much for-profit detention costs U.S. taxpayers is public information and readily available on the ICE website (https://www.ice.gov). The budget proposal for fiscal year 2019 indicates a decrease in the average daily population of detained refugees to 47,000, which includes a limitation of 2,500 family beds. The average daily rate for the family beds is $318.79 per person per night, a number "calculated by dividing the total funding requirement of $290.9M by the projected ADP [average daily population] of 2,500."[11] The per-person cost, billed to taxpayers, is justified in the name of national security. The United States spends a ton of tax dollars locking up families who are seeking asylum, most of whom have family members living in the United States who would happily host them for free.

The cost to lock up children is much higher. It was nearly $800 per day per child at the Tornillo facility in the desert. Comparatively, it costs $53–$55 per day to have a child in foster care in Texas.[12] An advocate for children said, "These for-profit facilities are in the business of making money from detaining children (and adults). It's a huge profit machine." An immigration attorney who advocates for the rights of detained children said, "The concept of detaining children is deplorable, however you want to conceive of things—religious, theological, ethical, or humanitarian. I'm committed to ending the detention of children, but the for-profit nature is the impediment to ending detention of children."

ABUSE OF POWER

The abuse of power the families and children experience resonates with an argument from ethicist and theologian Reinhold Niebuhr. He proposes, "Since inequalities of privilege are greater than could possibly be defended rationally," the powerful ones in the system look for creative ways to justify any unjust actions, often relying upon their place of privilege to be sufficient justification.[13] Demeaning or demonizing the families situates the guards as more privileged. The actions of the guards will continue to be exonerated as long as society accepts and justifies the ill treatment of the families. The social privilege of the resident guard over the dehumanized migrant continues to justify itself and this injustice continues. Individuals such as judges, guards at a CBP facility, and employees at a for-profit immigrant family detention center would say, "I'm just doing my job. I'm just following orders," conveniently shifting all responsibility up the bureaucratic food chain to the commander-in-chief. Individuals at the bottom are also culpable for the injustice dictated from the top. The collective whole may be more immoral, as Niebuhr proposes, but each person is accountable. Hitler set the agenda, but he didn't enact the evil actions by himself. He had lots of state-funded support. His minions were guilty, too.

PHILOSOPHICAL PERSPECTIVE: DETENTION CENTERS DETERMINE MORAL DNA OF A NATION

Historically, philosophers have examined life in the city to understand the moral DNA of contemporary life. Recently, that context in affluent nations has been replaced with the refugee camp or detention center because these facilities represent, shape, and ultimately determine the public view of a particular state. Hence, how a nation cares for refugees is the essence of who and what the nation values (or does not value).[14] The denial by presidential administrations that there's anything inhumane or unjust about the treatment of refugee families seeking asylum has made immigrant family detention an acceptable norm, lowering the ethical, moral, and philosophical standards of the United States because of how we, as a nation, treat refugees who are desperately seeking asylum.

II

U.S. IMMIGRATION POLICIES AND PRACTICES

4

The Messy Immigration Matrix

The normative international structure that organizes the world into clearly bounded states dates back to the Peace of Westphalia in 1648, which ended the Eighty Years' War. The peacemakers brokered an agreement that determined which lands would remain Catholic, Lutheran, or Calvinist. The agreement also divided Europe into administrative units for political jurisdiction. This was the beginning of the concept of sovereign borders, which ultimately became the basis for the current nation-state organization, which basically gives authority to each state to govern what happens within its borders, including who is allowed admission. We have no say regarding our origin or place of birth. It simply is what it is. Wherever we live is a reality of the moment. The international state system works fine when the Powers That Be govern their subjects justly.

People should have the right to remain in their own homes, but when circumstances beyond their control force them to evacuate against their will, they have the right to seek asylum, the right to be protected through their connection to global citizenship. The international community is supposed to step up to help its global citizens when someone's home country fails to do so. Instead of readily offering aid to people who are seeking safe asylum, affluent nations like the United States use terms like "alien" or "illegal" to maintain their irrefutable claim to who is—or is not—allowed inside their sovereign and sacred borders. Refugees challenge the very notion of how much sovereignty a country should claim, over against what a nation actually does claim as its right.

Figure 4.1. The ACLU hosts a rally in front of the federal courthouse in Brownsville, Texas, on June 28, 2018, to protest family separation.

INTERNATIONAL PROTECTION
FOR REFUGEES SEEKING ASYLUM

Following World War II, the United Nations High Commissioner for Refugees (UNHCR) created the Universal Declaration of Human Rights, which recognized the right to seek asylum from persecution in other countries.[1] Current international refugee protocol includes two fundamental components: the 1951 United Nations Convention Relating to the Status of Refugees, which is a multilateral treaty, and the subsequent Protocol Relating to the Status of Refugees, adopted in 1967, which is simply referred to as the Protocol. The United States is a signatory nation, which means we agree with the parameters specified in these international documents regarding our moral, ethical, and legal responsibilities for refugees seeking asylum. The Convention defines asylum as possible for persons who are unable or unwilling to gain protection from their homeland due to well-founded fear of persecution based on five specific categories:

- race
- religion
- nationality

- political opinion
- membership in a particular social group

The classification "inept government" is not currently identified as guaranteeing an international right to asylum. Nevertheless, government ineptitude is a key contributor to families and unaccompanied minors becoming forced migrants, embarking on what a professor of forced migration and international affairs has termed "survival migration."[2]

Since 1967, the Convention has been a technical tool to determine refugee status around the globe. The Protocol establishes protection for asylum seekers on two critical points: (1) asylum seekers should not be punished for seeking asylum in another country, and (2) based upon the core norm of nonrefoulement, signatory nations should not return asylum seekers to their home country without determining whether or not they have a valid asylum claim. "Nonrefoulement" means asylees should *not* be returned if their lives would be at great risk. Signatory states of the UNHCR Protocol agree to follow up with an asylum policy that offers an option for safety and security for people, like the families from the Northern Triangle, whose lives are in danger. Asylum laws are supposed to prioritize what's best for those seeking safety, over against anything else a receiving nation might want to emphasize. It's not about us. It's about the needs of people desperately seeking asylum.

Glitches in the International Refugee System

A notable glitch in the refugee system is that individual governments remain in control of defining and limiting who and how many people may enter their bounded state. The same governments that are in agreement about the rights for refugees as signatory nations of the Convention, including the United States, also insist that the right to seek asylum does not equate with a nation being required to actually grant asylum. The international state consensus seems to be, "You can ask for asylum, but we have the right to say no." State sovereignty doesn't mean that each nation has the freedom to do whatever it chooses. Rather, each nation is morally constrained. Also, just because a nation has the sovereign authority to make a particular decision, that decision isn't automatically moral, just, or legal. History presents us with plenty of examples otherwise.

Another complication is that there's no international enforcement to back up the Convention's definition of persons whom the international community owes safe asylum. There's also no international entity that holds states accountable when they violate the UNHCR Convention or Protocol. There needs to be some tool for enforcement; otherwise the Convention is a pretty ideal, but without any substance to make the necessary difference in the lives of so many displaced persons.

Asylum seekers from the Northern Triangle also suffer from the double standard that they're forced to show individual fear and threat to life, yet they're lumped together with the violence in their homelands and therefore accused of being a potential "security risk" to the United States. Their unwanted status is further justified by the "illegal entry" they make in their desperate quest to seek safety. Of course, as you will discover in the ensuing chapters, the United States tightens access, changes the rules, and looks for ways to prevent refugees from entering through legal ports of entry.

GLOBAL TRENDS IMPACT FIRST WORLD RESPONSE TO REFUGEES

Global trends impact how affluent nations respond to refugees. The managing director of the Center for Law and Religion and Harold J. Berman Senior Fellow in Law and Religion at Emory University, Silas Allard, highlights what he calls "five legal developments" that are shaping conversations about transnational migration and how the affluent West responds to persons facing impoverishment, violence, and natural disasters in developing or third world countries. He suggests the following five legal developments are about the integrity of a nation construed as nationalism: (1) Brexit, which is driven by migration—the impending exit of the United Kingdom from the European Union; (2) President Trump's push for a wall at the U.S.-Mexico border; (3) restriction of migrants to designated U.S. ports of entry, which are staffed by ICE and CBP personnel; (4) proposal to end birthright citizenship; and (5) externalization of border controls, whereby the vetting of migrants is done outside of a country's own borders (for example, proposals to conduct European asylum screening in Africa). Allard believes these changes impact the demarcation of jurisdiction, of who has responsibility in which territory. He clarifies, "It's about who has responsibility if you are five feet on this side of the line or not." The root of all five legal developments is the concern about security and what to do when there is any sense of threat. He suggests that the securitization argument can be about existential or nonexistential threats.[3] In other words, these trends are based on real or perceived security threats; they could be fact or fiction.

The United States quickly jumped on the bandwagon of enhanced restrictions for asylum seekers. Chapter 6 explains unjust "metering" and other practices the United States has employed to limit access for asylum seekers. Under the "Remain in Mexico" policy, for example, seekers wait on the other side of our border until they're actually granted asylum (if they are). The *Wall Street Journal* reported that this practice became the new norm in December 2018 when the United States "shifted" its border policy to return some migrants to Mexico while their asylum claims slowly creep forward in the U.S. system.[4]

THE MESSY U.S. IMMIGRATION MATRIX

The nature of the life-threatening emergencies facing asylum seekers means they must take decisive action immediately. Lives are at risk. There's no time to dilly-dally. When death is imminent, they start walking north. Before they even cross the international border between Mexico and the United States, they enter what I call the immigration matrix, which pushes against them with a radical *un*welcome that violates the ideals of the international protocol for refugees. I use "immigration matrix" in the most expansive sense, to include literally any person, agency, or entity that interacts or intersects in any capacity with immigration. The largest mass of the matrix encompasses government entities and their employees from the top down; nonprofit agencies; U.S. immigration laws, policies, and practices; lawyers; judges; interreligious faith traditions that do (and do not) assist these families; and the media, regarding how accurately they do (or not not) report the news about refugees seeking asylum. It also includes elected officials and registered voters and all the lobbyists who work for special interest groups to push their agendas through Congress.

The American public is included in this massive matrix. *We the people* are part of it, too. At some point, we must take responsibility for our actions and *in*actions. "We" includes every single employee of for-profit detention centers and government agencies (i.e., ICE and CBP), elected officials from the top to the bottom, and the American public, including registered and eligible unregistered voters. In this chapter, we'll consider the key participants that refugees interact with during their initial hours, days, and weeks upon arrival to the United States. We'll look at some of the other immigration matrix participants in later chapters.

U.S. Immigration Principles vs. Practices and Policies

The United States became technically and officially in compliance with the 1967 Protocol when President Ronald Reagan signed the Refugee Act into law in 1980; it specifies that someone seeking asylum must be physically present in the United States to apply for, and prove, credible fear of "well-founded persecution." The 1980 Refugee Act also stipulates the concept of nonrefoulement, the Convention and Protocol protection priority not to return anyone back to a country where they would face direct threat to life. The language in immigration law includes specific technical terms that define the parameters of who is which type of immigrant. The technicalities contribute to whether or not a migrant is allowed to remain in the United States. In the technical language, an "immigrant" is anyone who seeks to relocate to another country, whether permanently or short-term. The Immigration and Nationality Act (INA) broadly defines an immigrant as "any alien in the United States, except one legally admitted under specific nonimmigrant categories" (section 101(a)(15)). Overall, depending on whether a refugee or asylee has received permission to enter another country, they also may be labeled an "undocumented," "unauthorized," or "illegal" migrant. Remember that a refugee files the paperwork before they enter the United States, and an asylum seeker makes the claim upon arrival.

Immigration to the United States is based on the following principles: the reunification of families, admitting immigrants with skills that are valuable to the U.S. economy, protecting refugees, and promoting diversity. Since the 1920s, family reunification has been the key principle guiding U.S. immigration policy, admitting immigrants based on family relationships. Family reunification was formalized into law with the 1952 INA, with the 1965 amendments (P.L. 89-236) eliminating national quotas, which were seen as discriminatory. Congress passed the Immigration Act of 1990 (P.L. 101-649), which increased total immigration and provided a "permanent annual flexible cap of 675,000 immigrants, and increased the annual statutory limit of family-based immigrants from 290,000 to the current limit of 480,000."[5] There is no predetermined or prescribed cap for refugees or asylees; rather, that limit is set by each sitting U.S. president, in consultation with Congress. On July 18, 2019, the Trump administration began lobbying for an unprecedented zero refugees for 2020.

Family members are prioritized based on the legal status of the petitioning U.S.-based relative and the age, family relationship, and marital status of the prospective immigrant. Congress sets the legal immigration limit for each category of allowable worldwide immigration to the United States. Congress also sets a per-nation cap. As of November 1, 2017, the "visa queue" for family-based immigrants awaiting the numerically limited visas was just under four million people. Congress sets the numbers for the INA, which must be changed through legislation.[6]

THE *FLORES* SETTLEMENT: PROTECTION FOR UNDOCUMENTED CHILDREN IN U.S. CUSTODY

U.S. laws include special protection for children who are undocumented. Hope Frye, an immigration and human rights attorney for more than forty years, explained, "In 1985, fifteen-year-old Jenny Flores was held by the legacy Immigration and Naturalization Service (INS) in a dilapidated hotel in East Los Angeles, along with adults of both sexes, an inappropriate arrangement for anyone, least of all children. Jenny's aunt wanted to sponsor her release, but INS allowed only parents to serve as sponsors. Carlos Holguin, a brilliant human rights lawyer, brought a lawsuit on behalf of Jenny and all the other detained children."[7] The government settled the case in 1997, after taking it to the United States Supreme Court. The government calls it the *Flores* Settlement Agreement and refers to it as FSA. Frye explained, "We call it the *Flores* settlement because we remember the case was about individual children who were represented by a girl whose name was Jenny Flores." The *Flores* settlement sets the nationwide terms and conditions of the detention, release, and treatment of children in immigration custody.[8] It's the rule of law for how undocumented children are supposed to be treated in the United States. The legal definition for "children" in immigration is that they are age seventeen or under. Whether they are traveling with their families or unaccompanied, *Flores* sets the parameters for nominal care immigrant children are to receive when in U.S. custody. The second that children turn eighteen, they age out of ORR and instantaneously become "adults" in the immigration matrix. The protection they were supposed to be afforded as minors in U.S. custody automatically disappears.

Flores sets specific parameters for the maximum allowable number of days (twenty) an undocumented child may be detained. Children also are supposed to be provided with basic necessities. An immigration attorney specified, "Children are to receive basic things like food, water to drink, and hygiene necessities like soap and a shower. *Flores* is basic and doesn't suggest or require that children be housed in the equivalent of a resort or a fancy hotel. They are supposed to receive basic things that constitute humanitarian care. That's not happening." The spectrum of mistreatment at for-profit facilities, which have been contracted under ORR, includes inadequate food, forcing children to take psychotropic medications without parental consent, and children being held for long periods when there are sponsors willing to take them.

In 2015, Judge Dolly Gee of the United States District Court of the Central District of California found that DHS, ICE, and CBP had breached the *Flores* settlement. Frye explained, "Among its many prior and ensuing attempts to minimize culpability, the federal government took her decision to the Ninth Circuit Court of Appeals and argued, among other things, that *Flores* applied only to unaccompanied children. It is important that the Ninth Circuit found that *Flores* applies to all children, whether they arrive with family or unaccompanied." The judge found that CBP had continued its practice of detaining children in "deplorable and unsanitary conditions," which included inadequate access to food and drinking water; inadequate hygiene (e.g., access to a bathroom, soap, towels, and toothbrushes); cold temperatures; and inadequate sleeping conditions, including twenty-four-hour continuous light exposure. Court documents indicate the judge found that CBP failed to advise children of their rights under the *Flores* agreement. CBP also interfered with their right to counsel, failed to make and record ongoing efforts aimed to release these children, commingled children with unrelated adults for extended periods of time, and kept children in locked and unlicensed facilities for weeks or months. Judge Gee gave the government one year to remedy all the violations she found and to comply with *Flores*. Testimonies from migrants and advocates affirm that these *Flores* violations continue.

Trump Administration Attempts to Change *Flores* Stipulations

To circumvent the legal parameters and limitations established by *Flores*, the federal government proposed new regulations on September 7, 2018, regarding the detention of children, which would apply to unaccompanied minors and to children traveling with an adult parent or guardian. Like his predecessor, President Trump justifies this long-term detention of mothers, fathers, boys, and girls as being a deterrent for future immigrant crossings, to ensure appearances at immigration court proceedings, and to protect the legal resident communities from security threats. All three of these trumped-up excuses will continue to be counter-argued by lawyers, advocates, and anyone who has ever personally interacted with refugee families seeking asylum.

As expected, the Trump administration's attempt to circumvent the time limits *Flores* places on holding minors in immigration detention facilities immediately was challenged by lawyers, advocates, and stakeholders who compiled detailed objections to the proposed regulations, which would put *Flores* out of business and keep kids locked up interminably. For example, see the case put forth by Project Lifeline, a nonprofit advocacy group. The overview summary of objections argues, "The Trump Administration maintains that the proposed regulations 'parallel' the 'relevant and substantive terms' of *Flores* and 'implement the substantive and underlying purpose of' the FSA, while departing at times from its 'literal text.' Nothing could be further from the truth." Project Lifeline maintained that, if finalized, the proposed regulations would:

1. permit the indefinite detention of families;
2. cause children to remain in the custody of DHS or the Office of Refugee Resettlement (ORR, a unit within HHS) for longer periods of time, if not indefinitely;
3. make it more difficult, if not impossible, for children to be released from ORR to family sponsors (parents and other relatives); and
4. change the standards of care a facility needs to provide for its resident children, creating unsafe, unhealthy, and dangerous conditions for children.[9]

The comments also charge, "Moreover, this dismantling of protections for children would also incur significant financial costs," which, of course, the U.S. taxpayer would be required to fund.

Flores Violations: Time and Treatment

The current administration is not adhering to the *Flores* settlement regarding the length of time children may be detained. There also are blatant violations of the nominal conditions for basic care the children are required to receive. Court actions against the U.S. government indicate that children are being detained six months or longer, including children who have a close family relative who wants to sponsor them. Frye emphasized, "Children are supposed to be in the system twenty days max. That's not happening. The trend that started in mid-2016 has been to detain unaccompanied children longer and longer." She explained, "The *Flores* agreement says very clearly what the government has to do. It even specifies what they have to do when there is an influx of unaccompanied minor children. The government has never complied throughout any of the administrations since 1997, when the settlement was enacted." She emphasized that *Flores* covers "the basic aspects of care we give all children: food, water, warmth, and adequate medical care. It's about safe and sanitary conditions. It's not, as some suggest, about creating fancy environments."

The presumption under *Flores* is that a child should be in and out of processing as quickly as possible. Frye explained, "Children are to be moved as expeditiously as possible through the detention process so that they arrive, ideally, with their sponsor in less than twenty days. They are only supposed to be held by CBP for seventy-two hours maximum. I've spoken with children who were held by CBP for five days and have been in ORR custody for over nine months and counting." She added, "You'll never hear me say 'detained children,' because that puts the emphasis on detention. Instead, I will say 'children who are detained.' We all need to be aware of the language we use. Sometimes I call the children I meet with 'babies' to emphasize that these are just kids, just like your kids or mine." We don't treat these children like kids; we treat them like criminals.

The Center for Human Rights and Constitutional Law (CHRCL), as class counsel in *Flores*, is responsible for monitoring the government for its compliance with *Flores* and seeking enforcement from the court when the government fails. CHRCL sends lawyers and doctors into detention facilities that hold children to inspect the facilities and to talk with the children about their experiences in detention. What the children say is written into declaration forms. These declarations are the evidence placed before the court that proves governmental noncompliance with *Flores*. Declarations used in court become public when the court papers are filed. Frye leads many of these all-volunteer teams of lawyers and doctors who collect *Flores* accountability testimonies. She explained that they use trauma-informed interviewing to learn how the children are being treated. Then they read the declarations to them in Spanish and the children sign them. Teams visit multiple facilities, and the lawyers and doctors might interview thirty children at each one.

CHRCL then analyzes the testimonies collected from the various facilities, which are located across the United States. Frye explained, "They [the children] don't know each other, and they came from different countries and different points of entry. You might get different details, but the overall responses are consistent when it comes to the children telling what happened since they arrived in the U.S." The name of the court case is always *Flores* vs. whoever the current U.S. attorney general is. Frye added, "The details of what happened to each child are different, but the underlying problems are the same. For example, this child had a cold 'mystery meat' sandwich at one border patrol detention center while another child at a different CBP had uncooked ramen soup." Frye noted, "The judge believes what the children say because of the consistency."

All cases related to the *Flores* Agreement are in the same court. For example, in the June 29, 2018, United States District Court of Central California, Western Division, court case known as *Jenny Lisette Flores, et al.*, [captioned Lucas R.] *v. Jefferson B. Sessions, Attorney General, et al.*, CHRCL includes declarations of children who testified that they were forcibly administered drugs while being detained at the Shiloh Residential Treatment Center, formerly operated as Daystar Treatment Center, in Manvel, Texas, located south of Houston. Frye explained, "Many of these children have come from regular ORR facilities into this nightmare of long-term detention in highly restrictive environments. The children are considered to have mental health or behavioral problems when many simply were depressed, desperate, and confused so they have acted out in ways we would understand. Giving them drugs and putting them in these hellholes is so wrong in every way. It is immoral and criminal." Frye testified before Congress on July 10, 2019.[10]

The stories seem too outrageous to be true; yet there are multiple examples of abusive treatment of children who are detained. Southwest Key ORR facilities in Arizona faced charges for the sexual abuse of minors in their care, including one employee who was convicted and sentenced on January 14, 2019, to serve nineteen years in prison for seven counts of abusive sexual assault with male detained minors. Another employee has charges pending for inappropriately kissing and touching a teenage girl.[11] We add to the injustice when we ignore, disregard, or accept this inexcusable treatment of children.

The suffering of children who are detained is exacerbated by the extensive length of time they're locked up, particularly children who have family members who are ready, willing, and able to sponsor children in their homes. Frye said, "We have obstructed our way to ending children being detained because it has become a big for-profit business." The prison companies are among the biggest lobbyist groups in D.C.[12] Essentially, they lobby for the dehumanization of migrants in order to capitalize private prison companies. Frye added, "Faith-based leaders, and people of conscience, need to stand up and say, 'We see you. We call you out. In the United States we don't lock up children.'" She believes that everyone, no matter what religious or political belief each holds, should share this view. She said, "I heard a pastor in a church that opposed abortion because of the 'sanctity of life' chide the congregation for being inconsistent. The pastor said that sanctity of life means from beginning to end." The pastor called them, as people of faith, to oppose the detention of children and condemn the government for its practices.

Terminal Limbo: Long-Term Detainment of Children

Children are being detained much longer than the very clear stipulations specified in the *Flores* agreement, some as long as nine months. This includes many children who have a relative who has applied to become their sponsor. This unnecessary detention comes at a massive financial cost to U.S. taxpayers. The number of children detained dramatically increased after President Trump took office, hitting a record of 14,000-plus in November 2018.[13]

The excessive number of children and length of time they're detained is directly related to presidential policy changes. On the pretext of fulfilling its obligations to release children into a safe and suitable environment, which is what *Flores* always has maintained, the Trump administration changed the rules and required everyone living in the destination household to be fingerprinted and to have a background check. ICE used the information it collected to arrest and deport undocumented persons in the household that had been planning to sponsor an unaccompanied minor. Instead of helping out their relative and providing free room and board at no cost to U.S. taxpayers, these family members were arrested and deported themselves. No previous administration investigated a potential sponsor's immigration status as part of the consideration for custody of an unaccompanied minor.[14] The zero tolerance policy extended to longtime residents of the United States and prevented unaccompanied minors from being released from the for-profit detention facilities.

A few elected officials directly opposed this policy. The Shut Down Child Prison Camps Act was introduced in the U.S. House and Senate on December 20, 2018. It ordered the governmental agency that has oversight for unaccompanied, undocumented children, the U.S. Department of Health and Human Services, which oversees ORR, to empty out and close two unlicensed detention centers effective immediately.[15] Two days earlier, on December 18, 2018, the administration had lifted its fingerprinting policy for everyone in the household of a sponsor for an unaccompanied child.

While due process was slowly creeping its way to justice for unaccompanied children seeking asylum in the United States, these children were locked up for months in massive facilities, like the "concentration camp in the desert" located in Tornillo, Texas. For example, one teen was locked up at Tornillo for eight months even though she had an aunt who was perfectly willing and able to take responsibility for her. The cost of her detention: approximately $800 per day, for a whopping total of $24,000 per month and $192,000 for her eight-month detention. Multiply these numbers by the 3,800 beds at Tornillo, and the per-day price tag billed to the U.S. government, funded by U.S. taxpayers, was staggering. At the beginning of the 2018 hurricane season, DHS covered the bill by shifting almost $10 million from the Federal Emergency Management Agency to ICE.[16] After months of public outrage and bad publicity directed against the Trump administration, Tornillo finally closed the first week of January 2019.[17]

CRUELTY TO CHILDREN EXTENDS WITH 2019 SECURE BORDER ACT

The Trump administration's cruelty against children ramped up with its 2019 Secure Border Act provisions on immigrant children. In an open letter to friends, colleagues, and advocates for refugee children, attorney Frye explained the ramifications of this government edict for children seeking asylum:

Over the past year immigrant children have increasingly become targets of the Trump Administration's anti-immigrant campaign. Thousands of children have been forcibly separated from their parents (many still not reunited with their mothers and fathers), thousands have been held in cages (the children call them "dog cages"), at least two minors in U.S. custody recently died, and the number of detained unaccompanied minors has skyrocketed to 15,000, not because of a new influx but because this Administration now unreasonably delays releasing them to parents or relatives living in the U.S. Among other tactics that delay and prevent the release of children who are detained, the ORR informs parents and relatives seeking children's release that they will be turned over to ICE for possible arrest and deportation.

I want to let you know about the most recent assault on this vulnerable group.

Dueling bills to end the government shutdown failed in the Senate. Last Friday, agreement was reached to end the shutdown until February 15, 2019. Congress and the White

*House committed to negotiate over the next three weeks border security, relief for DACA
and TPS recipients, and the treatment of immigrant children from Central America. The
issue of Central American children was injected into the shutdown discussion by President
Trump in a January 4, 2019, letter to Congress, and again last week in the Senate's End
the Shutdown and Secure Border Act of 2019 ("2019 Secure Border Act"), that received
fifty votes in the Senate.*

*The 2019 Secure Border Act provisions on immigrant children are illegal and immoral and would lead to the persecution, torture, and undoubtedly the death of Central
American children who seek asylum in the United States.*

*The Act makes children from El Salvador, Guatemala, and Honduras ineligible to
apply for asylum in the United States by providing that they can only apply for asylum
outside of the U.S. at a "Designated Application Processing Center in Central America."
Before applying for asylum there, a child must first apply for asylum with the United
Nations High Commissioner for Refugees (UNHCR), or a non-governmental organization designated by the Secretary of Homeland Security (no details are provided about this
process), and the UNHCR or the non-governmental must advise DHS that the child "is
likely to be eligible for asylum . . ."*

*Even if the child's asylum claim is approved by a U.S. Application Processing Center,
the child will still not be admitted to the U.S. if he or she was previously denied asylum
(even if new facts warrant a different decision) or does not have "a qualified parent or
guardian [living] in the United States capable of taking custody and care of the minor
upon arrival in the United States." About sixty percent of unaccompanied minors do not
have parents or legal guardians living here.*

*Unbelievably, the Secure Border Act requires the immediate deportation of any Central
American child unless the child is the victim of human trafficking.*

*The Unites States is bound by the terms of the 1967 United Nations Protocol Relating
to the Status of Refugees. The Protocol prohibits the deportation of any person, including children, to countries where they face persecution. Our laws governing asylum are
modeled after and conform to the dictates of the Protocol. By denying Central American
children the right to seek and be granted asylum in the United States, the Secure Border
Act violates domestic law and our obligations under international treaties.*

*It's hard to believe that there is so much enmity and vitriol towards children— any
children. That the president would dare to offer these cruel ideas as part of a solution to
any problem is an indictment of the American soul.*

Please feel free to share this email.

Hope[18]

Dismantling the laws that protect migrant children creates an irresponsible response
to the question of how the United States lives up to its legal and moral obligations
per a mouthful of acronyms: IIRIRA, INA, ORR, and UNHCR. The proposed
regulations also disregard U.S. international responsibilities to the Convention and
Protocol. Each presidential administration leaves its thumbprint on the dysfunctional matrix of U.S. immigration control.

5

National Leadership Shapes U.S. Immigration Policies and Practices

A quick surf on social media regarding the southwest border, particularly the migrant caravan stuck in Tijuana because the United States blocked admittance, nets a flurry of comments against the migrants. Typically, they're accused of being "illegal" and violating our rule of law. The reality is quite different. International and U.S. laws are set in place to protect asylum seekers, but these laws are violated with the innovative tactics the various presidential administrations implement to prevent people from pleading their case for asylum on U.S. soil. As immigration attorney Hope Frye explained, "International law says that if they enter and seek asylum, we cannot detain them. The receiving nation must allow them to enter. If they can't make their claim successfully, then they can be ejected. First, they must be allowed admittance, and they must be allowed to make their claim."[1] The United States then has the moral and legal responsibility to provide a reasonable pathway for asylum seekers to make their case for asylum.

The current messy immigration matrix didn't emerge overnight. It's been shaped through the decades, particularly during the past forty years. Policies and practices that interpret U.S. immigration laws change with each sitting U.S. president, the laws and policies enacted by Congress, and how these procedures are interpreted and enforced.[2] Presidential bias makes a tremendous difference in how our immigration laws are interpreted and applied. Frye explained, "Attitude impacts how the rules are interpreted and applied. Not necessarily what they actually say, but the consequences of how the rules will be implemented." For perspective, here's a cheat sheet of U.S. presidents during the past forty years:

- Donald Trump, since 2017
- Barack Obama, 2009–2017
- George W. Bush 2001–2009

- Bill Clinton, 1993–2001
- George H. W. Bush, 1989–1993
- Ronald Reagan, 1981–1989
- Jimmy Carter, 1977–1981

PRESIDENTIAL LIMITS AND U.S. IMMIGRATION LAW: HOW IT WORKS AND HOW IT'S ADMINISTERED

Annually, Congress and the president determine a number for refugee admissions. A newly elected president can negate what his predecessor had established for accepting refugees. The fiscal year 2016 cap for refugees was 85,000.[3] On September 29, 2017, President Donald Trump issued a presidential memorandum to the secretary of state, setting the refugee admissions cap for fiscal year 2018 at 45,000, less than half the cap of 110,000 set by the Obama administration for fiscal year 2017, and a further diminishment from the 50,000 limit Trump had already set in his March 6, 2017, Executive Order 13780. The 2018 cap was the lowest refugee limit since 1980.[4] The Trump-Congress decision to cut the refugee number by almost 60 percent is indicative of an ongoing issue with international response to provide neighborly welcome for global citizens who are in harm's way. Overall, U.S. immigration has always been a very restrictive system of requirements and numerical limits. It's tightly constrained. The legal system isn't available to regular people. Limiting access to the United States, particularly for Latino/a migrants, by using the excuse that they're all "drug dealers, criminals, and rapists"[5] unilaterally denigrates the Hispanic community. It also disregards that, as immigration attorney Frye asserts, "There's an enormous amount of vetting that goes on. We have mechanisms in place to prevent criminals from entering the U.S."

Although the asylum category in U.S. immigration does not technically have a cap, the presidential protocol for cutting the refugee limit suggests a similar unwelcome for asylum seekers. In fiscal year 2014, 23,533 individuals were granted asylum. The actual determination for asylum is made through the U.S. Immigration administrative court system, which is part of the Department of Justice (DOJ). The U.S. attorney general appoints immigration judges and members of the Board of Immigration Appeals, who may or may not have experience in immigration law.

EXPEDITED REMOVAL

Immigrants crossing the Mexico-U.S. border historically were processed by what was termed "catch and release." When migrants were caught who were determined not to be a threat to national security or to the local community, they were immediately released with a notice to appear in immigration court. Those who were considered a threat or unlikely to appear before a court were ejected as soon as they were captured and deported back across the border. Rather than owning our international moral and legal responsibilities to and for asylum seekers, the United States has created laws to ensure that we reject and eject as many migrants as we can, as quickly as possible. Expedited removal was added to INA by the Illegal Immigration Reform and Immigrant Responsibility Act of 1996 (IIRIRA). Before IIRIRA, immigration inspectors didn't have the authority to force arriving noncitizens to leave the Unites States. Expedited removal makes it "legal" for DHS officials to eject or deport noncitizens who come to the United States without proper authorization. The expedited removal laws also specify that asylum seekers are subject to mandatory detention until an asylum officer makes the preliminary determination that there is credible fear (see chapter 7). The point of mandatory detention is to verify identities and to ensure asylum seekers appear for their hearings or removals.

IIRIRA was not intended to limit or deter legitimate asylum seekers from entering the United States at any legal port of entry so they could then make their case for asylum. When expedited removal initially was implemented in March 1997, the DOJ applied it only to arriving noncitizens at ports of entry, which expanded in November 2002 to apply to undocumented non-Cubans who had entered the United States by sea within the prior two years. Less than two years later, in August 2004, DHS applied expedited removal to all undocumented non-Cubans who were apprehended within fourteen days after entry within one hundred miles of the U.S. international land border. The procedures that supported expedited removal initially were executed in the Laredo, Texas, and Tucson, Arizona, sectors. Then, in September 2005, expedited removal applied to the entire southwest U.S. border.

It's no surprise that the countries with the largest number of noncitizens deported through expedited removal are Mexico, Guatemala, Honduras, and El Salvador. Skimming over annual Immigration Enforcement Actions reports, available online through the DHS Office of Immigration Statistics, confirms that these four countries bear the brunt of deportations due to INA and U.S. immigration policies and practices, accounting for as much as 98 percent of expedited removal deportations in recent years.[6] The title for current U.S. immigration policy could simply be "Central Americans NOT Welcome." Whatever remaining catch-and-release was being done, it officially ended in 2006 under the George W. Bush presidential administration. Later policies instituted during the Barack Obama presidential administration have been labeled catch-and-release, but there was more catching than releasing. The stage was set to ramp up detaining mothers and children, initially together and later splitting children apart from their mothers and incarcerating them separately. The Trump administration's spin on immigration procedures upped the ante from catch-and-release to catch-and-*detain*, as President Trump tweeted in late 2018:

> Migrants at the Southern Border will not be allowed into the United States until their claims are individually approved in court. We only will allow those who come into our Country legally. Other than that our very strong policy is Catch and Detain. No "Releasing" into the U.S. . . .
> 3:49 PM–24 Nov 2018

Migrants are detained only long enough for expedited removal.

The term "expedited removal" makes it sound clean and neat, but it's actually a very complicated administrative process. Acronyms can become dizzying, so here are the full names of the key players with the abbreviations afterward: Expedited removal is carried out by multiple agencies of the U.S. Department of Homeland Security (DHS). U.S. Customs and Border Protection (CBP) makes the preliminary determination at the border during a "screening" interview. U.S. Immigration and Customs Enforcement (ICE) detains (locks up) asylees and makes parole decisions about when/if to release asylum seekers from detention. For asylum seekers, due process also involves U.S. Citizenship and Immigration Services (USCIS), which conducts the asylum interview and decides whether each migrant has credible fear of persecution. The Executive Office for Immigration Review (EOIR) and the U.S. Department of Justice (DOJ) also are involved. Persons who are not deemed "arriving aliens" are eligible for bonds, and an immigration judge within the EOIR, a branch of the DOJ, may review the bond amounts. Most asylum seekers can't afford to hire an attorney, and the court doesn't appoint one for them. They must make their case on their own, including unaccompanied children.

Once an individual has passed through the initial hoops at the border and moved up the food chain to "detainment," generally in a for-profit prison facility, an immigration judge is responsible for deciding whether the asylee will be deported. The key factor is to prove credible fear of persecution or torture if they were to return to their country of origin. If the asylum officer determines that the person doesn't have credible fear of direct persecution and threat to life, the person is deported via "expedited removal" without first having had the opportunity to appear before an immigration judge. Any asylum seeker who does not pass this initial credible fear examination by immigration officers at the border/point of entry to the United States is "barred from returning to the U.S. for at least five years (but often much longer)."[7] A second attempt to cross "illegally" guarantees an extended sentence in a for-profit prison.[8]

OPERATION GATEKEEPER

Operation Gatekeeper began October 1, 1994, with the DHS strategy to increase the number of border agents at the busiest crossing points along the U.S.-Mexico border while also increasing the amount of fencing used in the highly traveled sections. It began with George W. Bush but became streamlined during President Obama's tenure. It's called a "consequence delivery system," which punishes migrants for coming into this country, but also makes it more difficult for ejected migrants ever to come back.

John Fife, pastor of Southside Presbyterian Church in Tucson, Arizona, when it became a sanctuary church in January 1982 for refugees from Central America, explains that the strategy behind Operation Gatekeeper was to block the heavily traveled urban sections of the border by building eighteen-foot steel walls and adding four times the number of border agents. By blocking the most popular border crossing areas, migrants would be forced farther out into the desert. The theory was that the risk factors of the desert would deter migrants from making the much more life-threatening crossing.[9] Instead of two and a half days, the migrants suffer the risks of the desert for four to six days. Instead of being a deterrent, Operation Gatekeeper causes more migrant deaths, as the Red Dot Map in Arizona attests.

OPERATION STREAMLINE

The rule of law of any nation is not a guaranteed good thing. It can't be overstated that history shows that the powerful make unjust laws all the time. Slavery was the law. Disenfranchisement of women and people of color was the law. Segregation was the law. It's an inappropriate argument to stand on the rule of law alone. Just because something is a "law" doesn't mean that it's even remotely about justice. Rather, it can, and often is, intended to keep the powerful in power and the weak marginalized and without voice.

Operation Streamline is a perfect example of current injustice done in the name of the law. This government initiative criminally prosecutes unauthorized border crossers. Streamline began in Del Rio, Texas, on December 16, 2005, and expanded to

Figure 5.1.   A sketch of Operation Streamline proceedings in Tucson, Arizona, on August 27, 2018.
Courtroom sketch by Helen T. Boursier.

every border state except California. When the Trump administration's zero tolerance prosecution policies began in 2018, a new Streamline court was added in San Diego.

Before Operation Streamline, most migrants were in civil deportation proceedings, while criminal charges were reserved for repeat offenders and for people who had real criminal records. Operation Streamline courts are criminal courts. In Streamline courtrooms, unlike most federal prosecutions, judges condense the entire criminal proceeding—including initial appearance, plea, and sentencing—into a few hours on a single day. Although it's the current rule of law, Operation Streamline is assembly-line *in*justice that focuses on rapid deportation and/or filling up privatized for-profit prisons. Every migrant who goes through Streamline is considered a criminal. The United States provides a court-appointed attorney, which the judge makes a point to tell the accused is "at no cost to you." These court-appointed attorneys meet with their client during the morning for about thirty minutes. They're seated at tables in an open room that offers no client-attorney privacy. In fact, the human trafficker who "guided" a migrant across the border could be seated at an adjacent table, affording no sense of safety to the migrant sharing self-testimony with an attorney. The group court proceedings are held during the afternoon of the same day. Convicted migrants are either deported or brought to detention centers at the close of the court session.

It's a stunning experience to observe Operation Streamline. Defendants are shackled at the hands, waist, and feet and brought en masse into a Streamline courtroom. In Tucson, the shackles are removed before the line of seven defendants enters the courtroom and stands behind the microphones placed across the front of the courtroom. All are advised of their charges, waive their constitutional rights, plead guilty to entering at a place other than a port of entry, and are sentenced. The option of asylum rarely is a consideration in a Streamline courtroom because it's a criminal courtroom that functions completely separately and independently from U.S. Immigration.

Mass-Production Injustice

Operation Streamline is a fast track to deportation preceded by filling the pockets of private detention facilities, which profit at the expense of taxpayers and the gross injustice against primarily Central American migrants. In two to three hours, up to one hundred migrants are judged, sentenced, and deported or sent to serve more time in prison. First-time border crossers are charged with illegal entry, which is a criminal misdemeanor, punishable by up to six months in prison. First-time border crossers in Streamline usually get a sentence of time served, and will be deported quickly back to their home country. If they're from Mexico, they'll be sent back to Mexico immediately after the court proceedings conclude. If they're from Guatemala, El Salvador, or Honduras, they'll be put in for-profit detention centers until there's enough migrants from one country to fill a government plane, which drops them off in their home of origin.

Repeat crossers get a minimum thirty-day jail sentence. An advocate for migrants in Arizona explained, "If they previously have been in the U.S. and have a driver's license, that pumps up the days. If they entered in Texas and now they reenter in Arizona, that is considered 'lateral repatriation' and they get another thirty days tacked on to the sentence. They also will be charged with illegal reentry, which the government knows because they scanned the [finger]prints. That bumps it up to becoming a felony, which carries two to ten years with a ban for reentry for ten additional years."

Most first-time border crossers who are charged with illegal entry plead guilty and get a sentence of time served, which means the time that they have been in Border Patrol detention before going to court. They're deported with a criminal conviction on their record. It's only a misdemeanor, but it's considered a "criminal record" nonetheless. Those charged with illegal reentry are offered a plea bargain. If they agree to plead guilty to the lesser violation of illegal entry, the felony charge of illegal reentry will be dropped. An Arizona advocate said, "The migrants take what the attorneys offer, which generally is to reduce it to a misdemeanor for 30–180 days, six months max, and be deported. Or they risk ten to twenty years." After serving the sentence, immigrants will be deported to their home country with a criminal conviction on their record, which means that they probably will never be eligible for any path to citizenship because of this "criminal" record of "illegal entry." Another Arizona advocate for migrants said, "On the off chance that someone asks for asylum and is deemed eligible for asylum, they would be held at the private for-profit detention center at Eloy [Arizona], located in the middle of nowhere." With the massive backlog of asylum cases pending, those relegated to any privatized detention center will be stuck behind bars for several years.

Operation Streamline in Tucson

The migrants arrive at the Evo A. DeConcini U.S. District Courthouse, located at 405 West Congress Street, at 9 a.m. shackled together. They spend the morning there, where they will eventually be interviewed by one of the court-appointed lawyers. There are sixteen lawyers who will each have four or five clients to meet with during the morning. After lunch, the hearings take place seven at a time in the courtroom. A volunteer who witnesses Operation Streamline proceedings in this Tucson courtroom every Monday explained, "They used to bring the migrants in [the courtroom] shackled, but now they unshackle them, so they have more U.S. marshals there to offset the possibility of [hostile action by] these 'dangerous' criminals." The witness continued, "Generally, about half will be charged with a misdemeanor for 'illegal entry' and the other half will be charged with a felony because of an illegal reentry." This witness and advocate said that when three people in one felony group asked for a classification of credible fear, the prosecutor stood up and said, "You cannot have 'credible fear,' but you could have 'reasonable fear,' which requires more documentation."

The following are verbatim excerpts from the Operation Streamline proceedings I witnessed at the federal courthouse in Tucson on August 27, 2018. The defendants entered in single file through the doorway on the right side of the courtroom, each one stopping to stand behind one of the seven microphones placed in a straight line before the judge's bench. They turned and faced the judge and held their hands behind their backs. It was unsettling to see a hospitality table located just out of reach of the row of defendants. The table contained pitchers of water and stacks of paper cups. It's water these migrants desperately needed during their journey through the Sonoran Desert, and it represents hospitality they did not, and will not, receive in the United States. Meanwhile, the lawyers stood behind their clients and whispered among themselves while the judge rapidly mumble-read the charges and rights to each defendant. They were required to respond in Spanish (even if they spoke English).

Judge: Do you understand your rights?

Migrant: *Sí* (yes).

Judge: Do you waive your rights to a trial?

Migrant: *Sí* (yes).

Judge: Do you understand the rights, consequences, and convictions?

Migrant: *Sí* (yes).

Judge: We have before the court the following individuals . . . All of you are represented by lawyers at no cost to you. You have to decide today how you want to plead. Do you understand these rights and consequences and do you waive these rights? All of you are guilty. Counsel, you may step back.

When one migrant opted to plead not guilty, instead of taking the plea bargain, the judge asked, "Do you understand it is sixty days?" The migrant responded, "*Sí*" (yes). The judge clarified, "Do you want to go to court?" The migrant responded, "*Sí*" (yes).

Through a translator, a defendant who'd been sentenced to six months in jail said, "I apologize a thousand times over, but I have severe claustrophobia and I fear I will make an attempted suicide." The judge responded, "I can only tell you that you will find the strength to make the sixty days. If you plead not guilty, your incarceration would be much longer. You lost the right to be free when you made the illegal entry to the U.S." Then the judge asked the lawyer standing behind the convicted migrant, "He previously has been in custody for only a short period of time?" After the lawyer responded "Yes," the judge looked at the migrant and said, "Try to make it."

When a lawyer called the judge on being out of order with his questions to another row of seven migrants standing before the microphones during the same Operation Streamline proceedings, the judge had the court reporter read back his questions and then he asked them again. After the questions had been reread in the correct order, through a translator, the defendant said, "I accept my responsibilities." After this row of seven had been convicted within a ten- to fifteen-minute period, the migrants walked back out of the courtroom single file, and a few minutes later another other row of seven migrants filed into the courtroom to stand behind the microphones and make their short responses to the judge in this mass-production deportation system of so-called justice. The process builds up the criminalization of migrants and pushes a civil violation into a criminal violation.

A summary of the proceedings for Operation Streamline, filed on the Green Valley-Sahuarita Samaritans website for this particular day, includes the following report documented by volunteer Katrina Schumacher:

Magistrate Judge Bernardo P. Velasco, 1:40–3:00
15 attorneys, Christopher Lewis Federal Prosecutor
Observers: Pastor Randy and about 70 plus assorted clergy from all over the United States. Amazingly, all were able to fit using the seats in the middle as well as those on the left.

75 migrants were on the docket including 9 women. There were 57 Mexicans, 8 from Guatemala and 5 from Honduras. No country of origin was given for the 4 dismissed at the beginning. 27 people were arrested near Sasabe, 13 near Nogales, 9 each near Naco, Douglas and Lukeville and 1 each near Ruby and Hereford. 10 migrants were arrested 5-6 days after the date they gave for entrance into the country. One woman's entry date was 9 days before her arrest.

4 people were dismissed at the start of proceedings—most likely for language.

Sergio Melgoza Barbosa 18-32148M (Atty either Fernanda Muñoz or Jessica Ruiz—a substitute) was continued until September 17th at 9:45. Mr. Melgoza wanted to request asylum.

The 28 remaining misdemeanor cases were all sentenced to 'time served.'

The 45 migrants charged with 1325-1326 had no asylum requests.

Robert Oriel Figueroa Martinez 18-32124M (Atty Bert Vargas) from Mexico made a statement to the court. He said he had severe claustrophobia and could not control it. He apologized many times. He said he was afraid if he was incarcerated it might lead to suicide. Judge V. said, "your ability to remain unconfined ended when you were arrested." The judge essentially told him to stay strong. The statement is on the record. Is there any way of finding out where he is and sending someone in to evaluate the situation? 60 days.

This group was sentenced to 2,340 days of incarceration. At $161 per day that's $376,740 of our tax dollars at work. Several migrants made requests which were granted but the judge can only recommend—the Bureau of Prisons has the final say.

I had on earphones and heard [Judge] Velasco say just before he came back to answer questions [from the visiting clergy], "I'll be Daniel in the lion's den." The questions [from the clergy] were wide ranging. Was due process possible in this setting, could he have done something else with the claustrophobic man? How about quotas? Answer: "We elected a president who wants increased prosecution. Here we are. Here we are."[10]

Following the rapid-fire convictions of all seventy-five migrants, the judge graciously held a short question and answer session with this courtroom filled with advocates for migrants. I asked the judge, "What would it take so that it might be possible for an asylum claim to be considered in the same context as this illegal entry charge?" He responded, "It is not possible. You have to keep questions about asylum and immigration enforcement separate." I followed up and asked, "Is it possible for the two related concerns to ever meet at some point in the future?" The judge said, "No. Not possible. One is criminal court and the other involves immigration court. The two are separate with distinct laws, parameters, and functions." He added, "We elected a president who wants increased prosecution and that's what we get. The majority of Americans voted. The majority said we want this. It doesn't matter what it costs for the attorney fees or detention. If the American people vote for it, it is what they are going to get." He concluded his Q&A session with the packed courtroom of advocates by saying, "I try to get you to go out and gather up political support and still you keep coming to see me. I am just upholding the law as set by the politicians in Washington." The American people have a very expensive mass-production system of injustice that costs taxpayers a bundle. As the judge pointed out, we voted for it. We also pay for it.

Whopping Costs to U.S. Taxpayers

It's impossible to determine exactly how much Operation Streamline costs U.S. taxpayers, but the sum total of all the options would be a whopper.[11] The tally would cover costs for courtrooms, prosecutors, defense attorneys, U.S. marshals, court interpreters, transportation, and detention center beds per person per night. A report from Grassroots Leadership estimated that incarceration costs for all of the Streamline convictions for the first ten years (2005–2015) totaled $7 billion.[12] Factor in the billions of dollars we spend on militarization of the border, detention, and deportation, and there's a ton of taxpayer money that could be spent on humanitarian assistance instead.[13]

ZERO TOLERANCE AND FAMILY SEPARATION

Announcing the zero tolerance policy at a law enforcement conference in Scottsdale, Arizona, then attorney general Jeff Sessions declared, "If you are smuggling a child then we will prosecute you, and that child will be separated from you as required by law."[14] The caveat "as required by law" was a Trump administration innovation to justify its subsequent family separation policy and practices. An immigration attorney explained, "Zero tolerance means that every adult who crosses the border at an unauthorized place will be prosecuted. So they're prosecuting seventy people a day who don't have any idea why they are being prosecuted." The attorney added, "Essentially, zero tolerance means prosecution." When he announced the zero tolerance mandate, Sessions specified, "If you don't like that, then don't smuggle children over the border," which indicates the Trump administration has very little knowledge of, or respect for, the violence that forces families to flee their homelands to seek asylum in the United States. Instead these families disappear from public sight with trumped-up legal language to justify violating the Convention and Protocol as families are separated and locked in separate for-profit detention facilities.

A volunteer who sits in the federal courtroom in Tucson once a week to document Operation Streamline deportation hearings explained that when zero tolerance and family separation were implemented, the defendants who entered the courtroom were sobbing. The volunteer said, "The first day nobody knew what had happened. The judges didn't know and the lawyers didn't know." As the injustice continued through the ensuing few months, the volunteer reported that some of the lawyers were not cooperating. Instead, "They were showing civil disobedience and dragging their feet."

The policy to force children to part from their parents is a chilling parallel to Nazi Germany and the thousands of children who were separated from their parents across Europe.[15] In his memoir *Night*, Elie Wiesel immortalized his painful forced separation from his mother when he was a teenager and his family arrived at Birkenau, reception center for Auschwitz: "'Men to the left! Women to the right!' Eight words spoken quietly, indifferently, without emotion. Eight short, simple words. Yet that was the moment when I was parted from my mother."[16] Much more recently, Russian president Vladimir Putin has been accused of taking children from their parents as a form of state terror.[17]

As a result of these two policies—unilaterally enacted without the constitutional due process Americans would expect as normative for such grandiose policy and procedural changes impacting thousands of refugees seeking asylum—children were forcibly separated from their parents for months. Babies, young children, and teenagers were packed off to separate facilities, including siblings being locked up in different facilities and cities across the United States. Advocates and media focused their attention on 2,337 as the official number of children who were separated, but the *Wall Street Journal* reported, "Thousands more children were separated from their parents by U.S. immigration workers at the border."[18] The actual number remains unknown. A human rights attorney said, "Instead of calling it 'family separation,' call it what it is: kidnapping children, which is exactly what Hitler did." By the time the fiasco was beginning to be corrected, some parents already had been deported and others could not be located within the massive system of immigrant detention.[19] The emotional scars on these separated families will last a lifetime.

INCONSISTENCY AND IMPROMPTU RULE-CHANGING

As you can see, the rules change on a whim, not the laws per se, but how one person in office decides to interpret and apply previously existing statutes. Zero tolerance and family separation were created by the Trump administration. Congress didn't change any of our immigration laws. Federal law doesn't require separating families at the border. The Trump administration unilaterally enacted these "laws" on May 7, 2018, for families crossing the southwest border "unlawfully." Random acts of inconsistency also seem to be the norm, including when, how, and how many families are released from government facilities at the border and allowed to continue on to their relatives in the United States. Following a flood of unexpected mass releases during October and November 2018, which came in anticipation of the massive migrant caravan's arrival at the Texas-Mexico border, a doctor who volunteers at a clinic for migrants at that border said, "I believe this is planned chaos. We are not ready. No backup supplies. Not enough volunteers. We are running out of meds." Immigration practices have been more dictatorship than democracy, which means all participants in this democracy are culpable for not fulfilling our requisite roles in the checks and balances that keep a democracy honest, forthright, and truly by the people and for the people.

OPERATION FAITHFUL PATRIOT

In a show of presidential force with Election Day 2018 approaching, President Trump ordered the Pentagon to deploy U.S. troops to the southwestern border to stave off the migrant caravan that was slowly making its way through Mexico. More than 7,000 active duty troops were deployed to assist CBP and the 2,100 National Guard soldiers who already had been sent to the border. The troops installed barbed wire fencing along the border and camped out in anticipation of mothers, fathers, boys, and girls arriving somewhere along the Texas-Mexico border to request asylum. They ultimately arrived Thanksgiving weekend in Tijuana, Mexico, at the Mexico-California border. What began as Operation Faithful Patriot to "defend" the nation against the caravan of migrants became known as "border support" when the Pentagon later announced it had nixed the original name because an operation was specifically a military event, and assisting at the border did not qualify.

The outcome of the operation turned border assistance remains pending as the asylum seekers are stuck south of the border while the United States maneuvers to keep these refugees seeking asylum out of the country. American response to the migrant caravan is a magnification of a double delusion: (1) the migrants are "illegal," and (2) this "one nation under God" upholds the law with honesty, integrity, and justice. A reality check verifies that U.S. policies and practices continue to push against, and violate, U.S. *and* international law for refugees seeking asylum.

6

Reality Check

Blatant Violations against Asylum Seekers at the Southern Border

Theoretically, human sacredness is at the core of the principles, policies, and practices governing the United States, including refugees seeking asylum here. The families and children seeking asylum experience a very different version than the ideal enshrined in the founding documents for this nation. Instead of justice, they often experience flagrant violations of national and international laws regarding the treatment of refugees seeking asylum.

HOW THE U.S. ASYLUM PROCESS IS SUPPOSED TO WORK

With the 2019 End the Shutdown and Secure the Border Act, the Trump administration is pushing the asylum process so it begins outside of the United States.[1] Meanwhile, the asylum process is supposed to begin when an asylum seeker enters the United States and tells a border agent that they're seeking asylum. The U.S. official should document this statement and follow procedures to ensure that the immigrant's asylum request is evaluated fairly. The complex process includes an initial screening known as a "credible fear" or "reasonable fear" interview (see chapter 7), which is conducted by a U.S. Immigration official, sometimes at the border point of entry and other times after the asylum seeker has been locked up in a for-profit detention center. Persons who flunk this initial screening are deported. Technically they may appeal the ruling, but it is more likely that they will be deported back to their country of origin without any option for recourse.

The process for persons who pass the initial screening varies dramatically with no particular rhyme or reason to the pattern. Some are sent to a for-profit detention facility and locked up at taxpayer expense for months or years while their case slowly makes its way through the backed-up immigration court system. Others are released into the custody of a family member or close friend who has passed the vetting process, not unlike a U.S. citizen being released on bail into the custody of a family member. Some are required to wear ankle monitors, what the families refer to as a *grillete* (fetter or shackle) for the duration of the pending asylum process; others are released without the *grillete*. Americans fancy up this monitor by calling it an "ankle bracelet," like it's a piece of jewelry, but it's not pretty or comfortable. It's yet another way for corporate America to profit at the physical and emotional expense of migrants.

A mother from Honduras whose children were taken from her when she crossed the U.S.-Mexico border to request asylum said, "The rules change all the time." She explained that she paid $1,500 in bond money and was released without having to wear the *grillete*, but eight days later she saw a large group of mothers who had *grilletes* on their legs and they'd paid the bond money, too. Maria (not her real name) said, with a laugh, "I paid the money. They can throw my *grillete* in the trash." Other families are released from border facilities and allowed to continue on to their family members in the United States without being locked up in detention facilities and before passing the credible fear interview, but with the *grillete*. A volunteer with refugee families responded to an October 2018 update about mass releases with the ankle monitor, stating, "They act like the credible fear interview decides everything, yet they release families from the border all the time without them!" Sometimes they do; sometimes they don't. There doesn't seem to be any consistency as to which policies are enacted at the border, on whom, or for what reason.

Whenever the asylum seeker's case finally makes it to the courtroom, they must prove that they have the "well-founded fear" requirement per the UNHCR Protocol and U.S. Immigration parameters noted earlier. The process to become an authorized refugee is complicated, tedious, and painfully slow. In the simplest terms, using acronyms for the key players, the process goes like this:

> Adult: CBP → ICE → USCIS interview for credible fear →
> notice to appear → release or deportation → appeals
> Unaccompanied Minor: CBP → ORR (twenty-day max
> hold per *Flores*) → release to sponsor

That's how it's supposed to work, but it often doesn't. Instead, injustice begins before an asylum seeker even enters the United States, as our government officials use several strategies, authorized from the Powers That Be higher up in the immigration matrix, to turn back migrants who are deemed "inadmissible." Ethicist Joseph Carens cautions that, instead of focusing on how much "burden" we as a nation are expected to bear in welcoming and assisting refugees seeking asylum, "the much more important issue is the moral wrong involved in the use of techniques of exclusion to keep the numbers within bounds."[2] In other words, we need to be looking at the harm, injustice, and moral horror that we perpetuate at our southern border in the name of rule of law, a rule of law that our government opts to tweak, adapt, invent, and/or flat disregard at will.

FLAGRANT INJUSTICE AT THE BORDER

Soon after family separation began, two volunteers from the Interfaith Welcome Coalition (IWC) in San Antonio traveled to the Texas-Mexico border on a fact-finding mission to discern what was and what was not being reported by the media. They went to the McAllen-Hidalgo International Bridge. Their eyewitness account reported, "As we walked to the Mexican side of the bridge we saw and took pictures of three CBP officers blocking the U.S. Port of Entry (POE) on the other side." After they completed their visit to a refugee ministry in Mexico, the witnesses relayed, "We saw the CBP officers standing and blocking access at the middle of the bridge at the U.S./Mexico line." There was a young mother with four children on the Mexico side of the line, seeking asylum in the United States. One of the volunteers spoke with the mother to confirm that she was seeking asylum and had been denied access. The other volunteer told the two CBP officers that mother was seeking asylum and was legally allowed to enter the United States. Both officers responded that they could not let the mother enter because the facility was already overcrowded. The volunteers found a shelter for the mother and her children in Mexico, and then continued through the checkpoint to the United States. The volunteers said, "We observed only seven people in the waiting area described as 'overcrowded' by CBP supervisors."[3]

More and more, stories have slipped through the gatekeepers' net that suggest an inconsistent and even flagrant disregard for the international right these families have to seek asylum. For example, a mother walked across the bridge at Matamoros, Mexico, on February 2, 2017, with her three-year-old son and presented herself to the U.S. Border Patrol at Brownsville, Texas, to request asylum; she recounted that the border patrol gave her two options: (1) sign a piece of paper saying she was *not* afraid to return to her home country, and then they would reunite her with her son (who was not with her during that interrogation session) and release both of them back to Mexico; or (2) sign that she *was* afraid to return to her home country, and then they would send her on to continue the asylum process, but they would keep her son. It was a *non*-choice: she signed that she was *not* afraid and they were deported. These refugees from Honduras—mother and son—walked back across the bridge to Mexico.

The Mexico side of the international border is not a safe place. When refugees seeking asylum are blocked from legal access, they become prey to horrendous dangers, as described by a 2017 Human Rights First report: "Cartels, smugglers, and traffickers—who control areas around border crossings and wait outside some ports of entry where they see migrants and asylum seekers as easy prey—have kidnapped, raped, and robbed asylum seekers wrongly turned away by the U.S. government."[4]

Amidst this appalling moment-to-moment threat to life, this mother and son managed to survive while they stayed just across the border in Mexico for a week or so. Then they walked *back* across the bridge and presented themselves to CBP a second time. The mother told the border patrol that if they were going to deport them, they needed to deport them back to her country and *not* back to Mexico. The border patrol sent them both to the *perrera* and from there to the family detention facility at Dilley, where the mother passed the credible fear interviews and continued on with her son to her brother, who lived in Dallas. I asked the mother how she knew to present herself again. Had someone told her to do so? The mother replied, "No, but the idea of walking all the way back to Honduras was too horrible to consider, so I presented myself again." I responded that she had *mujeres cojonas* and the mother laughed.[5] How many (unknown) others have had a similar experience? The immigration agents at the border who make the determination that a staggering number of those who seek access to the United States are, in fact, "inadmissibles," suggests that due process is being disregarded.[6] The mother and son had presented themselves for asylum at a "legal" point of entry, yet they were treated in the same demeaning manner as "illegal aliens" who "sneak across" the border.

Blocking Bridges and Turning Back "Inadmissibles"

The eyewitness account of CBP blocking the McAllen-Hidalgo International Bridge and the threats and coercion against the mother and son from Honduras exemplify the current official policy and practices of blocking bridges with what CBP calls "turnbacks" to prevent "inadmissibles" from applying for asylum in the United States. Congress, through IIRIRA, specifies that "inadmissibles" include anyone who presents fraudulent or no documents.[7] Human rights advocates first noticed and challenged the turnback practice in March 2016. It's become an increasingly common policy and practice along the southern border.[8] It violates the international moral and legal obligations of nonrefoulement (see chapter 4), which the United States has as a signatory nation of the UNHCR Convention and the 1967 Protocol. Nonrefoulement applies to any refugee seeking asylum, whether they enter the United States through a "legal" or "illegal" point of access. It also applies to refugees attempting to seek asylum, while they're standing on the other side of the bridge and asking to be let in.

The increasing turnback practice also violates U.S. immigration law, which specifies the right to ask for asylum in the United States. INA creates the legal parameter that "any alien who is physically present in the United States or who arrives in the United States (whether or not at a designated port of arrival and including an alien who is brought to the United States after having been interdicted in international or United States waters), irrespective of such alien's status, may apply for asylum in accordance with this section or, where applicable, section 1225(b) of this title."[9] In 1996, Congress added the phrase "whether or not at a designated port of arrival" as part of IIRIRA, which broadens the access for refugees to seek asylum to include "illegal" points of entry, but without the "illegal" label, which has been charged against families seeking asylum by the current presidential administration.[10]

An independent study conducted by Human Rights First at several U.S. ports of entry along the U.S.-Mexico border documented individuals and families who were "wrongfully denied access to U.S. asylum procedures." The report specifies, "In the wake of the election and President Trump's January executive orders relating to refugees, CPB agents have in some cases claimed the United States is no longer accepting asylum seekers." Examples of CBP officer explanations include "Trump says we don't have to let you in" and "[Christians] are the people we are giving asylum to, not people like you." The report is based on 125 cases of individuals and families that CBP wrongfully denied access to make a formal asylum application. Instead, they were rejected outright and logged as "inadmissibles."[11]

These new border access controls are part of CBP's "metering" or "queue management" effort, so-called legal practices that violate preexisting U.S. and international laws. *The Guardian* reported detailed examples of asylum seekers who attempted entry at various remote ports of entry along the southern border, and the irresponsible and unjust response of border officials who outright rejected these vulnerable families seeking asylum. One example after another confirms U.S. complicity in a spectrum of offenses meted out against asylum seekers, denying them access to the United States to file their formal claim.[12]

For example, after visits to Nogales and Ciudad Juárez, Mexico, the Southwest Conference minister for the United Church of Christ (UCC), Bill Lyons, sent an email update on border and migrant assistance ministries. During his visit, the United States was gearing up in response to the infamous migrant caravan from Honduras. He confirmed that there were more than forty-eight families waiting in Nogales, Sonora, Mexico, for their turn to apply for entry into the United States. Lyons wrote, "Department of Homeland Security (DHS) agents are deliberately slowing the application process and accepting only two families per day. Migrants are forced to find food and shelter for a long wait at the ports of entry." The wait time in Nogales was approximately twenty-four days, but it was up to forty-two days in Tijuana. The long delay forced migrants to seek access to the United States at unauthorized points of entry. Lyons reported, "Migrants are not sneaky about it; in fact, the majority of them seek out border patrol agents to which they surrender, hoping that their basic needs will be met and that agents will be forced to process their entry applications." Instead, the "illegal entry" nets an Operation Streamline fast track to deportation.

Lyons's report indicated that the migrant shelters he visited in Mexico were full and working to open additional bed spaces. He said none of their ministry partners expressed being overwhelmed. Instead, they were "working hard retooling to accommodate the backlog of migrants being created by DHS's delay tactics." He relayed the insights he gained from migrant stories and from the medically documented conditions of the seven-hundred-plus migrant families welcomed in one week at churches throughout Arizona. He reported,

> We learned that while they were in detention migrants received inadequate nutrition, inadequate medical care, and were exposed to harsh environmental conditions that left them sick and weak upon release. Almost everyone released [from immigrant detention] required medical attention. A number of children required hospitalization (some of them in ICU). Several babies were near dehydration because their parents were not provided with adequate water and formula to give them. Some parents reported dipping toilet water to give their children in order to keep them hydrated.[13]

Government officials may justify their actions by saying that they're not denying access to asylum but simply processing applicants as space allows. However, our government is using unjust and illegal practices that harm refugees seeking asylum, forcing them to wait an average of two to three weeks on the very risky, life-threatening Mexico side of the border. So much "illegal" focus is pushed onto migrants seeking asylum that these grievous and grandiose illegal practices by CBP against migrants have been virtually disregarded, dismissed, justified, and/or exonerated in the name of "legal" law enforcement and the rule of law. The same standard of legality needs to be applied to our unjust policies and practices that illegally limit access to the United States for refugees seeking asylum.

The increased deviant treatment of refugees before they even step foot on U.S. soil was exacerbated with the zero tolerance policy (see chapter 5), which violates international and U.S. immigration law. Jeff Sessions's unjust and illegal proclamation was magnified on November 9, 2018, when by presidential proclamation Trump declared that asylum would be denied to persons who enter the United States between official ports of entry. They would be prosecuted for (and convicted of) "unlawful entry" and deported with a "criminal" record. Ten days later, U.S. District Judge Jon S. Tigar of San Francisco issued a nationwide restraining order barring enforcement of the policy.[14] The Ninth Circuit Court of Appeals ruled in favor of the restraining order. Pushing a personal agenda to close borders, build walls, and illegally deny access for asylum seekers to legally enter the United States remains an ongoing presidential focal point at the time of this writing.

While the legal battle is being duked out over whether or not asylum seekers can access the United States between official points of entry, the U.S. government has taken aggressive action to close down many of those "legal" locations. A 2018 report cosponsored by the Robert Strauss Center's Mexico Security Initiative indicates, "Despite CBP's assertions that asylum processing is available at all 328 U.S. ports of entry, in multiple border cities, processing only takes place at specific ports of entry. For example, in the ports of entry connecting Tijuana with San Diego's border communities, there are three ports of entry for pedestrians but only one is currently processing asylum seekers."[15] In October 2018, Southern Poverty Law Center filed a civil complaint against then secretary of homeland security Kirstjen Nielsen and others, regarding the border turnbacks, specifying examples from fourteen ports of entry. The complaint argues that this unlawful practice violates "the Immigration and Nationality Act (INA), the Administrative Procedures Act (APA), and due process under the Constitution's Fifth Amendment." The accusations also include "that CBP officers did not just alert asylum seekers regarding a lack of processing space but also used lies, threats, intimidation, coercion, verbal abuse, and physical force to block their access to U.S. ports of entry."[16] The international plot of deception thickens. When asylum seekers are turned back to wait in Mexico for their turn to be allowed admittance, Mexican officials demand money to let migrants pass and/or to have their names put on the official list, which gets them the possibility of eventual access to make their case for asylum on U.S. soil.[17]

A preliminary report by the DHS Office of Inspector General indicates, "CBP regulated the number of asylum-seekers entering ports of entry, which may have resulted in additional illegal border crossings."[18] When the legal access point to enter the United States and seek asylum shuts down illegally, the families turn to the river to bring their children to safety. Then, of course, they are termed "illegal" and deported because they have a "criminal" record. Injustice runs rampant as the United States abuses the responsibilities that come with state sovereignty and the moral and political obligation to the UNHCR and refugees seeking asylum. The deterrents make it much more difficult to obtain asylum, but, more important, testimonies of the families and volunteers who assist them verify that it's increasingly difficult to have the opportunity to make a formal application for asylum.

Admittance to the United States Nets More Injustice at the Border

The 2005 and 2016 USCIRF reports verify similar accounts of injustice at the border from refugees seeking asylum and the volunteers who assist them. USCIRF is an independent, bipartisan, U.S. federal government commission created by the 1998 International Religious Freedom Act (IRFA) that monitors the universal right to freedom of religion or belief abroad. It adheres to "international standards to monitor religious freedom violations globally, and makes policy recommendations to the President, the Secretary of State, and Congress."[19] The findings from the 2016 study don't differ significantly from the 2005 report, both of which document key problems in U.S. immigration policies and practices with refugees seeking asylum. The key problems documented in the 2005 study include:

- incorrect interviewing and unreliable record-keeping practices by immigration officers at ports of entry;
- failures to refer asylum seekers for credible fear determinations;
- inappropriately punitive detention conditions;
- wildly varying rates of parole (release) of asylum seekers from detention; and
- inconsistent asylum adjudications by immigration judges.[20]

The 2016 study specifies additional concerns related to the increased family migration from Central America with mothers and children requesting asylum, including "concerns about CBP officers' interviewing practices and the reliability of the records they create." The findings report "flawed Border Patrol internal guidance that conflates CBP's role with that of USCIS." Concerns include cynicism and disbelief about the veracity of the claims asylum seekers make in their need for asylum, and too much reliance on technology during the interview process, which generates efficiency at the cost of identifying the underlying concerns of the asylum claims and protecting the asylum seekers' safety. There's also nominal, if any, privacy for asylum seekers while they give their personal stories of horror, which are their catalyst to seek safety in the United States.

The report also cites the facilities ICE continues to use to detain asylum seekers, both before and after their credible fear interviews, as "inappropriate penal conditions." The document charges ICE with "failure to develop uniform procedures to determine bond amounts" and raises "serious concerns" about ICE's "extensive use of ankle bracelets over other alternatives, and without individually assessing each asylum seeker's non-appearance risk." The report also is critical of the "U.S. government's detention of mothers and children in Expedited Removal who expressed fear of return," which the report determines "is inherently problematic." It specifies that "several courts have found that the facilities used do not comply with the U.S. government's own standards for child detention as defined in a 1997 legal settlement, the *Flores* Agreement."[21] The report provides nonpartisan documentation for the same types of complaints against government agents and officials that families seeking asylum have made to volunteers assisting them in diverse capacities and contexts along our southern border.

U.S. mistreatment also includes disrespect for the nominal property a migrant carries across the international border. For example, an advocate for migrants in Arizona explained that the point of arrest is CBP, and then migrants are transported to private prisons. The advocate clarified, "The belongings stay at the arresting agency. If you have a backpack with a phone and a list of phone numbers, you might never see your belongings again. There literally are trailer after trailer of migrant belongings because of the ineptitude of all these agencies. They are supposed to keep the belongings for thirty days and then [the asylum seekers] are supposed to get them back. That doesn't happen." The few precious personal items a migrant carried through the desert are stripped away and forever lost to CBP bureaucracy in an unknown storage facility at the Arizona-Mexico border.

FAMILY SEPARATION: ILLEGAL ACTIONS AGAINST REFUGEES SEEKING ASYLUM

The U.S. violated international refugee protocol when President Trump and then attorney general Jeff Sessions began separating children from their families as a barbaric tool to force the Democrats in Congress to bow to the president's will regarding funding the wall along the U.S.-Mexico border. A Roman Catholic sister who helps with the hospitality ministry for refugees in San Antonio shared the story of the mother of a six-year-old, a little girl who was lying in her mother's lap with a blank look on her face. This child had been taken by a gang in her homeland. They burned her wrists and then dropped her back off at her mother's house. The mother had no choice; she picked up her child and ran to the United States. It took twenty days of walking. When she arrived, she was shackled and her daughter was taken away from her. She didn't know why. She didn't know where they'd taken her daughter. They were reunited in the *perrera*. The Catholic sister asked, "Why did they take the child? There is a misguided view that if we separate the families that others would not come, but that's not true. Their country is horrible. They will be killed if they stay." So they come here asking for safety.

Families seeking asylum suffer excruciatingly. The Trump administration intensified the practice of separating children from their parents, but spouses already had been separated at the border, and children already had been separated from their mothers while in one of the typical holding facilities used by CBP, including during the Obama administration. A mother who was forced apart from her husband at the border and detained with their three children while he was locked up in an adult-only facility said they didn't expect to be locked up at all. They expected to be living together as a family at her brother's house. She explained, "I arrived in the United States on Friday, October 13, 2016, and I didn't know that so much time would pass without being together with my husband and my family in the U.S." She didn't know where he was incarcerated, and they hadn't had any communication since they'd been forced apart at the border. Separating children longer-term adds another level of agony for families seeking asylum, but they'd already been suffering greatly from U.S. policies and practices implemented along the southern border.

Maria and Juanita Share Their Stories

I spoke with mothers who had been caught up in the family separation fiasco when they crossed the southern border to request asylum. Maria and Juanita (not their real names) shared their experiences because they wanted their voices to become testimonies against the injustice that so many families have experienced. Juanita was separated from her son, age six and a half; she left her five-year-old and her twenty-one-month-old with her mother in Honduras. Maria was separated from her two children, ages ten and twelve, who had traveled with her to the United States. I visited with Maria the day before she was reunited with her children. She said, "The most important thing is my children. We've been apart for too long, and it's so very difficult. I didn't know any of this would happen. I thought I would go to be with my family." She shook her head back and forth and said again, "I didn't know any of this would happen." Maria added, "It's difficult to continue each day."

Maria had no idea what was happening along the U.S. border and was stunned that she was separated from her children. She explained that her boyfriend had made the journey ten months earlier. He spent fifteen days in detention, and then he was released to be with his grown daughter who lives in Ohio. Maria left Guatemala April 4, 2018. She worked her way through Mexico to pay for the trip. She made empanadas and tortillas in Chiapas and then she worked for two weeks mending clothing in Reynosa. She didn't use a *coyote* because it was too expensive, so she just crossed the river with her two children on June 11, 2018. ICE immediately separated her from her children. She said, "When I left my country, I didn't know this would happen to me. They put me in one place, my daughter in one place, and my son in another place. We've been separated one month and one day."

She explained that there were seventy-five adults who initially were detained with her in the *hielera*, and they also were separated from their children. After the *hielera*, she spent twenty-six days in detention, where there were four units with seventy-five women in each unit. All of the mothers had had their children taken away. She kept repeating over and over, "Muchos gentes, muchos gentes" (so many people, so many people) while she shook her head back and forth as she described the Port Isabel Detention Center in Los Fresnos, Texas. This detention center is owned by ICE, but private industry profits, because its guards are provided by Ahtna, Inc., a group of businesses overseen by the Ahtna, a federally recognized Alaska Native people.[22]

I spoke with Juanita, age twenty-six, the morning after she was reunited with her son. While she shared her story, tears ran down my face as I silently wept for this mother's pain. They left Honduras on May 20, 2018, in an emergency. She didn't warn her brother in the United States that she was coming. She quickly left her homeland because she had a death threat hanging over her head. ICE took her six-year-old son the very first night they were in the *hielera*. She said she'd been there for only a few hours when the officers came in the wee hours of the morning. Her son was sleeping in her arms. One officer yelled at her to wake up her son. She said no, that he was sleeping. The officer yelled at her again. This mother gently rolled her son off of her to place him on the concrete floor beside her. The officer grabbed her son and took him away on a bus. Juanita said, "When they took him I was crying, and he was crying too." She said, "They kept telling me that I would see him 'tomorrow . . . tomorrow . . . tomorrow,' but that was June 6 and I didn't see him again until July 12, 2018." From the *hielera*, they took her to the *perrera* the next day and then to court. She was at the courthouse all day. Then, late at night, they took her back to the *perrera*. Then she was sent to Port Isabel. She passed the credible fear interview on June 19 (see chapter 7). She said, "Then waiting, and waiting, and waiting. Finally, thanks to God, I was released."

She wasn't allowed to speak to her son by telephone until she'd been at Port Isabel for sixteen to eighteen days. They finally allowed her to speak with her son four different times, for ten minutes on Mondays and Wednesdays for her remaining two weeks in detention. She said her conversation with her six-year-old was always the same. She said she could hear the sadness in his voice as he asked his questions.

Son: Hi, Mom. When are you coming to get me?

Juanita: Soon. I will come to get you soon.

Son: When am I going to see you again?

Juanita: Soon. We will be together soon.

Son: When are they going to let you out?

Juanita: Soon. They will let me out soon.

Son: Are they feeding you? Are they feeding you enough?

Juanita: Yes. They are feeding me. They are feeding me enough.

Son: I want to be with you. I want to be with you.

Juanita: Soon. We will be together soon.

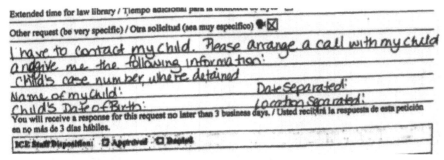

Figure 6.1. A detained mother's request on government form I-870 to contact her seven-year-old son, who was taken from her when they arrived in the United States and requested asylum.

She explained that she could barely get any words out because there was such a knot in her throat. When she hung up, she would just cry and cry and cry. Juanita's release paperwork includes her handwritten request: "I have to contact my child. Please arrange a call with my child and give me the following information: child's case number, where detained." The name and contact information never were filled in by any government agency. When she was released from detention, she was left to figure out how to locate her child on her own.

What a Mother Expected

Juanita arrived at the U.S.-Mexico border when family separation was headline news because of the international outcry against this Trump administration policy. I asked her what she expected would happen when she arrived to the United States. She said, "I was hoping to get to the U.S. to stay with my brother for protection. I had no idea this would happen. My brother didn't know I was coming until I called him when I arrived in Reynosa." She started weeping as she said, "I woke up one morning and left. The problem that I had there was too great. It forced me to leave. I had no time to plan. I left in emergency." Her greatest desire, the only thing she wants in the whole world, is to bring her other two children to the United States so that they can live together in safety as a family. I visited with Juanita the morning after she received her son back, and I asked, "How is he?" With her arms wrapped around her son in a loving motherly hug, she said, "He is the same." She said she really admires his bravery. She asked the social workers if he cried, and they said no. She personally asked if he cried, and he said, "No, Mommy, I didn't cry." She added, "Even when he was a little child and hurt himself, he didn't cry. He is strong."

A pastor who provided transportation for the reunification of Juanita and her son described the experience in a July 13, 2018, Facebook post:

I spent yesterday doing the sacred work of driving this sweet boy's momma around San Antonio as she anxiously awaited his release from one of the centers detaining children here. I'm still trying to process all I encountered . . . The lines and lines of children going outside to play on the small blacktop outside the building [on a sweltering hot Texas summer day], *this little boy dashing out of the line to hug his momma and then being told to get back in line, the immigration attorney who flew in from Sacramento at no charge to advocate for this mother and her son and who told me she was not leaving until he was released, the tears of so many (myself included) when their reunification finally happened, watching his mom look at him over and over as he sat behind us in my car, sitting across from them at Pizza Hut as they enjoyed their first meal back together (I wish I could post the picture I took of their smiles), the church that is providing housing for them (and others) graciously and fearlessly, and so much more. I'm grateful to Helen Boursier for telling their story. It needs to be heard. Over and over. This is not okay. Not ever.*[23]

Maria became very animated as she spoke with passion about her experiences. She'd not yet been reunited with her two children, but the pro bono attorney was hopeful that she would have them returned to her soon (they were reunited the following morning). Maria explained that when she first arrived at the detention center after her children had been taken from her, she realized that it was the president who wanted to take her children away. She said she realized that she alone couldn't make the president change his heart, so she prayed that God would intervene and change the president's heart.

As the time approached that she was to be released from the detention center, she asked facility officials about her children, but they never said anything. She said, "I kept asking about my children. Nothing. Nothing about my children." The day she left the detention center, there was no mention of her children, where they were or how she could find them. She said, "They just let me go and that was that. It was only the [pro bono] lawyer who worked hard to locate my children."

The children were detained at separate ORR shelters for children in greater San Antonio. Maria was staying at a sanctuary church in San Antonio while the lawyer pursued the due process to get her children returned. The day before Maria finally received her children, the pastor whose congregation hosted Maria said, "Even now, she's not allowed to know exactly where they're located. There's something in D.C. that has to happen there; there's no door to bang on in San Antonio. It's in D.C., so she waits and waits and waits to be reunited with her children." The pastor's message to her congregation the following Sunday included the testimonies of the mothers. She said, "Neither of these mothers had any idea what would be waiting for them, that their children would be taken away, that they would be treated as criminals, even though requesting asylum is in no way illegal. They told me last night how completely surprised they were by the harmful and violent way their families were received by the United States."

When I visited with Maria, she wanted to make it very clear that the day she left detention they didn't tell her anything about where her children were. She said, "I feel very strongly that I had the right to know where they were. I am their mother!"

When she specifically asked for the information, they told her that she couldn't have it. The news reports at the time made a big deal to explain that the families were given a tear sheet with information about how to locate their children, but neither of these two mothers received such notice. The DHS Office of Inspector General confirmed this lack of information in its September 2018 report *Special Review: Initial Observations Regarding Family Separation Issues Under the Zero Tolerance Policy*. The document overview concedes that "inconsistencies in the information provided to alien parents resulted in some parents not understanding that their children would be separated from them, and made communicating with their children after separation difficult." "Difficult" is a gross understatement; "impossible without diligent and vigorous legal intervention" would be much more accurate.[24]

The mothers were incensed about the treatment they received, not only that their children were ripped from them in the middle of the night and the subsequent lies and manipulations, but especially that they weren't given any information about how to reunite with their children after the mothers had passed their credible fear interviews and been released from detention. They gave me permission to review their stack of discharge paperwork to see if there was anything that gave any indication of how to locate their children. There was absolutely nothing in their official government paperwork about where their children were or how to locate them. And, of course, the entire stack of papers was 100 percent in English. Maria said that confirming the current status of her children, who were about to be released to her, was entirely the lawyer's doing. She said, "God sent the lawyer because otherwise I really don't know what I would have done." She added, "Your president plays with the feelings of people. It's very hard, and it hurts deeply."

ROTTING IN JAIL: LONG-TERM (FOR-PROFIT) DETENTION

In addition to the current violations against unaccompanied children who are detained far beyond the twenty-day limit specified in *Flores* (see chapter 4), with the backlog in the immigration court system, children and families traveling together literally could languish behind bars for years. In fact, on February 27, 2018, the U.S. Supreme Court ruled that immigrants could continue to be detained indefinitely while a determination was made regarding their "legal" status in the United States. The 5–3 decision reversed the Ninth Circuit Court of Appeals decision that immigrants had to receive bond after being detained six months if a ruling had not yet been made. The ruling on *Jennings v. Rodriguez* applies to illegal and legal immigrants, including permanent residents.[25] The precedent-setting case was based on Mexican immigrant Alejandro Rodriguez, who had been detained for more than three years without a bond hearing. The Supreme Court decision will keep adult refugees seeking asylum incarcerated interminably at taxpayer expense. Currently, families traveling together are partially broken apart, typically the father being separated from his wife and children to be incarcerated individually while the mother is "detained" with their children. The ultimate injustice is to deny their credible fear for asylum and then deport the vulnerable right back to the violence they are fleeing.

U.S. CULPABILITY FOR FEMINICIDE
IN THE NORTHERN TRIANGLE

If family separation wasn't harsh enough, Sessions also unilaterally mandated that families couldn't use gang or domestic violence as justification for a credible fear claim, the two biggest factors that most of the families are fleeing. Sessions declared that this violence against women and children no longer "counts" as a viable testament for asylum.[26] The severity of their threat to life is not heard, understood, taken seriously, and/or respected. Fortunately, a federal judge blocked several of the Trump administration's policies on December 19, 2018, including Sessions's edict that domestic violence and gang violence didn't "count" for asylum claims. U.S. District Judge Emmet G. Sullivan called these policies "arbitrary and capricious and contrary to law" and demanded that the government immediately stop their unlawful enactment.[27] Because of this "arbitrary and capricious" edict, how many innocent victims already had been denied asylum and deported back to the probable death that they were fleeing?

The United States becomes a key player in feminicide, bearing culpability for the brutal killing of women and girls because they are female, each time we deport at-risk women and girls back to the very violence they are fleeing.[28] The mothers don't name femicide in their testimonies, but they've lived in a culture of violence and have been victimized by the gangs. They know what happens to women and girls. The mothers have described precursors to femicide, horrifying experiences that became their motivation to seek asylum.

A twenty-two-year-old mother from Honduras explained the abuse she received from her partner. She said, "He beat me with a corrugated cable, and he would not give me food. He said if I left him, he would kill me. I hid. Enough! I do not want to continue to live in a country where there's so much delinquency and where I fear for my life." By "delinquency," she means, of course, the prevalent violence against women and children, all of it unchecked, unstopped, and unpunished because the government does nothing. Another mother explained, "They did evil things to my daughter. Then they said they would kill her if I didn't pay the rent, the fee they determined in exchange for my daughter's life. That was when I organized my trip. I'm here to ask for help. I'm asking for asylum to protect my daughter."

Remember, the UNHCR core norm for refugees, known as nonrefoulement, mandates that, instead of forcibly returning asylum seekers to their homelands, where their lives will be at great risk, the United States needs to create ways to embrace the bigger picture and welcome asylum seekers as neighbors who become friends.

7

Credible Fear for Asylum

Asylum seekers are supposed to be given a preliminary screening at the border to determine whether they might qualify for asylum. If they pass this initial conversation, the next step is to pass the formal credible fear interview, where they must demonstrate through their testimony that they have legitimate or credible fear due to one of the five parameters of the UNHCR, which U.S. immigration laws also affirm: race, religion, social group, political opinion, or nationality. How an asylum officer interprets their story determines whether or not a claimant meets the "nexus" of any of the five specified options.

As chapter 1 illustrates, migrants are fleeing gang-related persecution, violence, extortion, and death threats. They are persecuted because they refuse to succumb to the immorality, death, and destruction that rules in violently dangerous nations. The majority of these asylum seekers have profound faith in God, which grounds their moral compass as they seek to live honorable, moral, and just lives. They refuse to succumb to the rule of violence, which is the way of the land in the Northern Triangle. A volunteer who assists refugees explained, "The families are being held to their moral code in a lawless society, so in a way, they're being persecuted for their religious beliefs."

THE CREDIBLE FEAR INTERVIEW

These mothers, fathers, and children aren't lawyers. They don't know U.S. immigration law, and they don't have a lawyer present at the initial screening or during the formal credible fear interview. The one thing the families do understand is that everything hinges on whether or not they can prove credible fear. They clearly understand that if they don't pass the interview, they will be deported. The detainees experience overwhelming anxiety as they seek to prove their credible fear, particularly because very few pass this momentous interview. Maria and Juanita, the mothers described in chapter 6 whose children were separated from them at the border, were told before they went into their interviews that only three or four out of one hundred would pass. Maria said, "Three passed. Everyone else is being deported." Juanita added, "They are being asked whether they want their child to be deported with them or if they want them to stay in the U.S. with a family member." Their kids are welcome; the parents are not.

Passing the Credible Fear Interview

The credible fear interview includes two sets of questions, with additional follow-up questions by the asylum officer for clarification of the details. The asylum officer should have been given detailed notes from the initial screenings conducted with the asylee during the border station processing, including the point of entry to the United States and whether the person initially claimed fear of torture or persecution. The first set of questions covers general background information like birthday, home country, and whether the individual has any family relationships in the United States. The second set of questions addresses the detainee's fear of return to the home country. When the detainee gives a reason for fear, the interviewer asks follow-up questions for elaboration about that fear. Each asylee must have a very specific response with a "significant possibility" for one of the five UNHCR/U.S. fear factors to be able to prove during a hearing before an immigration judge. The applicant also must pass what are referred to as "bars." Answering affirmative to any of the points will result in being barred from receiving asylum. The bars include:

- You have persecuted others on account of race, religion, nationality, membership in a particular social group, or political opinion.
- You have been convicted of a particularly serious crime.
- There are serious reasons for believing you committed a serious nonpolitical crime outside the United States.
- You have engaged in terrorist activity, are likely to engage in terrorist activity, have incited terrorist activity, or are a member or representative of a terrorist organization.
- You were firmly resettled.
- There are reasonable grounds to believe that you are a danger to the security of the United States.[1]

Generalized fear because someone lives in a dangerous environment is insufficient for a credible fear claim. The threat must be directed specifically toward each particular applicant. A pro bono attorney who regularly works with refugee families observed that the chances of being granted asylum are much higher for those who already have experienced violence. In other words, "just fear" of targeted violence is not as impressive as already having endured and survived actual violence to oneself and/or one's children. There also are factors at the subjective discretion of the official at each phase of the asylum process, from preliminary screeners at the border to immigration judges in federal court.

Discretionary Factors

The discretionary factors might include the degree of previous persecution or torture, whether the applicant entered the United States using false documents, whether the point of entry was legal or illegal (i.e., whether the migrant "sneaked in" or walked across a bridge at an official port of entry to request asylum with a border official), whether the applicant could go to *another* safe country, age and health, whether the applicant has close family connections in the United States, whether the applicant has committed any minor crimes (including illegal entry), and whether the applicant has shown good character. Although refugees who don't have direct familial connections in the United States are at a disadvantage, that factor is a point of encouragement for the refugees from the Northern Triangle because virtually all have close family here. U.S. Immigration traditionally has favored family reunification, which is a strong draw for the families who want to be reunited with relatives already in the United States.

Variables that are beyond the control of any asylum applicant include the experience and background of the asylum officer and immigration judge, racial bias, political agendas being enforced under a particular presidential administration, and the applicant's country of origin.

With the race to push as many asylum seekers back across the border as possible, the expedited removal process requires that asylees must quickly "navigate a lengthy and complex labyrinth to have their asylum claims considered."[2] The Trump administration made legal due process more challenging and unjust when it suspended funding for legal orientation programs at detention centers. The only source of legal advice for most refugees seeking asylum disappeared in April 2018 when the DOJ cut off the millions of dollars in grant funding that had supported these programs. The vast majority of migrants don't have access to an attorney. The legal orientation program was how they gained an overview of due process and legal options for asylum. Now that's been taken away, so their legal journey to asylum is that much more difficult. Trump even cut funding for legal aid for children in shelters.[3]

Obstacles to Self-Testimony

Without a lawyer, witness, or refugee advocate present, everything hinges upon the reliability of the applicant's self-testimony, but the obstacles to overcome are daunting. The self-testimony experience adds a new layer to their already traumatized selves. The families did not surf the Internet prior to coming to the United States to read up on what would be required of them upon their arrival. They fled violence, which necessarily includes leaving quickly, without advance preparation

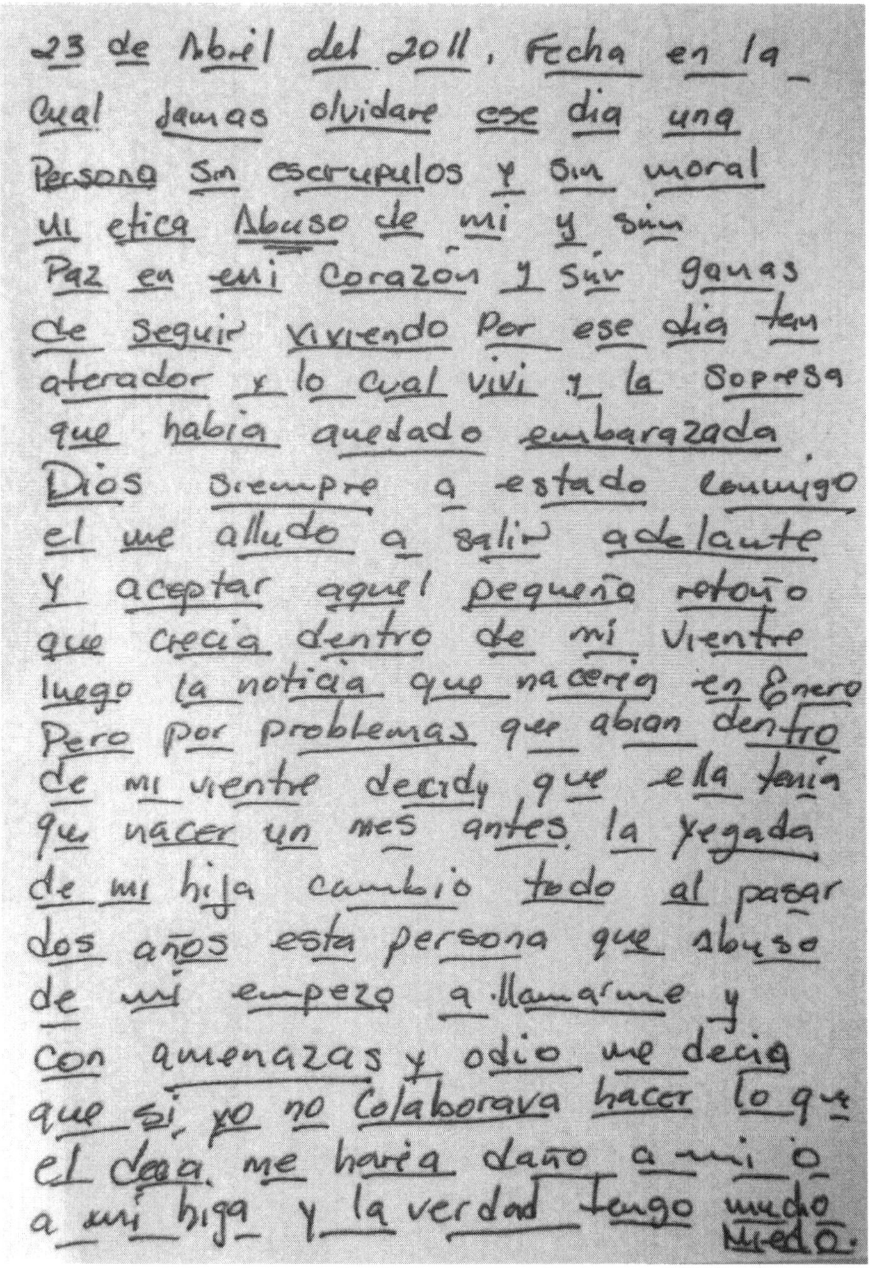

23 de Abril del 2011, Fecha en la
Cual jamas olvidare ese dia una
Persona Sin escrupulos y Sin moral
ni etica Abuso de mi y Sin
Paz en mi Corazon y sin ganas
de seguir viviendo Por ese dia tan
aterador y lo Cual vivi y la Sorpesa
que habia quedado embarazada
Dios siempre a estado conmigo
el me alludo a salir adelante
Y aceptar aquel pequeño retoño
que crecia dentro de mi vientre
luego la noticia que naceria en Enero
Pero por problemas que abian dentro
de mi vientre decidy que ella tenia
que nacer un mes antes, la yegada
de mi hija cambio todo al pasar
dos años esta persona que abuso
de mi empezo a llamarme y
con amenazas y odio me decia
que si yo no Colaborava hacer lo que
el deca. me haria daño a mi o
a mi hija y la verdad tengo mucho
miedo.

Figure 7.1.   A detained mother wrote "My Case for Asylum" as part of an "art as spiritual care" session inside Karnes County Residential Center on September 14, 2016. The underlined words indicate the key points in her self-testimony. She wrote about being raped and becoming pregnant. After her daughter was born, a "person without scruples and without morals" started calling and threatening her, saying that if she did not comply with his demands, "there would be damage to me or to my daughter." Her testimony concludes, "and the truth is I have much fear."

or forethought. They have limited access to interpreters, particularly for some Guatemalans who speak only the indigenous languages. The overall procedure also is tedious, with multiple delays, which are attributed to the overloaded immigration system and the backlog of cases. Instead of building walls and funding for-profit detention facilities, taxpayer dollars would be better invested reducing the 746,049 pending cases in the immigration court system (the fiscal year 2018 backlog through July 31, 2018).[4]

The most emotionally painful obstacle to overcome is the necessity to confront and share the applicant's personal trauma with uniformed strangers who are in the position of power, and who have the authority to accept or reject their self-testimony. The USCIRF report *Barriers to Protection* affirms that there are not enough female agents or officers to interview all the women and children and that many children flat don't want to talk to uniformed male officers. There's also a lack of privacy for the families to give their personal witness of suffering and trauma. This report also indicates that officers collecting credible fear testimonies haven't had trauma-informed training for interacting with these vulnerable women and children seeking asylum.[5] The mothers and fathers, sons and daughters, must find a way through their pain to make a public witness to their suffering. The statistics may be corporately compiled of the violence, death, and feminicide in their homelands, but their individual stories are painful and emotionally distressing each time they are remembered and shared. It's never easy. Self-testimony often requires finding words to express what conscious memory cannot recall, what has been internally silenced as a measure of safety and protection from the trauma the asylee experienced.

Another one of the hidden hurdles refugees must navigate is the assumption that anyone and everyone who crosses the southern border is completely after the fabled "American Dream."

DEBUNKING THE MYTH THAT
EVERYONE WANTS TO LIVE IN AMERICA

Political rhetoric and popular U.S. opinion assume that all migrants want to come here because this country is so fabulous and their countries are so horrible, so of course they want to "sneak into" the United States. It's simply not correct. As a volunteer with refugees said, "Our assumptions get in the way of what we *think* we know. We also have assumptions about things we don't know anything about." Assumptions interfere with documented truths on why refugees are seeking asylum. The assumption that asylum seekers are really out to beat the system rather than escape violence emerges from the relative affluence of northern America compared to the impoverishment of Central America. It's incorrect and a mistake to believe that most asylum claims are fraudulent. Such a convenient assumption manifests itself in negative and stereotypical judgments against the marginalized. Although the majority of some six thousand asylum seekers that I've interacted with are literate, they aren't educated in U.S. immigration law. Given the direct threat to violence explained earlier, it's more likely that they do have a valid claim for asylum.

People don't want to leave home. They like their homes, their families, the colors that surround them, the food. They don't want to leave, but they cannot stay. These families are coming from lawless countries where the violence gets worse and worse. There's no help for them. An advocate emphasized, "They like their food, family, and culture. They accept their circumstances. They don't want to leave, but they have to, so they come here."

Hope Frye explained that as a young lawyer, she represented a lot of Persians during the Iranian crisis (late 1970s through mid-1980s). The Ayatollah had taken over and they were all vulnerable. She represented one family from Tehran. They were all college educated and had been very successful, but they had to flee for their lives. This family was in deportation proceedings, and the parents were both desperate to stay in the United States, as people on both sides of their families had been tortured and killed. Frye remembered, "I won the case. Afterwards, this man was weeping. I tried to comfort him by reminding him that now they were safe. He responded, 'You don't understand. This means that we can never go home.'" She said it was an important lesson early in her legal career that asylum seekers and refugees would rather stay home. She specified, "They love their church and their community and their family and friends. Basically, they leave everything behind that they love and run for their lives. Listening begins by realizing that it's a myth that everyone wants to come here. They don't."

This assumption that everyone wants to come to the United States binds Americans within the limitation the assumption contains. Frye explained, "If you are pro-immigration and you believe this, then your view is, 'Aren't they lucky they were allowed to stay?' If you're against immigration, then you don't want anyone allowed in because they're only coming here for the 'sweet life.'"

"Aren't they lucky to be here?"

↑

————Assumption everyone wants to come to the United States————

↓

"They just want the 'sweet life' in America."

Before an asylum claim can be fully heard, first we need to dispel this myth that America is so great that everyone wants to live here. Frye said, "It simply isn't true. We need to dislodge this false narrative." For example, a mother said:

> *I Seek Safety*
> I seek safety from abuse:
> > physical
> > psychological.
> I seek safety
> > for my children.

We are escaping:
    drugs
    alcohol
    violence
    persecution.
I am afraid for my life.

Mother, February 24, 2016
From Fear to Freedom[6]

This succinct testimony is something volunteers hear again and again. Some mothers and fathers share more of the grim details behind their escape to safety in the United States, but the bold-type theme remains drugs, gangs, guns, extortion, violence, persecution, and femicide. A volunteer with refugees explained that CBP and ICE often say, "Their stories can't be true because they are all so similar." The volunteer clarified, "Their stories are so similar because they're all going through the same horrible experience." She added, "When people share their stories with me, they have no reason to lie to me. I see and I hear their suffering." I've had friends, neighbors, colleagues, and strangers challenge my testimony of these families seeking asylum, often with the cryptic remark, "And you believed them?" I've always responded, "Yes, they have no reason to lie to me." Perhaps a more appropriate response would be, "Why don't you believe their witness, which you've heard through me?"

Children Suffer from the American Dream Assumption

Unaccompanied minors also are recipients of the American Dream assumption, but they get dumped on vicariously through accusations against their parents for being "so heartless" in sending them off to America to fend for themselves. A pediatrician who volunteers with children who are detained said, "The public perception is, 'How can parents do that to their children? They must be horrible parents to subject their children to this.'" The doctor added, "Of course, if they are 'horrible parents,' then it's easier to lock up their children into eternity without offering any recourse for the safe asylum these children so desperately need."

Historical perspective is needed to understand that the parents are simply trying to give their children a chance to live. The pediatrician mentioned above, whose father fled Nazi Germany and settled in Guatemala, said, "Parents are sending their children away to save their lives." This Guatemalan, who is now a U.S. citizen, compared the migrant children fleeing his homeland to the trainloads of children that were sent out across Europe in an attempt to protect them from Nazi Germany. He said, "All of these parents, then and now, are doing what they have to do to try to keep their children alive." We need to push our assumptions aside so that we can hear the witness of the families. The following two examples are verbatim reports from the credible fear findings documented on government form I-870. Both applicants passed the credible fear screening, while ninety-seven others who requested asylum during the same session were rejected and deported.

MARIA'S CREDIBLE FEAR CLAIM

Maria (not her real name) is from Guatemala. Otherwise, the identifying points have been removed from her interview report to protect her privacy and safety. The report indicates, "The interview started at 0922 CST and ended at 1145 AM CST."

Maria was a housekeeper; she cleaned and did laundry in her boss' home and also at two small business locations. Maria and her children lived with the boss. The boss threatened to kidnap Maria's two children if she did not give her children to her willingly. The boss's daughter was unable to have children and the boss wanted Maria's children for her daughter. She said the children would have a better life. She threatened Maria two times. She endured verbal abuse, but no physical abuse; her children were not abused.

Future Harm

Officer: What do you think will happen if you return?

Maria: I will be killed because they threatened to kill me if I didn't give them my children.

Officer: Who would do this to you?

Maria: [My boss] and her daughter.

Officer: Why would they want to do this to you? What motive do they have to do this to you?

Maria: To get my children.

Officer: How did you get away?

Maria: When [my boss] left for church I took my children and left for another town.

Officer: Were you safe in the new town?

Maria: No, they were looking for me. Two men came to my new house. They were the same police officers from my old town who I filed the report with. They said if I didn't give them my children in 24 hours, that they would kill me.

Officer: What is the name of the town?

Maria: [Town], Guatemala.

Officer: How do you know they were the same police officers from before?

Maria: I recognized them as the ones I tried to report [my boss] to.

Officer: When was that?

Maria: April 4, 2018.

Officer: When did you leave Guatemala after this?

Maria: I left the next day before they could come back.

Officer: How far away was this new town?

Maria: Twelve hours away.

Officer: The same two police officers that you gave a report to before found you in a town twelve hours away?

Maria: Yes.

Officer: Do you fear anyone else?

Maria: No.

Officer: Could the police or government protect you from the people you fear?

Maria: No, they are helping [my boss].

Officer: Can you live in another part of your country and be safe?

Maria: No, we tried already.

Officer: When did you leave Guatemala?

Maria: On April 4, 2018 [sic].

Convention against Torture (CAT) Investigation/Involvement

Officer: In the past, have you ever been threatened or harmed by the government, police, or authorities in your country?

Maria: Yes, from the two I already told you about.

Officer: Are you afraid of the government, police, or authorities in your country? Why?

Maria: Yes, because they threatened to kill me and take my children.

Consent

Officer: Are you aware of any connection between the people you fear in your country and the authorities/public officials of your country?

Maria: Yes, [my boss] works with the police.

Officer: Do you have any reason to believe the people you fear have connections or are working with the authorities/public officials in your country?

Maria: Yes.

Officer: How do you know this?

Maria: Like I told you before.

Acquiescence

Officer: If you return, will you be harmed by anyone who has the permission or consent of the authorities?

Maria: Yes, the police will kill me and take my children to [my boss].

Officer: If the government or police knew that you were to be harmed, do you have any reason to believe that they would look the other way and let the harm happen?

Maria: Yes, they would be the ones harming me.

Questions on Torture

Officer: Do you have fear of being tortured in your country?

Maria: Yes.

Officer: Who will torture you?

Maria: The police will kill me.

Additional Nexus

[The officer asked the five questions that relate to the five terms for asylum. Maria answered no to all five questions, a typical example of mothers not making the connection that they are being persecuted because of their religious/moral/ethical code.]

Summary of Testimony

You testified that you are afraid to return to Guatemala because you have been assaulted by two men when you were thirteen, your children were threatened to be kidnapped by your boss, and you were threatened to death by two police officers if you didn't willingly give your children to [your boss].

You testified that you were attacked and suffered an attempted rape by two unknown men when you were thirteen years old. One of these men was arrested and went to jail for the crime.

You testified that your old boss [first name] insulted you and called you names. You were a housekeeper for her and your children and you lived with her in Guatemala City. She said that your children would have a better life with her and her daughter rather than with you. She threatened to kill you if you didn't give your children to her. When [your boss] went to church on 3/25/18, you took your children and fled to a town 12 hours away. On 4/4/18, the same two police officers from Guatemala City came to the new town [town name]. They threatened to kill you if you didn't give your children to [your boss] within 24 hours. You fled Guatemala the next day with your children.

You believe that if you return to Guatemala your children will be taken and you will be killed and that the government cannot protect you.

Officer: Is this summary correct?

Maria: Yes.

Officer: Are there any changes or additions you would like to make?

Maria: No.

Officer: Is there anything else that is important to your claim that we have not yet discussed?

Maria: No.

JUANITA'S CREDIBLE FEAR CLAIM

Below is the witness of Juanita (not her real name) from Honduras, who was detained at the Post Isabel Detention Center in Los Fresnos, Texas. Identifying details have been removed to protect her safety and privacy. She brought her six-year-old son to the United States, but they were forced apart at the border, and he was being detained in "transitional foster care." She left two children with her mother in Honduras. Her brother is a U.S. citizen and lives on the East Coast, and he will sponsor his sister and nephew.

Fear Claim

Officer: Why did you come to the United States?

Juanita: I was fleeing my ex-partner.

Officer: Did you come for any other reason?

Juanita: No, just the threats of my husband.

Officer: Have you been physically harmed in your country?

Juanita: Yes.

Officer: Have you been threatened by anyone other than your husband?

Juanita: No, just my husband.

Officer: Who has physically harmed you in your country?

Juanita: My partner.

Officer: Has anyone else, including a family member, threatened or harmed you in your country for any reason?

Juanita: No.

Officer: How many times were you threatened in your country?

Juanita: Many times.

Officer: Why did your partner threaten you?

Juanita: Because I did not accompany him when he was involved in all those things that were political harm. They were burning things like tires and I didn't go with him.

Officer: Did he threaten you for any other reason?

Juanita: Because I decided to leave my house and he said I don't have his permission to leave the house. He said if I left the house without his authorization he would kill me.

Officer: How many times did he physically harm you?

Juanita: Many times.

Officer: Why did he physically harm you many times?

Juanita: Because I didn't do what he said. Many times he grabbed me by the hair and he beat me. Many times he took me by force because he said I didn't do what he told me to do.

Officer: Are you referring to [name of husband]?

Juanita: Yes.

Officer: When was the first time he threatened you?

Juanita: April 15, 2017.

Officer: Did you live with him?

Juanita: Yes.

Officer: When did you begin living with him?

Juanita: December 2016.

Officer: What was the threat he made to you on April 15, 2017?

Juanita: He said that I shouldn't try to escape from him and that he will always find me and he will kill me when he finds me.

Officer: If he threatened you, why didn't you leave him?

Juanita: I left him and I went to live somewhere else, but he found me through his friends and when he found me, he threatened me and he beat me up again.

Officer: When did you leave him the first time?

Juanita: January 20, 2018.

Officer: What was the worst physical harm he did to you?

Juanita: Bruises on my body.

Officer: Did you ever require medical attention from any harm you received from him?

Juanita: No, none.

Officer: When was the last time he threatened or physically harmed you?

Juanita: May 18, 2018.

Officer: What happened on May 18, 2018?

Juanita: He threatened me and beat me up. He dragged me to the toilet and told me not to escape again and "if you do I am going to kill you. Don't try to escape again, because you are mine."

Officer: What did you do after he threatened and beat you on May 18, 2018?

Juanita: I fled. I left his house and I took this way to come here. I made the decision to come here.

Officer: Did you leave the house right away?

Juanita: No, two days later. That is when he left.

Officer: Who are your two other children with?

Juanita: My mother.

Officer: Where is the father (of the child who came with you)?

Juanita: In the United States.

Officer: Did your partner threaten to harm you for any other reason?

Juanita: No, just because of that and because I didn't help him to use drugs.

Officer: Did you report any of the threats or harm to the authorities?

Juanita: No, none.

Officer: Why not?

Juanita: Because he always threatened me and told me it would be worthless if I went to the police and opened a claim against him because he would always look for me to kill me.

Officer: On what date did you leave your country?

Juanita: May 20, 2018.

Officer: Are you willing to return to your country?

Juanita: No.

Officer: Why are you unwilling to return to your country?

Juanita: Because he will be worse.

Officer: Is there any other place you could live safely in your country?

Juanita: No.

Officer: Why not?

Juanita: I tried already.

Officer: When you left the first time, how far away did you live?

Juanita: Four hours away.

Officer: How did he find you four hours away?

Juanita: He has many friends in many different parts. That's what he does. He travels a lot.

Officer: What do you think will happen if you return to your country?

Juanita: First he is going to mistreat me and then he is going to end up killing me.

Officer: Why would he kill you?

Juanita: Because I have fled and if I return, he is going to be worse.

Officer: Have you received any threats since you left your country?

Juanita: No, none.

Officer: Is there any other reason you are afraid to return to your country?

Juanita: No.

Convention against Torture (CAT)

Officer: Do you believe the police or your government can protect you?

Juanita: No.

Officer: Why not?

Juanita: In Honduras there are many things happening and nobody protects us.

Officer: Ma'am, do you think the police can protect you specifically?

Juanita: No, because in Honduras, they don't do anything for us.

Officer: They don't do anything for whom?

Juanita: The government doesn't do anything for anyone.

Officer: Ma'am, are there people in jail in Honduras?

Juanita: Yes, many.

Officer: So, why don't you believe the police can protect you?

Juanita: Because many of them sell themselves.

Officer: How do you know that?

Juanita: Because my sister went to report her husband and her husband only stayed two hours in jail. When they released him he laughed at her and told her that he gave them 200 Lempiras and they released him.

Officer: Do you believe that the police are connected to your ex-partner?

Juanita: Yes.

Officer: Why do you believe that?

Juanita: Because he told me that if I file a report, nobody will listen to me.

Officer: How does that connect him to the police?

Juanita: Because he has a lot of friends.

Officer: How does that connect him to the police?

Juanita: He has friends and he has a cousin that works at the police.

Officer: How does having a cousin that works for the police connect your ex-partner to the police?

Juanita: That is what he said.

Summary of Testimony

You left your country because you were threatened and beaten many times by your ex-partner. Your ex-partner harmed you because you wouldn't help him do political harm, do drugs, and do everything he said. He also beat and threatened you because you left him. You fear returning to your country because you would be harmed or killed by your ex-partner because you left him and disobeyed him. You did not report any of this to the police because the police don't do anything. You left your country on May 20, 2018.

Officer: Is all of this accurate?

Juanita: Yes.

The interview began at 10:16 a.m. and ended at 11:22 a.m.

BARRIERS TO PROTECTION

The excerpts from the credible fear interviews of Maria and Juanita offer only a glimpse of the interactions between asylum seekers and U.S. officials. A USCIRF summary report on its broad-based investigation of U.S. immigration facilities, protocol, and practices, *Barriers to Protection*, indicates that the credible fear interviews this independent bipartisan group observed raise "concerns about CBP's interviewing and recordkeeping practices, including errors and inconsistencies in documenting what the claimant testified." The report includes examples of misinformation, assumptions, and incorrectly recorded data. It documents examples where the agent didn't follow up on pertinent information, and where the agent recorded something that the asylum seeker never said. Other examples show where critical self-testimony was ignored or, worse, altered by the agent who recorded the information.

The report includes several examples of CBP officials who denied noncitizens the chance to claim fear where there actually was clear evidence of credible fear.[7] The two examples included above are supposedly verbatim accounts, yet information is missing, especially in the summary for Maria, which includes details that are not otherwise recorded in the transcript of the credible fear interview. Also, the documents are in English, so the agent easily could incorrectly record the interview, and these two mothers wouldn't know. They don't read, write, or speak English.

With the baggage and bias of the American Dream embedded in the DNA of this nation, it's inevitable that it's also pervasive in CBP and ICE personnel, who are the front line of contact with migrants and responsible for whether they pass the initial screening and then the credible fear interview. *Barriers to Protection* explains the twofold role CBP has "first to ensure that inadmissible non-citizens are not permitted to enter the United States and second, to ensure that non-citizens who fear persecution or torture have the opportunity to seek asylum, even if they otherwise would be inadmissible." It specifies that "USCIRF was concerned by the skepticism some CBP officials openly expressed of asylum claims, either generally or from certain nationalities." In addition, the report indicates that border officials "appeared to have little recognition of the potential negative implications their skepticism might have for case processing."[8] The families suffer the consequences of the false assumption that the American Dream is the driving force behind migrants seeking asylum. When their testimonies aren't heard, they're deported right back to the violence they were fleeing.

A pastor who volunteers with migrants explained, "The walls go up against listening to the trauma of the refugee partly because it's beyond the scope of 'my' knowledge and experience, but also because their stories sound pretty awful, and do I really want to deal with it?" He added, "Americans are good at dodging pain. We avoid learning potential bad health news, and whatever other bad news. We don't want to hear it, and we dodge or avoid contexts which would force the issue. We're also used to hearing that our ancestors came for financial reasons, but we tend to overlook the political reasons that also contributed." A pro bono attorney emphasized, "We have blinders on because we only want to see what we want to see." The blinders need to come off so that the truth of the asylum seekers' self-testimony can pierce through the pervasive assumptions, baggage, and bias that America is so great that *everyone* wants to live here. They don't.

Documentation also confirms an overall lack of compassion, empathy, and/or knowledge or appreciation of the systemic violence that forces the families to seek asylum. For example, a legal aid who has worked primarily with asylum seekers reported, "From the months of waiting they endure, the bureaucratic inconsistencies they navigate, and the callous responses of government officials to the traumatic stories they're forced to tell again and again, it seems our immigration system is designed to discourage them, not welcome them." She shared a representative example: During an asylum interview, a young client explained the details of her case for asylum, which included the day her family had been ambushed by armed men who shot her sister in the head. The sister later died in her lap. The legal aide documented the response: "'But you weren't hurt?' the officer asked brightly. 'Well, weren't you lucky!'"[9] There's nothing "lucky" about holding your sister while she bleeds to death in your arms.

The government has a moral and legal responsibility "to ensure that officers in the agencies charged with implementing expedited removal and asylum strictly adhere to the regulations, policies, and laws that have been instituted."[10] When someone is in a position to be a decision-maker, it's important to bear in mind that this privilege comes with a great deal of responsibility. Given that the families are at the mercy of so many government actors, it's imperative that these officials have integrity and follow the prescribed rules to ensure vulnerable families actually are extended justice rather than bureaucratic inconsistencies and red tape.

BUREAUCRATIC INCONSISTENCIES AND RED TAPE

Refugee advocates have become data collectors for the inconsistencies and red tape that bog down the immigrant system and stymie the pleas for asylum made by the refugee families. One advocate said, "Which judge you are given, and which district your case is heard in, has proven to make a significant difference [in] whether or not you will be deported. The district with Texas is bad; the district with California is much better."

It's reasonable to propose that refugee advocates exist because of the red tape and inconsistencies that have propagated injustice. For example, a mother and her three children, ages ten, nine, and three, fled from El Salvador to seek asylum in the United States. The husband/father had come to the United States three years prior, when the mother was pregnant with her third child. He'd been threatened with death in his homeland. Because he didn't seek asylum within the one-year timeframe, he's not eligible for asylum status and lives as an undocumented immigrant. When the violence became directed at his wife and children, they also made the dangerous journey to the United States, and the mother filed formal asylum paperwork to begin the due process. She and her three children were locked inside an immigrant family detention center for thirteen months. The youngest son spent one-third of his life in what Texas refugee advocates have termed "baby jail," while an immigration judge tried to figure out what do with this "difficult case." It was deemed difficult because the husband/father was undocumented, so he couldn't be named as the responsible party for the mother and three children to be released on bond.

The mother had numerous court dates where she was in the courtroom virtually, through satellite, while her advocate-funded lawyer represented her case before an immigration judge. Each time, the judge made the determination *not* to release her because of the undocumented status of her husband, but the judge also wouldn't deport her because the mother had a strong and viable case for asylum. The judge also would not set a new court date. The family was placed in terminal limbo while remaining incarcerated in for-profit family detention. Hundreds of families came and went, but this mother and her three children remain locked up. The mother lamented to me when I visited her at the detention center, "The judge will not deport me, but he also will not release me." After months of inertia, a clergyperson who lives near the husband offered to be the official sponsor for the family. The judge finally determined that the clergyperson could qualify as the sponsor, but then the judge set the bond at a whopping $10,000. Refugee advocates rallied to get the necessary five hundred signatures to support the mother's appeal to have the bond reduced. Finally, thirteen months after the family was locked inside a baby jail, they were given permission to continue the asylum process outside of those walls.

Another mother fled Honduras with her small child because they repeatedly were targets of gang violence. They sought and received asylum in Mexico. When they became victims of gang violence in Mexico, they continued the journey north and sought asylum in the United States. Because they'd already received asylum in another country, they were considered ineligible for asylum in the United States. Although it was well-documented that the mother and child have credible fear in both countries, the mother was expected to choose one of these two locations for her deportation destination. The mother also had trouble locating pro bono legal representation because of the "technicality" of her having received asylum in one country, which makes her ineligible for asylum in another. Other refugees have been deported because they didn't seek asylum in a country located closer to their own before seeking asylum in the United States.

FEAR OF DEPORTATION LOOMS LARGE

Fear of deportation clings to the families. It surfaces in many of the conversations with volunteers. A volunteer who visits detained families documented this story: "Maria [not her real name] is still concerned about being deported. During our visit, she noticed someone from immigration talking with another woman; she then commented that it was not good when 'that man comes' because the women are always deported." Fear of deportation looms large on the horizon because of the almost daily reminder of someone who receives the notice that they will be deported within twenty-four hours. One mother simply expressed, "I feel very sad for I am unable to remain in this country. I go tomorrow to Guatemala. I obey God, and for this reason I will return to my country with my family, accepting that it is from God."

These regular deportation notices are unsettling for all of the mothers. Not all of them accept the news graciously. For instance, the art ministry I facilitated as a volunteer chaplain began with detained children, but it shifted to art as spiritual care for the mothers on June 5, 2015, in response to an attempted suicide (see chapter 1, figures 1.1 and 1.2). One of the young mothers had learned that she was to be deported the next day with her young child. She'd had a particularly horrific story of violence from her childhood through her marriage, and she and her son had absolutely nothing and no one to return to at "home." In her despair and hopelessness, she cracked her ID card in half and used the broken pieces to saw through the veins of her arms. It was chilling, tragic, and indicative of the vulnerability these families face.

The littlest children are somewhat exempt from the fear, but the older children understand the ramifications of deportation. A teenage girl whose father was killed by gangs explained, "I do not want to return to Honduras. There I am threatened to death. Here, already I have hopes and dreams. I am able to study [in family detention] and thanks to God I have hope for a new life."

Passing the credible fear interview isn't a guarantee that a judge ultimately will grant asylum, but it does move applicants one important step further along the tedious journey to asylum. The ultimate outcome could be one, two, or three years away, with the result depending on the policies and practices shaped by the rule of law and the language of injustice at our southern border.

8

The Scarcity Mentality and the Language of Injustice at the Border

The scarcity mentality or "never enough" syndrome that Brené Brown writes about in another context contributes to unwelcome at our southern border.[1] The feeling of "never enough" contributes to public fears that refugees, and all undocumented immigrants, for that matter, place a financial drain on U.S. taxpayers. The comment mentioned in chapter 3 that a CBP official made to a detained refugee synthesizes the scarcity mentality on an individual basis: "Go back. We don't want you; you are thieves stealing our jobs." A volunteer who frequently shares her experiences with refugees during impromptu conversations with people she knows or meets said too many people have no understanding of or compassion for what refugee families have gone through. The volunteer specified, "People have competitive and hateful attitudes toward the families. They feel like the immigrants threaten 'me' so that 'I' may not have enough work or enough money to care for 'my' family."

Misinformation contributes to the scarcity mentality. For example, consider President Trump's tweet amidst the migrant caravan's arrival in Tijuana during Thanksgiving weekend 2018:

> Illegals can get up to $3,874 a month under Federal Assistance program. Our social security checks are on average $1200 a month. RT if you agree: If you weren't born in the United States, you should receive $0 assistance.
> 5:57 PM–27 Nov 2018

He pushed his tweet out to his fifty-six million followers. It netted 43,276 retweets and 84,500 likes. A *Washington Post* article quickly countered Trump's erroneous tweet with a blunt "It's wrong." The reporter documented, "That $3,874 figure has been floating around. It appears to stem from a Facebook post in 2017, showing documentation of an initial payment to new residents in a country. But the payment wasn't to an undocumented immigrant, it was to a refugee who was participating in a resettlement program. Actually, to a family of five refugees. And the payment wasn't in the United States. It was in Canada."[2]

The financial "burden" reality for taxpayers is quite different than Trump's tweet. There is no federal funding or assistance programs for unauthorized migrants. Instead, the "cost" to U.S. taxpayers includes the billions of dollars for militarization of the border, detention in for-profit privatized facilities, Operation Streamline and the judicial and enforcement system, and the deportation of migrants to their country of origin. Migrants and asylum seekers are not benefiting from taxpayer dollars. Instead, taxpayers are paying top dollar to ensure that migrants and asylum seekers suffer. In his argument "Against Cruelty," a Boston College professor proposes, "The sign that we are getting political theology wrong is the cruelty which has been imposed to inflict suffering. When there is no kindness, compassion, then it is an indication we are getting political theology wrong." He specifies spiritual cruelty, bodily cruelty, emotional cruelty, and psychological cruelty.[3] Migrants experience all of these cruelties, but the Powers That Be use technical language to justify injustice at the border.

THE LANGUAGE OF INJUSTICE AT THE BORDER

The American Dream (covered in depth in chapter 7) is one of the master narratives deeply embedded in the American ethos, but there are others that contribute to the *un*welcome at our southern border. American DNA has embedded beliefs from the foundation of this "one nation under God," beliefs that cast their viselike grip on the soul of this democratic nation. This DNA has become our master narrative, acting like a demigod of our dominant culture. It takes a deliberate, conscious effort to break free from this inherited cultural baggage so we can create space for a new vision. The point is not to disconnect completely from the past, but to identify and let go of anything that has evolved into an inhospitable, unjust, or even evil perspective. The past brought us to the present, but it doesn't need to dictate our future. Confronting false assumptions and political rhetoric requires identifying the faulty terms that are laden with unhealthy and defaming ideology that degrades and dehumanizes refugee families and children before they even cross the border and step foot on our sacred soil.

Degradation of human dignity is integral to keeping foreigners labeled as strangers, what philosophers refer to as "Other," rather than as neighbors who become friends. Just because terms like "illegal aliens" and "national security" exist doesn't guarantee that they are, in fact, accurate, beneficial, fair, reasonable, or just. Social scientist Brené Brown warns, "When we hear people referred to as animals or aliens, we should immediately wonder, 'Is this an attempt to reduce someone's humanity so we can get away with hurting them or denying them basic human rights?'" Brown adds, "When we engage in dehumanizing rhetoric or promote dehumanizing images, we diminish our own humanity in the process."[4] When language degrades human dignity, it must be challenged and changed. The people around the world who are the most susceptible to human rights violations are women and children in general, and people of color in particular.

Terms like "international border," "immigrant," "refugee," "illegal," "undocumented," and "national security" are examples of what theologian Edward Farley calls "deep symbols" or "words of power."[5] These technical terms carry a deeper significance than their surface meaning as they command control over particular concepts about American values, beliefs, and ideals. The baggage around deep symbols is slowly collected and embedded over time until these terms become the norm without people necessarily consciously thinking about the significance beneath their surface value. Similarly to the technical terms the refugees use to describe the sociocide in their homelands (see chapter 1), the deep symbols and power words in American DNA have a deeper meaning than their surface value. We use these technical terms to justify excluding refugees from asylum.

THE INFAMOUS U.S.-MEXICO BORDER

The U.S.-Mexico border is one of the strongest deep symbols in the current immigration debates. This international border isn't just ours; it's also theirs. The shared river that separates much of these two nations along the Texas-Mexico border is called the Río Bravo del Norte or Río Bravo looking north and the Rio Grande

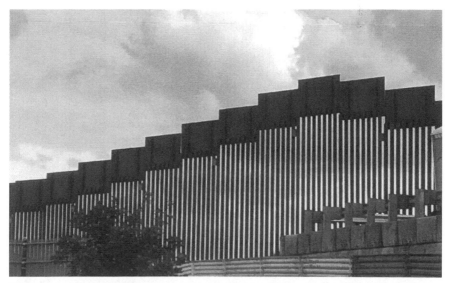

Figure 8.1. The U.S.-Mexico border near the San Ysidro border crossing; view from the California side. Behind the camera, out of view, is a massive factory outlet where Americans and Mexicans were happily, peacefully, and normally shopping on a Saturday afternoon in January 2019. There was no chaos, fear, or violence present.

looking south. This international line of demarcation is more than the literal 2,000-mile (3,200-kilometer) border separating one nation from another. As a deep symbol and power term, the U.S.-Mexico border symbolizes the authority and might of one nation over against another, which is used by each sitting U.S. president to prove to the world that the United States is the big, badass nation that is stronger and mightier than all the rest. For instance, President George W. Bush sent 6,000 troops to Texas, New Mexico, Arizona, and California in 2006, and President Barack Obama sent 1,200 military personnel to the southern border in 2010. President Trump raised the ante with his Operation Faithful Patriot (see chapter 5). The presidential message could adapt the official "Don't mess with Texas" slogan to international border rhetoric: "Don't mess with the U.S."

CRIMINALIZING MIGRATION

A receiving nation's assumptions tend to be louder than the testimonies of truth shared by refugees seeking asylum. The public in general, and political rhetoric in particular, focus on the "criminal" action of "sneaking" into the United States, labeling asylum seekers "illegal" or "illegal aliens." We conveniently disregard our unjust and illegal practices at our southern border, like metering, queue management, and blocking access to a port of entry (POE). Then we lump the families and children together as equal in crime to, for example, the human traffickers who smuggled them across the border and the drug cartel members who perpetuate violence. Elie Wiesel challenges the notion of anyone being called "illegal" with his question, "How can a human being be illegal?" He points out that actions might be termed "illegal," but not the person. People are people. There is no such thing as illegal *people*. "Illegal" is something the Powers That Be invented to distract attention from our own unjust and illegal actions against refugees seeking asylum. After all, if the powerful United States calls these "trespassing" migrants "illegal," then the high-and-mighty, holier-than-thou *we* can exonerate everything else *we* do to the illegal *them*.

Some of the families attempt to walk across one of the bridges connecting Mexico to the United States and present themselves to border officials at an authorized POE to request asylum. When we block legal access, many turn to the river in desperation to reach the safety of the United States. Others, usually at the mercy of the human trafficker they hired to guide them through Mexico, cross the river "illegally" and then look for U.S. Immigration officials once they arrive on U.S. soil. The perspective of power is that they "sneaked in," but most of the families would say they crossed the international border the best way that was available to them and then looked for Immigration. They view this contact as a successful completion to their arduous overland journey to request asylum. For instance, one mother explained that after the group she was with had crossed the river, which took approximately one hour, a patrol car approached with its siren screaming. She said, "He told us if we wanted to stay healthy then we should stop immediately. Then my heart calmed down because I knew that, for the first time in my life, I was doing something illegal to be there. But I did not have another option." She realized that she was doing something illegal for the first time, but that she needed to do so in order to bring her family to safety. The calm came to her because she knew she was doing the right thing, even though she was technically breaking the law by crossing the border illegally. She crossed the best way that was available to make her legitimate claim for asylum. With criminalization of migrants running rampant at our southern border, we brand her "illegal" and categorize her as a "criminal."

The "illegal alien" or "illegal immigrant" label remains permanently affixed to each human being seeking asylum for the duration of their due process. A woman from Romania shared her experience getting a green card. She said she came in "the front door" with the legal process. When she was standing in the line for her due process, she was in the same room with people who had entered "illegally." She said she was uncomfortable with how badly the "illegals" were being treated by the government officials. They were in the same room and following the same process. She said she was "treated like a princess" while the others were treated like substandard "illegals." She explained that when she picked up the small, fussy child of an "illegal" mother while the mother waited in line, an employee told her harshly to put the child down. The child then became more fidgety and agitated. As she was sharing her story, this Romanian started weeping. She said, "I am a woman. We comfort; that is what we do. But I wasn't allowed to help this mother." The Romanian said she also let a few of these young "illegal" mothers get in line in front of her because, again, they had young children who were fussy. The staff again criticized her. The Romanian asked an official why they were treating the others so differently, so much worse than her. When she said that she was here to get a green card just like these other mothers, the agent immediately responded, "Do you still want that green card?" The employee who gave the harsh response is indicative of the earlier point that peons at the bottom also are culpable for the injustice dictated from the top. The agent embodied the injustice of the bigger system in a very personal interaction with people directly impacted.

The Romanian said that when she got through the process, she was grateful to have the little plastic green card, but she also felt like she didn't deserve and shouldn't have received it, because of how badly the others were treated in the same room. She said, "Don't get me wrong. I am grateful every day for what I have been given. But in that room, I felt like I was back in Romania and under Communist rule. I felt unworthy to be treated well when the others there were not." The others were not deemed worthy because they had violated *our* rule of law.

RULE OF LAW

The rule of law is a powerful symbol in the United States and has been part of the DNA of this nation from its formation. Claiming the rule of law to justify or exonerate an action requires considering *whose* law and *which* interpretation. Although the rule of law is held up in its own right to speak against "illegal" immigration, the exact same term could and should counter the "illegal" rhetoric when the democratic process establishes and legitimizes unjust laws. Again, it's important to remember that simply because something is a law doesn't mean it's automatically just or enforced in a just way.

When responding to critics about his involvement in desegregation and civil rights, Martin Luther King Jr. defined a just law as a code made by humanity that "squares with the moral law or the law of God." An unjust law is one that conflicts with the moral law. Laws that build up "human personality" are just, and laws that degrade human personality are unjust. King argued that any law that "distorts the soul and damages the personality," which would include current laws supporting immoral immigration policies and practices, is an unjust law.[6] Left unchecked and unchallenged, the so-called rule of law undergirding the increasingly negative laws, statutes, and presidential edicts formulated against immigrants in general worsens with the anxiety-raising rhetoric of "national security."

NATIONAL SECURITY RHETORIC

The political debate in Washington about the humanitarian crisis of refugees seeking asylum zealously focuses on security risks to the United States. Even renaming Customs and Border Patrol to Customs and Border Protection is an intentional tactic to validate whatever CBP does as being in the name of protecting our national security. Securitization at the border is an extension of the scarcity mentality. We need to ensure that we are safe enough. Anything outside of our own nation creates a perceived threat to our safety. At some point, there needs to be a reality check about we're afraid of and what actually threatens the safety of the United States. The families are not a security risk. They're mothers and fathers seeking safety for their children. They're coming here to live peaceful, safe lives where their children can play outside without being tormented, violated, and/or killed. The parents are here to work to provide the basics for their families, often doing the types of jobs that Americans are unwilling to do. They're not here to plunder our nation, steal, or cause any sort of havoc. They've left violence behind. They simply want to live peaceful lives.

MILITARIZATION OF THE U.S. BORDER

Militarization of the U.S. border, a spin-off of the security rhetoric, is an internationally irresponsible response to the global crisis of mass migration. A respondent during a seminar on the refugee families asked, "What gives the government the right to change the way the border looks and how it is protected/guarded? Why don't the people in the nation have a voice and a vote in what the border looks like and how it is protected?" The questions were not intended to be rhetorical. The respondent reminisced about being able to casually go back and forth across the U.S.-Mexico border when he was a child. He also recalled going to Big Bend National Park and swimming the Rio Grande over to Mexico. He said there was no evidence of law enforcement anywhere, much like it still looks along the U.S.-Canada border.

There's no longer an easy back-and-forth across our southern border. Security and militarization have become the order of the day.[7] The Trump administration continues to dramatically alter the "look" of the border by stacking up rolls of concertina wire, as many as six separate coils of wire, on the U.S. side of the border in Nogales, Arizona. The *Washington Post* reported that a resident said, "This is overkill. It's way over the top." Residents and business owners have lamented "that it makes the town feel like a war zone."[8]

Militarization at the border enables, empowers, rationalizes, and exonerates violations by this nation. We justify our unjust actions in the name of national security and the rule of law, which is enforced through militarization at the border and any "necessary" actions used to enforce unjust laws that have been mandated without going through democratic due process. Militarization also generates fear, shame, and despair in the criminalized refugees. After witnessing a mass sentencing in a federal courtroom in Brownsville, Texas, an advocate said, "The fear, shame, and humiliation were palpable. You could literally feel their despair." The obvious hypocrisy is the double standard that claims the rule of law as justification to emphasize the "illegal" aspect of migration, while simultaneously disregarding that the rule of law also must hold the Powers That Be accountable to justice. Of course, all of the security rhetoric and militarization at the border is not about keeping *us* in. Rather it's about keeping *them* out. Power and fear collide at xenophobia, the fear of difference. The very stability of what King called "the large world house"[9] begins with examining, challenging, and eradicating racism at our southern border.

RACISM AT THE BORDER

Structural *isms* represent an "institutionalized abuse of power."[10] They include racism, "xenophobiaism," sexism, genderism, and any other *ism* that posits one group of people as having power and authority over another. Racism is passed down from generation to generation. It seems to be an elemental part of the human condition that takes a twelve-step-type recovery process to overcome.[11] The *isms* are exacerbated by the common tactic of the Powers That Be to justify the imbalance by blaming the victims, the oppressed, the marginalized, and/or persons of color for their own suffering. Conveniently shifting the blame, and dismissing any culpability, keeps the powerful in power and the marginalized at the margin. Political rhetoric uses the "low" stature of being Hispanic and "illegal" to justify why these asylum seekers shouldn't have rights to asylum, safety, or the most basic level of human kindness and compassion. The criminalization of refugee families "justifies" the racism of immigration-related personnel from the top down who treat these families as caged animals rather than as human beings.

Racism at the border is nothing new. It's a systemic sin that has been present since the European invasion of the North American continent and the brutalities meted out against the Native Americans. The racial atrocities continued with the forced migration of Africans, and the consistent racial and religious slurs against anyone who migrated to the United States and was not white, European, and Protestant. The freedom and liberties generously granted to white Europeans have never been the norm for anyone of color. A quick search for "racist political cartoons immigration" in Google Images will net an unlimited array of racism, past and present, that illustrates this nation's prejudice at the border.[12] It's a tragedy and a travesty to see these defaming cartoons. Perhaps a way through the futility is to name the current racism at the border for what it is: brownaphobia.

BROWNAPHOBIA AGAINST LATINA/OS

Brownaphobia is fear of the brown-skinned other. This "browning of America" paranoia means that Latina/os receive the brunt of the anti-immigrant and "national security" rhetoric. For example, Donald Trump kicked off his presidential campaign on June 16, 2015, with a speech that clearly specified that immigrants from Mexico are "rapists" and "criminals." Multiple tweets during his presidency have reiterated these harsh terms against Central Americans coming to the United States to seek asylum, most notably and consistently as the massive migrant train was slowly making its way through Mexico to the U.S. border.

> There are a lot of CRIMINALS in the Caravan. We will stop them. Catch and Detain! Judicial Activism, by people who know nothing about security and the safety of our citizens, is putting our country in great danger. Not good!
> 1:42 PM–21 Nov 2018

Trump's public rhetoric and immigration policy make it abundantly clear: *we* do not want *them* because they are brown. A migrant from the Northern Triangle who was unsuccessful in his attempt to receive asylum in the United States and who now lives in Nogales, Sonora, Mexico, said, "I'm sorry to say this, but many people on the other side treat us as delinquents, like we're going to rob them. We're not going to commit crimes. But you lock us up in your detention centers and you treat us like criminals." He added, "We go to America to do the work that people on the other side are not willing to do. We go to work. We go to provide for our families." Left unchallenged and unchecked, the immigration matrix will continue to run amok, particularly when the top leadership uses racial slurs against the very people whom the government (and citizens) of the United States should protect, by virtue of our participation in the

1951 Refugee Convention. It's past time to remove how someone's citizenship status shapes the way that people are treated at our southern border.[13]

EXCLUSION FROM ASYLUM

Instead of complying with our ethical, moral, and legal obligations under the Convention to offer shelter to persons fleeing for their lives and seeking a safe haven in the United States, we indulge brownaphobia and hide behind the fake front of the rule of law to detain, cage, and/or shackle families on their journey. Although the transnational, multibillion-dollar immigrant and refugee detainment program is carried out by individual corporations, they are contracted by the U.S. government, which means that the incarceration or "detainment" is paid for by individual citizens through tax revenue. Taxpayers foot the bill for building, staffing, and operating the centers for refugees seeking asylum. Meanwhile, the vast majority of Central American refugees have family members or close family friends in the United States who have offered free hospitality in their personal residences. Instead of trusting these sponsors, the immigration prison complex gobbles up tax dollars while families are separated from their children and/or spouses for some or all of their asylum-seeking due process.

It's a social sin, and *we* are culpable because we are part of the system locking up mothers and fathers and girls and boys because they dared to enter the United States and request asylum. We are part of the problem, and therefore we must become part of the solution—not only in terms of how the families are treated while they are on U.S. soil, but also in consideration of the international principle of nonrefoulement, which should prevent these families from their fearful reality: deportation instead of asylum.

III

HOPE FOR A NEW VISION

ALTERNATIVE OPTIONS
AND PRACTICAL ACTIONS

9

The Bigger Picture

Embracing Refugees as Neighbors

Philosophers, ethicists, and theologians spend a lot of time and energy writing, speaking, and teaching about a better way of being fully human. They use different sources to support their various arguments and proposals, but ultimately they come to a similar view that human beings can be nicer, kinder, and more loving. When we're not nice, kind, or loving, we become selfish, unkind, angry, and hurtful. So the harm we extend to others in our less than graciousness, our less than kindness, and our less than lovingness doesn't just hurt the recipients of our nasty ugliness. It also hurts us. I offer suggestions here for a bigger-picture view of an alternative option for how our nation could and should respond to refugees seeking asylum. My proposal joins philosophers, ethicists, and theologians who prioritize kindness, compassion, and love. These ideals can help us begin to take practical steps to move from our current cruelty toward what philosopher Iris Murdoch calls the Good.[1]

Whether we're seized by the literal faces of refugees, gripped by their chilling testimonies, or embarrassed, ashamed, disturbed, or angry about our nation's selfish, insensitive, and unjust response, the call to action must claim our hearts and move us to response. Immigration ethicist Joseph Carens offers three reasons for our moral responsibility to admit refugees. They are causal connection, humanitarian concern, and the modern state system.[2] Causal connection occurs when a nation has created a direct or indirect cause precipitating the migration, like our connection with drugs, guns, gangs, and the U.S. big-business practices that impact Central Americans. Humanitarian concern is the connection of human being to human being. Asylum seekers need a safe haven and the receiving country has the ability to provide it for these human beings. Carens's third point might seem less obvious. Essentially, the current international state system is organized such that each person is assigned to a sovereign state, generally at birth. When the modern state system fails, as it does for asylum seekers, the other states then have an obligation to correct the "failures of a social institution."[3] Because the United States participates in the international system of state sovereignty for governance, the United States has a responsibility to help when that system fails others who participate in the same interconnected political relationship. It's not *their* problem. It's also *ours*.

A pediatrician who volunteers with unaccompanied minors who are seeking asylum said, "The U.S. prattles on about how these parents can be so irresponsible to allow their children to be in this position." After giving a brief history of the Northern Triangle and how parents have had to send their children away to keep them alive, he added, "The part of 'responsibility' that the U.S. disregards is our own responsibility to receive these people who literally are fleeing for their lives." Instead we violate our own rule of law, disregard and disrespect international agreements and traditions, and yank children from their parents and lock them in horrible state-funded and state-run facilities.

The gross injustice horrifies families and children and incenses the volunteers who hear their heart-wrenching stories of suffering at the hands of the U.S. government. We can't disown, ignore, or deny our responsibility and culpability. We are part of this massive injustice, whether we like it or not. The paradox of responsibility is that we have an obligation to respond, whether we like it or want it. It's a responsibility that precedes any conscious decision or commitment to help these families seeking asylum. *We* are responsible before we even realize that we're responsible. Whether we want to be responsible or not, we just are.

Individually and as a nation, we must move toward a more just and hospitable response, despite any uncertainty or misgivings, with a sense of what Danish philosopher Søren Kierkegaard calls "fear and trembling."[4] Reinterpreting Martin Luther King Jr.'s words, we might say, "The shirtless and barefoot refugees from Central America are rising up as never before. 'The families seeking asylum who sat in the darkness have seen a great light.'"[5] They followed that light to America. King's famous words resonate with these families: "We are now faced with the fact that tomorrow is today. We are confronted with the fierce urgency of now. In this unfolding conundrum of life and history there is such a thing as being too late. Procrastination is still the thief of time. Life often leaves us standing bare, naked and dejected with a lost opportunity."[6] The families are here now; their time is today. Deportation tomorrow probably would mean death. It's time to challenge and change the current unjust practices at the border before it's too late for these families seeking asylum here, today.

RADICAL HOSPITALITY FOR REFUGEES SEEKING ASYLUM

The response of hospitality includes a turning from and a turning to: turning from our own selfish desires and turning toward the needs of these mothers, fathers, boys, and girls who seek our nation's compassionate response. French philosopher Jacques Derrida offers one of the most well-known arguments for what he calls "absolute hospitality," what I refer to as "radical hospitality" or "unconditional welcome." Instead of absolute or radical hospitality, we practice conditional hospitality. We limit who we welcome based upon family, class, race, and personal experiences. We want an advance guarantee that anyone we let in will be just like us and that our safety, security, and finances won't be infringed upon. How do we move from conditional to absolute hospitality? Philosophers, ethicists, and theologians have wrestled with his proposal because of its wild and crazy radicalness. Derrida shapes his argument from the very essence of hospitality itself.[7]

The Welcoming Essence of Hospitality

The word "hospitality" literally means "to invite and welcome the stranger," both on the personal level with how one welcomes the other into one's home, and on a broader community or state level. Hospitality is more than a religious-ethical construct. It inevitably raises sociopolitical questions about asylum seekers in terms of quotas, family connections, self-sustainability, public welfare, education, "foreign" languages, and ethnicity.

Derrida's philosophical argument supports a somewhat less threatening understanding of hospitality as it relates to asylum seekers and immigration reform. In essence, Derrida proposes that the welcome a nation or individual extends to a guest is a "function of the power of the host to remain master of the premises." The host receives strangers and extends hospitality while simultaneously remaining in control. Derrida believes the idea of "having and retaining the mastery of the house is essential to hospitality."[8] Derrida plays off the etymology of "hospitality" and "alterity." He says the one giving hospitality (*hospes*) is someone who has the "power to host someone, so that neither the alterity (*hostis*) of the stranger nor the power (*potentia*) of the host is annulled by the hospitality, which preserves the distance between one's own and the stranger."[9] We don't surrender ourselves as a nation when we welcome refugees. The U.S.A. remains the United States of America. Instead of being fearful of the stranger, we become open and affirming. They help us to become a bigger, better, more inclusive *us*.

Hostility-Hospitality Tension

Derrida's interpretation of the hostility-hospitality tension means that there's always a little bit of hostility in all hosting and hospitality. This tension isn't a bad thing. Instead, it's this *"tension* built into hospitality" that ensures the host (person or nation) retains sovereignty. Instead of fear and trembling, the invitation to radical hospitality opens our nation to the possibilities these refugees bring to our country. Derrida originally calls hospitality *"the* impossible," and he suggests it's only by pushing against the threshold, or limits of hospitality, that hospitality becomes "a gift *beyond hospitality*."[10] Derrida's sense of "beyond hospitality" offers possibilities beyond the limitations that are so often associated with hosting refugees. Instead of seeing these mothers, fathers, girls, and boys as burdens to lock up and deport, actions that personify stinginess, hospitality anticipates the possibilities these families bring. These families are eager to live peaceful and safe lives. The adults desire to be hardworking, honest, and dedicated mothers and fathers who provide for their children. Instead of living in fear of what they could "take" from society, we can eagerly anticipate the gifts they will contribute to melting-pot America.

The Challenge of Hospitality

As long as the rule of law holds power over families seeking asylum, radical hospitality remains an impossible possibility. Welcome, therefore, must include pardon. The concept of pardon is a big theme for philosopher Emmanuel Levinas. He believes that "the lure of the future is essentially the lure of pardon."[11] Pardon does not force us to give forgiveness; pardon only begins to be experienced afterward. It's only in moving through the uncertainty of forgiving that we begin to sense the certainty amidst the uncertainty. Offering pardon for a past sin, grievance, or broken rule of law takes the injustice from the past (our injustice against these refugees seeking asylum) and makes a new future possible. Pardoning the "illegal entry" is a tangible step toward facilitating unconditional welcome, which then opens the possibility of a hope and a future for the families and for this nation. Absolving the misstep of crossing the U.S.-Mexico border at an "illegal" point of entry eradicates a giant block to asylum, one that the U.S. Powers That Be invented to keep these families out. Pardon includes tangibly undoing the legal mess that catches, and then refuses to release, these asylum seekers from the grip of our injustice, slapping a misguided "illegal" label on people who are simply seeking safety in a nation that purports to welcome people longing to be free.

When we pardon the "illegal," both the givers and the receivers of this unjust category that is designed to dehumanize these sojourners, there becomes a transformative break between the past and the future. The wrongs done to these sojourners at our southern border can become transformed through mutual pardon—forgiveness for their "illegal entry" and our wrong of narrowing the gate and clamping down access to their legitimate right to enter and formally request asylum. It isn't just about forgiving them for "unlawful presence." Forgiveness also can pardon our unjust policies and practices that harm the families and limit their international right to asylum. Overzealous xenophobia created the oppressive actions at the border that define human beings as "illegal." Mutual pardon can begin to undo the mess we've made at our southern border.

Obstacles to Hospitality

The hang-ups people have about giving and receiving forgiveness parallel the stumbling blocks for welcoming the immigrant other. The primary obstacles to unconditional hospitality include:

- Selfishness ("I do not want to share 'my' country with strangers.")
- Fear ("There might not be enough to provide food, clothing, shelter, and jobs for me/my family.")
- Pride ("I got here first.")
- Scarcity ("It will cost too much. We don't have enough resources ourselves.")
- Power ("We made the laws; they broke the laws.")

Instead of clinging to the stubborn strength that comes from pride of ownership, the "not enough for me" perspective, or the "I got here first" attitude, human kindness, compassion, and love invite us to let go of our fear of these mothers, fathers, boys, and girls so that we can create an opening, a place and a space that facilitates hospitality with and for sojourners. Wading through these obstacles to hospitality includes respecting that these mothers and fathers, boys and girls, are people, just the same as you and me.

An advocate for unaccompanied minors said it also helps to keep perspective regarding how much "burden" it would be to the United States to welcome the immigrant and refugee children who are detained here each year. Focusing on the children, she said, "We need to scale the perspective to the reality. A football stadium for a professional team holds 50,000 people, and there are stadiums all across the U.S. We're talking about 134,000 children. It's not a massive number of people." For this advocate, the question shouldn't be "How can we afford to take care of these children?" Rather, she insists, "The question is how can we *not* afford to take care of these children?" The "impossibility" of hospitality becomes possible when we embody an ethic of kindness, compassion, and love, welcoming differences as we welcome neighbors who become friends.

JACQUES DERRIDA'S *DIFFÉRANCE*

Derrida's term *différance* is probably philosophy's most famous misspelling. The deliberately misspelled word is not intended to define people or things that are "different." He combines the verbs "to differ" and "deferring" to mean that any position we take is deferred to the indefinite future. He uses the word to define an emerging sense of possibility amidst diversity and conditions where there seemingly is no common ground. His term has a futurity sense that pulls, or perhaps pushes, the possibility toward the newness ahead, including, or possibly because of, the people, concepts, ideals, and "things" that tend to hold one bound to the present or past. He understands that *différance* also produces "things" (notions), which differentiate meaning and contribute to generating (more) differences.[12]

Différance as unknown and pending differentness is something to be welcomed, not something to fear. In the context of developing a more radical welcome for refugees seeking asylum, *différance* looks for inconsistencies, brokenness, bias, and outright blatant lies and deceptions in our immigration policy and practices. Derrida's American interpreter, John D. Caputo, suggests that by defending the idea of *différance*, Derrida meant to say that a person makes sense under conditions that threaten to undo the very understanding we've already made—that is, thinking has to begin again. Our beliefs and practices aren't carved in granite. (Thanks be to God!) Rather, what we believe and do are always evolving so we're not stuck where we are now, including with the current messy immigration matrix. There's a hope and future for something better to come into being.[13] *Différance* is particularly evident in the face of the strange "Other," a word philosophers use to name strangers who come from foreign places far away. Again, they are Other to us only until we move through that strangeness to welcome them as neighbors who become friends.

Différance in the Face of the Other

It's this *différance* in the face of whom Levinas calls the Other that we have the opportunity to be in a right relationship, not only with the neighbor, but with the Wholly Other before whom everyone must stand. For Levinas, the Other is always posited as the poor and the stranger. In modernity, the Other (the weak, the foreigner, and often the marginalized) is repressed and forced inside of totalizing systems. The Other becomes the object of ethical concern; yet contemporary philosophers typically view the Other as a generic "different" *différance* that includes everything different, and yet nothing is specifically defined. It is, in fact, the nondefined or the difference in the Other that makes inclusive hospitality redemptive. Refugee families seeking asylum put a personal "face" on the trace of God in the Other. Their tangible faces also offer the invitation of embodying kindness, compassion, and love through welcoming the strange Other. Refugee sojourners are the Other only as long as a receiving nation labels them as such. *We* have the authority, capacity, and responsibility to remove this label and welcome sojourners as our friends.

A Trace of God in the Face of the Other

Instead of viewing refugees as uninvited and unwelcome, we look to see what Levinas calls a "trace of God," which transforms strangers into neighbors. When we acknowledge this dimension of transcendence in refugees seeking asylum, we're then able to take the risk to move away from all that's safe and familiar and reach out to genuinely welcome these strangers. Currently, we make the sacred soil of our sovereign nation holier than the Thou of the strange human being who dares to cross an international border and step upon the holy ground of "one nation under God." Instead, we should respect, cherish, and care for these mothers and fathers, boys and girls, with the same regard as we have for the dirt upon which their feet rest as they ask for safe asylum. When we label our neighbors seeking asylum as "illegals" or "aliens," we disregard the trace of God in their faces and our humanitarian relationship together as sisters and brothers. There is no more powerful act than to love our neighbor.[14]

Figure 9.1. A volunteer from the Interfaith Welcome Coalition walks a group of families to Travis Park UMC for respite during a long layover before their bus departs from the nearby Greyhound station in downtown San Antonio.[15]
Watercolor sketch by Helen T. Boursier.

Naming the Stranger a Neighbor

Love narrows the chasm from stranger to neighbor to friend, highlighting the nearness of the neighbor. Whereas some refer to "neighbor" as representing the generic human race, shifting the focus from stranger to neighbor who becomes friend provides the balancing point on the teeter-totter of embodied love. Welcoming the neighbor as friend balances out our overinflated sense of self. Hospitality for refugee families means welcoming the families as they are, not in another package that *we* might prefer. Unfortunately, as Caputo highlights, "Derrida's well-known analysis shows [that] normally it ends up meaning welcoming the same, inviting a short list of insiders while discreetly keeping the uninvited (the other) in the dark."[16] We want to welcome only those who are like us, homogenized such that there's no sense of being threatened by any element of differentness. When it comes to an international line demarcating *my* country from *yours*, sameness rules the day.

"Who, then, is one's neighbor?" It's easy to love our neighbor when we have control to define and limit *who* the neighbor is. Typically, we welcome people we already like, admire, or enjoy being with. We don't open the door for strangers; we open the door for friends. It's easy to love people like *us*, but naming the stranger as neighbor pushes us to love all creation. Kierkegaard's take on "neighbor" opens the reference so that neighbor is an extension of us. These families are what this philosopher-theologian would call "the *other you*."[17] These Central American neighbors also test what Kierkegaard calls the mirror of selfishness or "self-love."[18] Without the neighbor, it's too easy to succumb to selfishness, as an individual and as a nation. Welcoming the stranger as neighbor pushes aside selfishness and creates an opening for this nation to offer kindness, compassion, and hope for these families and children who are desperately seeking asylum.

Recognizing these sojourners as near neighbors means that, as a nation, we don't abandon our neighbors to suffer whatever consequences may arise from being labeled "illegal aliens" and unwanted "inadmissibles" in the name of "national security." Looking at our near neighbors through the lens of kindness, compassion, and love then calls us to challenge the rhetoric of border militarization, which fosters xenophobia in a nation where Lady Liberty purports to welcome the "huddled masses yearning to be free." Kindness, compassion, and love insist that we respect human dignity for all people. The automatic response for some people is to refute hospitality as an impossible ideal, but we must raise the bar to the highest level—perfect and radical and wonderfully welcoming hospitality. Once we have a vision for the absolute radical ideal, then we can compare that to what a slightly less than unconditional welcome might look like.

HOSPITALITY AS THE EVENT OF IMPOSSIBLE POSSIBILITY

The event of radical welcome can happen when we begin making changes to move in the direction of welcome through our attitudes, policies, and practices now, today. Using the language of Caputo, "Events do not exist; they insist. It is we who are called upon to give them existence."[19] The role of people of conscience is to insist the event of hospitality into being at its point just beyond the horizon of possibility. Insisting pushes the possibility beyond impossibility. Instead of saying, "No, that can't possibly happen," we look for ways to make this ideal come to fruition. We make the impossible possible, starting now, today. For people of faith, that possible possibility embraces the limitlessness of the God they worship. The very essence of faith purports that God, Jehovah, Yahweh, Jesus can and will make a way clear when the faithful see no possible possibility. To say that this task before us is too daunting, too big, and too impossible is to put God in a box and close the lid. If God is God, then nothing should be impossible for the God who makes all things possible.

Our response of kindness, compassion, and love today creates the possibility for refugees to be made welcome into the future. This possibility for radical hospitality affirms the nonrefoulement tenet of the Convention to not deport families back to homelands where their lives will once again be at great risk. When we respond in kindness, compassion, and love, then the families have the possibility to be welcomed and they also have the possibility to live safe and productive lives, contributing not only to the blessing of their own families, but also to the greater good of American society. We will be better together.[20]

MARTIN BUBER'S "I-THOU"

A holy encounter with the families resonates with German-Jewish philosopher Martin Buber's well-known proposal: "I require You to become; becoming I, I say You."[21] We need each other. We are fully *us* only when we offer a genuine welcome for *you*. Hospitality volunteers experience this fusion through letting go of self and being fully present with these families seeking asylum. For instance, during a debriefing session following a day with the families, one volunteer chaplain described a scene inside family detention when I had my arm draped around a mother while I offered a prayer. The volunteer chaplain said, "Your eyes were closed, and her eyes were closed, too. For a moment, it was like she was out of the room in a sacred place. It was a beautiful moment. Even with your struggling Spanish, you weren't worried about your limitations with language. Your prayer was spontaneous and selfless." Together, we experienced this seemingly simple moment as an unexpected gift. For the gift of love to be a gift, and for the giver of love to receive the event of gifting, the gifting back and forth must be free. It's what Kierkegaard calls willing the Good for the sake of the Good, his understanding of what it means to have what he calls "purity of heart."[22] The love exchanged unconditionally is a gift.

The "Economy" of the Gift

Gifting includes three key elements: the giver, the receiver, and a "thing" to give. For Derrida, the gift is invariably related to economy. If the gift is given, the gift in no way must come back to the donor."[23] The gift must not circulate or be exchanged. There's no requirement to "pay it forward" in the *cargo* sense (mentioned in the book introduction). The receiver doesn't receive with the obligation to give back, as this would negate the gift itself. It's in this sense that the gift, like radical hospitality, is "the impossible."[24] Gift is gift; hospitality is hospitality; welcome is welcome. There's no ulterior motive; there are no strings attached. The gift of hospitality is kindness for kindness's sake, compassion for compassion's sake, love for love's sake. Gifting hospitality is not to garner any reward for oneself or others, but simply for the essence of willing Good for the sake of the Good. It cannot be reduced to public policy, as important as that policy may be. People of conscience see the Good, will the Good, and take actions to help facilitate the Good. If there's any sense of gain through the gifting of hospitality, it would be that by caring for strangers the world brings the sacredness of the Creator of all humanity into the historical present such that the world becomes holy ground.

The Paradox of Hospitality for Refugees as Gift

The paradox of radical hospitality as gift must break free of any mind-set of the circle of economy. For unconditional welcome to become gift in the fullest sense of the word, it cannot look or feel like a gift. It simply is kindness, compassion, and love expressed as radical hospitality. The condition the gift shares with unconditional welcome is that neither can be calculated. For Derrida, certainty about the outcome is "social security, economics" but not justice because "justice and gift should go beyond calculation."[25] Of course, there must be some calculation for the sake of prudence, but one must recognize that, at some point, any sort of calculation for the worth or value of a gift, such as radical hospitality for refugees, inevitably reaches a point where it's impossible to discern in advance all the benefits. Any gift that comes with strings attached doesn't emerge from love or act for love; nor is it justice. Just as gift must be pure gift, kindness is purely done for the sake of kindness, compassion for compassion, and love simply as and for *love*.

OPENING THE GATE (BREAKING DOWN THE WALL) FOR REFUGEES SEEKING ASYLUM

How far do we go in extending hospitality? How radical is the inclusive guest list expected to be? Derrida's ideal of absolute understands that the politics of hospitality cannot be founded upon opening the border to anyone and everyone unilaterally and unconditionally. There must be some vetting, some way for the receiving nation to be hospitable while also being open to welcoming some asylum seekers. Derrida realizes, for example, that trying to establish criteria to discriminate between the enemy and the friend in border control security requires some limitations, so there cannot be unconditional or "pure hospitality."

Nevertheless, Derrida sets the bar high for perfect or ideal hospitality so that we can then see what less-than-perfect hospitality looks like. Building a wall and slamming the gate closed on everyone would be measured against the perfect or "radical" hospitality of letting everyone in. When compared to the *ideal*, it becomes poignantly obvious that there is a vast difference between perfect hospitality, where everyone would be welcome, and our current situation of the wall being pushed, refugees seeking asylum being detained for months and months at taxpayer expense, or the Trump administration deviant tactic proposed July 15, 2019, to deny asylum protection to migrants who had not first applied at a closer country.[26] The ACLU promptly filed a lawsuit the next day against the so-called third country asylum rule. The current treatment of refugees seeking asylum exemplifies the extreme opposite of any sense of hospitality or welcome.[27]

The only way to understand what hospitality means is to begin by describing unconditional hospitality, which has "openness to whomever, to any newcomer." We have to at least begin by defining what it means to have perfect, radical, or unconditional hospitality as the goal to shoot toward. Then, in comparison, we will have a sense of a less-than-perfect hospitality. For Derrida it's unreasonable to formulate in advance the "criterion to distinguish between the good immigrant and the bad immigrant." He advocates suspending the use of such criteria, but he also realizes that it's not possible to do so. Instead, he proposes establishing what "pure hospitality" looks like and using that to discern the difference between a limited hospitality and a *less limited* hospitality. Derrida insists "that I *give place* to them, that I let them come, that I let them arrive, and take place in the place I offer them, without asking of them either reciprocity (entering into a pact) or even their names."[28] Radical hospitality begins by erring toward welcome rather than xenophobic fear.

Each of us must address that "thing" that is blocking us from welcoming sojourners, to look in the mirror of our own soul and see what it is that we're afraid of. Then we must consider whether we want to be ruled by fear or limitation, whatever that fear or limitation may be, or whether we want to become people of kindness, compassion, and love. Instead of focusing on what we imagine these asylum seekers will "take" from us, we need to recognize, honor, and appreciate the gifts that they bring. Embracing radical hospitality begins with direct interaction with refugees seeking asylum, encountering a personalized experience of communion with these families, literally meeting them face-to-face.

10

Moving toward Responsible Response

The U.S. immigration matrix is broken. It clearly needs to be overhauled, renovated, and/or transformed. It's not a *them* or a *Washington, D.C.,* problem. For citizens of a democratic nation, it is *our* problem, *our* concern. Immigration is a nonpartisan moral issue that concerns us all. How *we the people* participate in the transformation of this complex broken system requires an intentional response grounded in ethical, moral, and compassionate action, what Dietrich Bonhoeffer, a German theologian and Lutheran minister who was martyred by Hitler shortly before the end of World War II, famously described as "responsible response." Bonhoeffer's understanding of response isn't based on politics, public opinion, or what's in the selfish interest of one nation or one person. It isn't about me, myself, and I. Rather, responsible response is an intentional decision that carefully, reflectively, and deliberately responds to injustice with actions that are morally grounded.

Moving toward responsible response begins with personal reflection. Each one of us needs to consider what we've done, intentionally or unintentionally, individually or institutionally, that's contributed to causing harm (at any level). We need to wrestle with that and then consider what we're willing to sacrifice. The worst response would be to deny the reality of our culpability for migrant suffering. German theologian Dorothee Söelle laments that the Germans exemplified denial during and following the Holocaust. She explains that "the denial of reality" was "repeated in a thousand places, [which] only made the shame more inescapable."[1] Volunteers with refugees seeking asylum in the United States are equally incensed in the current context of injustice and suffering against our southern neighbors. The denial of the suffering of asylum seekers here parallels Germany's denial of the Shoah. Denying our culpability doesn't make our responsibility magically disappear. We contribute to their nightmare. We make the horrors worse with our immigration policies and practices. Doing nothing, nonresponse, is response. Whether it's from lack of resources, time, or motivation, nonresponse is the choice to side with the existing policies and practices of the Powers That Be. How do we jump-start this nation's responsible response? Where do we begin?

At the conclusion of a panel discussion about the U.S. response to migration at our southern border, Sister Norma Pimentel asked the audience to consider what barriers were holding them back from volunteering and helping the families and from wanting them to be here in the first place. She asked, "What are these feelings or attitudes, and why do you have them in the first place?"[2] Part of our feelings or attitudes may come from a confused understanding about the reality of what's actually happening compared to what we've assumed or understood to be true about the factors contributing to these families seeking safety in the United States.

EDUCATION

An informed and inclusive education is an antidote to enlighten false assumptions. Remove any blinders you may have about the messy immigration matrix and how it impacts refugees seeking asylum. Don't take my word for granted! Check out the facts firsthand. For instance, I was part of a panel discussion on immigration issues, and one audience member couldn't get it through their head why detention of children is so bad. The attendee asked, "It sounds like the kids are well cared for and it's all bright and cheery inside. Aren't they better off there than somewhere else?" Two of the presenters explained why it's a bad thing to lock up children, but this participant asked the same question again: "What's so bad about detaining children?" If this is a concept that eludes you, then let your research and reading about children who are detained be your point of entry so you can make the response, "Children shouldn't be locked up. Children should be free."

Learning about the systemic issues we contribute to mass migration from the Northern Triangle is another place and space for education. For example, at a screening of his documentary film *Trails of Hope and Terror*, Miguel A. de la Torre said, "When we build roads into another nation to steal their product and get cheap labor, why should we be surprised that these same people take these same roads to come to our country when they are no longer able to earn a living in their own? When the vast majority of the resources go to the center of the empire, to the wealthy and powerful, the people on the edges don't get enough to support their families." He added, "It doesn't matter if we turn a blind eye to it. It does not make us any less responsible."[3]

Do some investigative background checking to learn and discern the reality of the violence the families are fleeing, U.S. contributions to the economic instability in the Northern Triangle, and our culpability for drugs, guns, and gangs. Attend and/or organize an educational seminar and invite a specialist in any of the topics surrounding U.S. injustice at the southern border. Do your own research on the UNHCR, Convention, Protocol, and U.S. Immigration policies and practices.

Figure 10.1.   The lanes for loaded trucks in California bound for Mexico to pass through CBP, which seem to go on to infinity, stand empty on a late Saturday afternoon in January 2019. Mexico is on the right side of the chain-link fencing and barbed wire "wall."

Learn firsthand about the suffering of these families in their homelands and the additional suffering the United States heaps upon them when they attempt to cross the U.S.-Mexico border and seek asylum. Education helps to reframe our assumptions. Then we can correct the language we use about the reality of the suffering and the reasons why these families flee their homelands. Education also frames migration as a humanitarian issue that has policy ramifications. When I change myself, I can begin to change the world.

BLESSING

Education brings us one step closer to compassionate response by offering our blessing to the migrants' plea for asylum by simply saying, "May things go well for you." Once we've given our blessing to something, it's more probable that we would then offer tangible help.[4] The blessing also confirms that we respect their claims to asylum. We believe the truth of their testimonies. Blessing affirms our individual and collective witness to and for the families and their claim to basic hospitality. A Central American whose attempt to settle in the United States failed two decades ago (he settled his family in Mexico instead) suggested to a delegation of seventy faith-based leaders who were visiting Nogales, Sonora, "When you go back to your places of origin and you see migrants from Central America, extend your hand." That simple greeting is a tangible form of blessing. Our blessing includes unhesitant willingness to walk with the families along the way, so that *their* journey becomes *our* journey. Theirs is ours; ours is theirs.

SOLIDARITY

Solidarity with the refugee families names their humanity and also Buber's "I-Thou-We" connection and the relationality of *them* being a piece of *us* just as *we* are part of *them*. We cannot be whole when *they* are locked up in dog kennels, refrigerators, and for-profit family detention centers. Solidarity prioritizes the universality of love for all humanity. Solidarity affirms that *we* are not more precious, more beloved, more cherished than *them*. Solidarity includes our responsibility to shoulder together their witness, amplifying their voices so that they're acknowledged, heard, respected, and compassionately responded to in the public square. We raise our voices in mosques, temples, and churches across the country, and also around the dinner table as our own families and friends gather to break bread together. Solidarity means we weep when the front pages of the newspapers highlight stories of mothers and children being ripped apart at the border because they "broke our laws" as they entered the United States "illegally."

Solidarity demands that we call, write, and email our legislators, holding them accountable to the role of love over the rule of law. Solidarity marches, pickets, stages nonviolent protests, and generally exercises whatever civic disobedience is necessary to challenge and change the unjust sanctions against these families so we become a nation of radical welcome. Solidarity doesn't allow a country to slowly creep down the path toward fascism or dictatorship whereby one day we wake up and it is too late, not only for the refugees whose very lives are at stake should they be deported, but also for the souls of U.S. citizens as our nation slides down the slippery slope with one injustice sleazily joining forces with another and another and another. Solidary says, "*Ya!*" (Enough!), calling every aspect of the immigration matrix to accountability. Enough is enough! Solidarity ultimately helps to carry the burden of responsibility for a nation to willingly welcome these families seeking asylum.

ALLYSHIP

Allyship is an active form of solidarity. It means to stand as allies with someone, not necessarily among or with the actual people you are being supportive of, but with and for their cause, plight, suffering, and/or right to compassion, mercy, and justice. You begin with the people in your own circle of influence, with those who already respect who and what you are about. I cannot speak in *your* world; I don't know you,

Figure 10.2. Clergy colleagues respond to my allyship invitation to offer hospitality and welcome to the families at the bus station.

nor do you know me. There's no mutual respect or rapport, so it won't help if I share my two cents with you if we're strangers. It won't help to step into your world and advocate or be an ally. Allyship means that your witness in support of these families goes forth to your own family, friends, neighbors, and colleagues (your circle of influence) in whatever context that you would normally have contact or connection.

Humanization is the key conversation point. If we focus on political policies and "issues," then we dehumanize these migrants. We need to remember that we're talking about real people, human beings like us. We need to shift from issues rhetoric to language that humanizes. Not everyone will agree with you; not everyone will want to hear about your experiences, but your circle of influence is the place to begin.

PERSONAL EXPERIENCE MAKES A BIG DIFFERENCE

An attorney who volunteers for *Flores* accountability inspections said, "Our listening is informed by who we know. If you know one person from Honduras, Maria, who cleans your house, you say how wonderful Maria is and too bad there aren't more people like Maria." It comes down to taking the effort to get to know the people who are seeking asylum in this country, meeting them face-to-face on a personal level, as the attorney added: "But if you know her family and her friends and more and more of her connectional group, then your listening is informed by this wider perspective. The more people we know of a population, the more we change our assumptions and the more we are able to really listen. We either assume Maria is an exception, one of the 'good ones,' or we can say, 'Wow! All of my assumptions were wrong.'"

The best way to understand asylum seekers is to come and see them for yourself. For example, a seminary student I brought with me to volunteer with traveling families at the Greyhound bus station in San Antonio exemplifies the personal connection. This student said the most powerful aspect of her day with the families was in their eyes. She said, "When I look into their eyes, it's clear that they aren't robbers, drug addicts, or sneaky people who are trying to get away with something." She said she noticed a depth of genuineness in their eyes. Some people showed hesitancy and uncertainty, but through gazing into their eyes, she found it obvious that they aren't here to take advantage of the United States or to "get away with" something. They clearly are kind, caring, lovely people who need help so that they can live their lives.

A native of Mexico who is a legal resident of the United States had a similar experience when he volunteered as a translator for a sanctuary church that hosted families during family separation/reunification. After we visited with the mothers and he heard their stories, he was flabbergasted about their experiences of injustice at our southern border. He said, "Until today, I had no idea that any of this was happening." Nothing takes the place of a firsthand experience with the families.

FROM COUCH POTATO TO ZEALOT
AND EVERYTHING IN BETWEEN

You'll discover your place on the "participation in responsible response" spectrum when you make the political personal through direct interaction with refugees seeking asylum, in whatever context and whatever capacity. You need to see the faces of these mothers and fathers, brothers and sisters, to make their lived reality yours. The spectrum of possibilities for response ranges from the couch potato who listens to (and believes) the talking heads on television and social media but does zero first-person investigation, to the other extreme of hopping on a plane to Mexico City to ride in the migrant caravan, sleep in the shelters with them, and experience the road trip firsthand. There's a large range of options between the extremes of couch potato and zealot. What's your spot in the spectrum?

On the entry-level range, one of the people in an immersion experience I attended in southern Arizona never had a passport. She's retired and in her upper sixties. She had to get an expedited passport in order to be able to attend the Mexico aspect of the week-long event. She didn't let the passport or her age, gender, or employment status inhibit her. A young woman from northern Vermont, who also spent a week of intensive on-site training in southern Arizona to learn and experience migration firsthand, said she knew absolutely nothing about border issues. She explained that her town is generally very active with social justice concerns. They sent her down to learn and to bring back what she found out so that she could enlighten her community from a firsthand experience.

Someone who advocates through writing said, "The oppressors must be held accountable, and we must continue to remind the world of the injustice through how we bear witness. We hear the cries and hold the oppressors accountable." History and justice demand that we document what's happening through writing, speaking, singing, and making art, so that we witness and document the suffering of these families. Witness is not just about recording what's happening today, but preserving it as a record for the future. For example, the Grass Valley–Sahuarita Arizona Samaritans have a writers group. In addition to writing the training materials that make it easy for others to learn how to help, they also write letters to the editor and proactively write positive things about migrants. A member of this group explained, "We do it as a group so that different names go out as the author and more articles get published. It's been a way to make a difference in our community." Two newspapers published editorials from this writers group during January 2018 in response to the "crisis" at the southern border and the government shutdown. One letter described the reality of the peacefulness at the Arizona-Mexico border, "which has among the lowest crime rates in the state. There's no panic on these border streets."[5] The other offered suggestions for specific ways to improve border security:

We do need border security.

We need more customs agents. They catch the drug smugglers. We need more agents to man the gates at ports of entry; only six of 14 gates are open due to lack of agents at Mariposa Port of Entry in Nogales. We need more gates manned to alleviate delays in commercial traffic and inconvenience to people crossing the border.

We need more immigration judges. It's inhumane and un-American to ask anyone to wait years to get a hearing. It's uneconomical to detain people who could be supporting their families or continue to be productive members of society. Unnecessary detentions and lack of immigration judges are a drain on taxpayers. It's an economic issue!

These are immediate needs. Eventually, we need immigration reform with consistent and enforceable laws![6]

Artists also find creative ways to document and witness for migrants. An anonymous installation artist known only as JR created an enormous outdoor picnic on both sides of the border fence that separates Tecate, Mexico, from Tecate, California, to depict a sense of radical hospitality. The artist painted the massive table with a pair of eyes, one eye on each side of the border. The crowd that gathered for the picnic shared the same food, water, and music, with half of the mariachi band playing on each side of the border.[7] Other artists have created ways to do art together with migrants, even something as simple as making Valentine cards with children on the floor of the bus station while traveling families wait to depart or making Christmas cards to give to families who are detained. Creative people look for creative ways to share their creative talents to make a difference with and for refugees seeking asylum.

Organized Actions in Federal Court

On the more extreme side of the spectrum, advocates have held actions in federal court to protest Operation Streamline and family separation. An advocate explained the obvious: "To do an action in federal court is pretty significant." A group of clergy went together to a courthouse. When the first migrant said, "Culpable" (guilty), someone stood up and said, "You are not guilty; this court is guilty, and this country is guilty," and then they read a scripture passage. A marshal hauled this clergyperson out of the courtroom. Then the next minister repeated the same. When the third faith leader stood and did the same thing, they had run out of marshals and had to go to another courtroom to get more. The advocate explained, "None of us got arrested, but we all got carted off." On another occasion, a group of high school students just stood up and turned their backs to the court as a silent gesture of protest.

Flores Volunteers

An ongoing flow of doctors, lawyers, and translators hold the government accountable to the *Flores* agreement (explained in chapter 4). A retired immigration attorney who makes multiple volunteer *Flores* visits to facilities where unaccompanied children are detained said, "Why do I do it? To help the children. I have the skill set, and I want to do something to make a difference in the lives of these children." She added, "I remember one indigenous child who was too traumatized to speak. No one spoke K'iche, and he didn't speak Spanish or English. He was completely shut out, unable to communicate. I will never forget his eyes and the depth of his pain. For some of the children, looking into their eyes is like looking into blank shells. There's nothing there. I don't sleep when I volunteer with the children. It's too haunting."

There's something for everyone to do. You can help in whatever context or capacity works best for you. What's your skill set? What are the gifts you have to share? How can you begin to make a difference in the broken immigration matrix to bring help and hope for refugees seeking asylum? There are a bazillion opportunities and points of entry. What is yours to do?

11

Making the Political Personal

Three Examples

The options for participation are limitless regarding how you can help these families seeking asylum. You might opt to take a short-term trip to a border state and volunteer with existing organizations already helping sojourners, or you could look for individuals, groups, and agencies offering assistance in your own community. Volunteers have their own stories about why they got started, the assistance they offer, and the lessons learned and insights gained. Here are three personal testimonies.

LONG-TERM HOSPITALITY FOR A
MOTHER AND SON SEEKING ASYLUM

Meg hosted a mother and son in her home for thirteen months while they were pursuing the formal asylum process. She decided to make this commitment after taking a group of high school students from her church to San Juan Bonito in the Rio Grande Valley in South Texas during the summer of 2017. They went to see immigration from a more human perspective and to put names, faces, and stories with what's happening. They went to La Posada Providencia, a shelter run by Catholic sisters specifically for people who are seeking asylum. Meg explained, "We heard a lot of people's stories, and La Posada shared that they were bursting at the seams and looking for people to host families." Some don't have any place to go and they've exhausted all their resources getting to the United States, mostly people from Cuba and the Congo, Meg explained, because those from Central America generally have family here. All of the families at La Posada are formally in the asylum system. No one is here that the U.S. government doesn't know about.

Meg said, "I stewed on it for a while, for a couple of months. I had a lot of work to do to get my house in shape so it could be inhabited by people other than just me." In September she called and talked to Sister Zita Telkamp at La Posada. Meg explained her experience:

> When I finally called to say I was ready, she didn't have anyone that would fit at the time, but she called me twenty-four hours later to say she had a mother and son, whom I'll refer to as D and D for privacy's sake. She asked if I could come in three days. So, four days later I drove an hour from Seguin to the Greyhound bus station in San Antonio to pick them up. They had no clue who I was, why they were there, or how long they'd be with me. They just got put on a bus from Harlingen in South Texas. They were sent up to me in San Antonio (three hours north). I didn't know them, and of course, typical me, I was late getting there, so the bus had already arrived. I just walked in and asked every mother who had a son with her, "D?" until a mother with a son said, "*Sí*." They had no idea what was going on, or who I was. I didn't speak Spanish, and neither of them spoke any English, though the son is fluent now. They just got in my car and I took them to my home.
>
> A friend who is fluent in Spanish came to the house later that day to explain the basic functions of the house, like how to use the shower and the washer and dryer. That's when I realized they didn't know why they were there or how long they would be there. The mother asked, "Why are we here, and how long are we staying?" Through the friend who was interpreting I said, "You can stay as long as you need to while you work on your asylum case."

I asked Meg what surprised her about her experience of hosting a mother and son for thirteen months in her home and what was the greatest challenge. She said, "I didn't expect the awkwardness from Mom D needing to be able to contribute to the household. She did a lot of cooking and cleaning, and I felt very, very uncomfortable for a very long time. I hadn't offered to host them so that she could cook and clean. I finally decided to let her do what she felt like she needed to do without placing any expectations." Mom D didn't have a work permit until eleven months into the extended-stay hospitality. Meg added, "I think it weighed very heavy on her. I paid for all the groceries and the expenses that came up."

When I met with Meg, D and D were flying to the East Coast the following day to continue the next phase of their asylum journey with a cousin who'd offered to host them. Their case had been denied because the judge determined that extreme domestic violence did not count as a valid reason for asylum and that being female was not enough to quality for asylum based on being in the "group" of abused women. The court case was heard during the timeframe that Jeff Sessions had mandated that domestic violence and gang violence weren't valid reasons for asylum (see chapter 6). After the devastating verdict and the impending deportation back to the violence D and D had fled, they chose to appeal the judge's decision. Meg said the hardest part was the boy leaving. "He's become my little buddy. We do our routine in the morning, then I take him to school and pick him up after. We've bonded over day-to-day living together. He's light. He's funny, smart, goofy, and energetic. You cannot help but be won over by him. They've also adopted my dogs. The dogs sleep in their room, and they will be devastated when D and D leave tomorrow." The greatest joy of this Lutheran minister who offered unconditional hospitality was that she baptized both mother and son the Sunday before their departure. "The mother had asked me to baptize her son, and then it turned out she hadn't been baptized either," Meg said. "And I did it all in Spanish, not well, but it's done."

For others who might consider hosting families, she has these words of advice:

> It's going to break your heart and give you life in ways you've never anticipated. It's going to be harder than you think, but also better than you think. You will feel angry and powerless during the process, and you're going to have to just live with that. The system needs to be overhauled. All we can do is find ways to honor the humanity of people and give them space to live and breathe in a time and place in their lives that is so horrible. The biggest lesson I've learned is that it's a broken system that perpetrates itself over and over again. I want there to be one person that I could point to and blame, but everyone's hands are in this system we have created.

Meg never formally asked her congregation for help, because it was her personal choice to offer hospitality. She explained, "That said, they all pitched in to help in countless ways, and they have been impacted by having this mother and son in their lives for thirteen months. They cried during the baptisms on Sunday." She added, "Now when they see stories in the news, it's not policy about faceless, nameless people. They see D and D. They also connect directly to the teachings in scripture. It's no longer abstract; it's real because of this mother and son."[1]

MINISTER FLIES TO MEXICO CITY AND JUMPS ON THE MIGRANT CARAVAN

During November 2018, Pastor Gavin Rogers flew to Mexico City and jumped on the massive migrant caravan while it was slowly making its way from Honduras to the United States. He's returned there several times to reconnect with the friends he made during his portion of their journey to Tijuana. He also participated in the December 10, 2018, ecumenical protest march with 250 faith leaders and activists who joined in solidarity to walk to the beach at Friendship Park in San Diego, which abuts the southern border with Mexico.

Here's an excerpt of the conversation that unfolded between Gavin and the guest host before a rapt audience of approximately sixty people who had gathered to hear his story firsthand. They were in the back room of the Friendly Spot Ice House in San Antonio for Pub Theology, a public outreach ministry sponsored by Travis Park United Methodist Church (UMC), where Gavin is an associate pastor.[2]

> Rey: How'd you get the idea to get on a plane to Mexico City and then find the migrant caravan? What gave you the idea and how did the caravan get to become a caravan?
>
> Gavin: I've worked with the homeless for a long time, and I've always cared about people who have been mislabeled, how we speak about them. Everyone assumed the caravan

was coming to Texas, so I decided to research where the caravan was—near Mexico City at the time. This is the kind of thing I would've done when I was younger, even just six years ago. It's fairly cheap to fly there, and I have a good friend who lives there, so I hopped a plane and flew down. I convinced my Airbnb host to drive me to find the caravan. It turned out to be in a soccer stadium in Mexico City. We asked some questions to get a sense of what was going on: "Is this the largest group?" "Yes." "When are they leaving?" "In about four hours." I put my bag in my friend's car and at 4 a.m. took the subway out of Mexico City as far as it would go with those on the migrant caravan. Most times I didn't have a translator and that forced me to figure out communication because I don't speak Spanish.

Rey: What did they call you?

Gavin: I quickly became "Gavino," who is a famous singer. Sometimes they called me Gavi, but mostly it was Gavino.

Rey: Did you reach a point traveling where you saw politics or theology differently? How did one or the other change because of this experience?

Gavin: As a Christian pastor, I worship a God who is a refugee. Faith-based people try to wiggle out of it. I don't see this as a political response. For me, it's a theological response. There can't be a different Christian or faith-based response around what country you live in. It's one faith-based response for all countries. It also doesn't matter what religious tradition you follow—they're all pilgrims: Moses, Abraham, Mohammed, Buddha, and currently the Dalai Lama still is a migrant living as a refugee in India. For people of faith, it shouldn't be a divided issue.

I met volunteers from [different agencies] who have very different religious and political views, but they were there to help the migrants the same as me.

Rey: Who are the migrants in the caravan hoping will help them? Nice politicians? Churches? Who?

Gavin: There was a lot of confusion in the caravan about where the administration stands. [Pause] We're confused. One of the biggest lies we keep telling ourselves is that there's scarcity and lack of resources. That's just not true. The migrants saw their act in coming here as one of complete transparency. They didn't hire *coyotes*. They were very forthright. They saw it as an act of legal action. They hoped people would see it as a legal act so that people would change their minds. When they first learned that I was a pastor, then they'd ask, "Do you know Pastor Johnson . . . or Pastor Smith . . . ?" Many of these people were evangelized by protestant pastors who went to Central America on mission trips and did evangelism there during the past forty years. Pastors cared enough to go to Central America to do evangelism, so why wouldn't these same pastors care enough to help them when these same people come to the U.S. for asylum?

Rey: The youth you traveled with who are from Honduras, do they get a sense of how they're depicted in the U.S.?

Gavin: They know that Trump is a wildcard. They have phones. Sometimes they work and sometimes they don't. But overall they don't have access to the same information that we have. I didn't get the sense that they took all the public/social media talk personally.

Figure 11.1. CBP agents surround faith leaders who are kneeling in the surf on the American side of the Pacific Ocean at Friendship Park at the California-Mexico border during a protest march on December 10, 2018. At least thirty faith leaders were arrested. Pastor Gavin Rogers, wearing the white robe, participated in the protest.
Photo by Mike DuBose, UMC News Service; used by permission.

Rey: What were their living conditions and what humanitarian aid is available to them?

Gavin: When they started leaving Guatemala to enter Mexico, agencies gave them tents. They used those no matter what shelter was available—so inside the soccer stadium and the indoor theme park or outside in parks or along the road. Each municipality had its response, so they would pitch their tents there—thousands of people. Some areas had more help available than others. It was a lot colder than people imagined. You'd hear people coughing. A lot of people got sick. I got sick. Tijuana was really bad. I'd planned to go back at Thanksgiving, but someone organized buses, etc., so the caravan arrived to Tijuana ahead of expectations. Tijuana wasn't prepared. Mexico did a great job along the way because the migrants were there only four days. But now, in Tijuana, they're stuck there.

Rey: What are some of your most memorable experiences with the caravan?

Gavin: People were in this together as a family. You could leave your stuff in your tent and no one would bother it. I left my backpack and no one bothered it. Once a wad of dollar bills fell out of my back pocket, and someone picked it up and handed it to me. They also watched my bag when I jumped off one of the trucks we rode on so I could run into the bathroom. Then I jumped back on the truck before it left for Cuerto.

Figure 11.2. The thirty-six-wheel truck Pastor Gavin Rogers rode during his journey through Mexico with the migrant caravan from Honduras.
Photo by Gavin Rogers; shared by permission.

We left Cuerto at 4 a.m. and we started walking to get to the toll station so we could try to get a ride on a truck. This day there was a huge thirty-six-wheeler that pulled up with steel beams on top. Someone asked the driver if he would accept riders, and he said, "Sure, get on." Hundreds of migrants climbed up. I had like ten seconds to decide, and at that point I didn't know anyone yet, and I didn't have any friends. I jumped on and squeezed in, and then the truck started to drive off. Immediately, the people around me wrapped their arms and legs around me to keep me safe. We were like a human pretzel, all in this intimate position. One had their arms wrapped around me and another had their legs completely around me and holding me tight. All of a sudden we were forced into community and hospitality together on this truck. I didn't know them. They didn't know me. I was a total stranger, and they treated me with complete and total hospitality. I wouldn't have become steadfast friends with them if it hadn't have been for that transformative moment when they immediately and completely took care of me, made sure that I was safe. We were on the truck like that for hours with our legs falling asleep, crammed in tight with everyone else. You really get to know people well when your bodies are draped all over each other, and you're doing all you can to hang on while the truck is moving down the road.

We got to the next shelter earlier than expected. The people I'd gotten to know, the ones who were riding close beside me, were all ages fifteen to twenty-five. They were all huddled up like a young adults group would be at church. We traveled six hours north of Mexico City at truck speed, not at car speed. A bunch of people got off at the shelter stop, but these young adults convinced the driver to keep going. I told them that it was crazy to keep going, but they wanted to so I stayed with them. That's when the truck started picking up speed and it got more dangerous.

Helen [from the audience]: What surprised you the most, and what disappointed you?

Gavin: No one has ever asked me these questions before. Their hospitality for me surprised me the most. Immediately they treated me with unconditional warmth. Throughout the trip, each time we got to a new mode of transportation, they made sure that I was there and that I was taken care of. They immediately gave such generous hospitality to me, a total stranger. I would expect them to take care of each other because they'd been traveling together for a while. But me? I was a stranger, and they welcomed me. It was right out of Exodus or Matthew in the Bible [Exodus 22:21, Matthew 25:35]. What was the other question?

Rey: What disappointed you?

Gavin: A lot of the Christian response has disappointed me. That's a copout answer, but true. If we would teach correct theology, then the bad theology about migrants will die down. When churches are reluctant to get involved because of the long-term future of these faith groups, I ask them what they are afraid of. What's the worst thing that can come out of this? I actually had someone respond that she fears getting hit by a drunk driver who's an immigrant. Maybe the better question is, What's the worst thing that can happen if we actually address immigration?

It's one thing to have a political debate over migration issues, including this caravan, but you cannot have a theological debate. I learned this from Helen: The migrants say they are coming here for a "better life," but they don't mean what we mean. They just want safety and the basic necessities of life.

Rey: How have you changed from this experience?

Gavin: A fifteen-year-old girl was traveling alone to reunite with her mother in the U.S. She hadn't seen her mother in years, not since she was a little girl. She was traveling solo, but she was safe in the critical mass of the caravan. She left with a small group of teenage girls, but her friends stayed behind in southern Mexico, so she joined with another group of young adults. She's like a sister to me now.

Rey: What are your parting words, your take-home message for us here tonight?

Gavin: Spend a day, two days, go to the border, meet with people. I guarantee something will change and probably for the good. Change will come when people personally meet people. It was a game changer for me, and it will be for you, too.

ATTORNEY PROVIDES PRO BONO
LEGAL ASSISTANCE IN TIJUANA

A California immigration attorney shared her experiences about helping the migrant caravan with legal assistance soon after it arrived in Tijuana. She wanted to share some of her thoughts about the experience there and, more important, to provide some clarification about the caravan and the asylum process, and correct some of the misinformation presented in the news and on social media.[3] Via email, she wrote:

I spent Thanksgiving weekend in Tijuana working with refugees in the caravan in the largest makeshift camp located at the Benito Juárez Sports Unit. As an immigration attorney, my role was to meet with people individually in the camp to explain U.S. asylum law and the asylum application process—which for arriving refugees will involve detention in harsh conditions, possible family separation, and a court case in which they will

*likely have to represent themselves because only about 20 percent of detained immigrants
are able to find representation.*

*First, the caravan is made up of refugees who are seeking asylum because they are
afraid to return to their home countries. The people I met were fleeing several forms of
persecution. There were political activists who took a stand against their own government
and were harmed or threatened as a result of their activism, Indigenous environmental
activists threatened for their work, people fleeing the civil war in Nicaragua, people who
experienced severe violence and death threats from gangs, domestic violence victims from
countries that do not offer any protections to women who want to leave an abusive partner, LGBTQ youth who faced persecution and acts of violence in their home country, and
parents who are trying to save their young children from violence.*

*Though the reasons people in the caravan are seeking refuge in the U.S. are diverse,
they are united by their desire to live in freedom and safety. They have made a journey
that is tremendously difficult because it was necessary for their survival. No one would go
through an experience like this unless they had no other choice.*

*Second, the refugees ARE following the legal procedures for seeking asylum in the U.S.
To seek asylum in the U.S. you must be present either inside the country or at a port of
entry. The caravan is in Tijuana to go to the San Ysidro Port of Entry to ask to apply for
asylum. The Port of Entry is processing arriving asylum seekers at a dangerously slow pace
so many will be forced to live in camps in Tijuana with limited to no access to drinking
water, food, or sanitary facilities for several weeks until they can turn in. From there,
they will be processed by CBP and left in a "cold room" (literally a very cold room full of
people, with no windows or clocks, where they will have to sleep on the floor with Mylar
blankets, no access to showers for at least a week, in the same clothes they arrived in,
given very little food . . . it's a terrible experience that should never occur in the U.S.).
Then, they will be transferred to ICE custody where they will be detained in a detention
center that is like a jail. Men and women are not detained together so many people will
be separated from their spouses. Children are sometimes removed from parents (especially
fathers). The refugees will likely do their entire asylum case while detained. And also ICE
takes all their personal belongings, which means if they brought evidence for their asylum
case that evidence may end up "lost" or "inaccessible." This is currently the legal way for
arriving refugees to seek asylum. It is truly a human rights violation and we all should
fight to change it. But, returning to my original point, the caravan members are following
our (inhumane) system for seeking asylum.*

*There is no "line" for people to wait in and that is true for other forms of immigration
relief as well. Any time I hear someone talking about the "line" and how people need
to wait in this "line," I am just astonished by how misinformed most people are about
immigration law. There is no magic line to come to the U.S. There are visas and forms
of relief based on a variety of complex criteria, each of which has its own wait time and
processing time. There's never been a line.*

*Third, granting asylum to people who qualify for it will not create an "invasion" or
"flood" of people. Refugees are involuntary immigrants, meaning that they are forced to
migrate for their own safety, not because they want to. I keep hearing people say things*

Figure 11.3. Wall at the California side of the San Ysidro Port of Entry at the U.S.-Mexico border. The massive migrant caravan remains stuck on the Mexico side.

like, "but everyone wants to come here so we can't just let in these refugees." As a refugee attorney, I can promise you "everyone" does not want to come here. Everyone does want to live in safety and ensure that their children can survive. Just like you probably don't want to leave your community to move to another country, most people also like where they're from as long as they can live there safely. You probably like living where you live because you feel connected to your loved ones, your community, your work, etc. Think about what it would take for you to decide to travel thousands of miles to a new country you've never been to before with your young children and only the clothes on your back. You're probably thinking it would take severe, life-threatening danger for you to get to that point. It is the same for refugees coming here. So many people I have met, including caravan members and refugee clients in the U.S., say their dream is that one day their country of origin will be safe enough for them to return. We need to get over this mentality of American exceptionalism that makes us believe that "everyone" wishes they could live in the U.S. and that we will be "overrun" if we simply welcome the people who are asking us for refuge so that they won't be killed. And while we're at it, let's stop using dehumanizing terms ("invasion," "flood," etc.) and be more respectful of everyone's humanity.

Fourth, there is no need to be afraid of people in the caravan or other asylum seekers. Obviously this should go without saying but given the current political narrative that we hear in the news every day, I think it is worth stating that there is no need to fear someone just because they come from a different country and speak a different language than you do. Asylum seekers are human beings and they want the same things for their life that you want for yours—things like the knowledge that their children are safe and the ability to express their political opinions without fear of government torture. This idea that we somehow should be frightened or intimidated by people who are seeking asylum is really bizarre and only intended to manipulate public perception so that certain groups can maintain political power.

Fifth, on the topic of safety, the only time I ever felt unsafe in the camp was when I saw military and CBP helicopters circling the camp repeatedly. When the helicopters got closer to the ground we could see armed soldiers sitting in the open doorways holding weapons. I realize that more than anything this is just a political stunt put on by the current administration (and one that costs millions of dollars), but it was still frightening to see. The only real result of the military presence was that refugees and aid workers in the camp felt intimidated but we had nowhere else to go, so we simply had to try to ignore it. It's deeply disturbing that our federal government is able to find millions for a political stunt that intimidates vulnerable people and yet somehow we lack funding for services like healthcare and education that actually would improve this country.

This immigration attorney closed her detailed update with a plea for tangible help to raise money for a bond fund for refugees seeking asylum:

Helping refugees bond out of detention means they can reunite with their families while their cases move forward on the non-detained docket. It also means that we have more access to evidence and more time to develop their case. These are life-and-death cases and on the detained docket they are completed in months if not weeks. That is simply not reasonable for a case with such high stakes in an area of law that is so complex. It is not an exaggeration to say that bond funds save lives so please donate if you can!

Another immigration attorney said, "Immigration court is like traffic court but with a death sentence." She explained, "Both have quotas to meet, but the consequences in Immigration court are literally the difference between life and death."

The personal stories included above might never be *you*, but that doesn't get you off the hook for participation in the immigration matrix. There are lots of other options for how you can begin to make a dent and a difference with humanitarian aid for refugees seeking asylum.

12

Help and Hope for Migrants

Humanitarian Aid on Both Sides of the Border

Directly engaging with the families through tangible acts of hospitality and welcome humanizes these families seeking asylum. A priest whose congregation helped reunite families in McAllen, Texas, said, "It's a good thing to come here and to see the families, to serve them, to touch them." The point is to find the best way to connect, a way that suits your interests, skills, time, resources, and/or location. There are numerous individuals and groups who volunteer their time, talents, and resources to assist sojourners on both sides of our southern border. This chapter offers a glimpse of some of the places and people who offer help and hope through humanitarian aid. The stories here are not meant to be inclusive or exclusive. Rather, these representative examples offer an alternative response to refugees seeking asylum. Instead of heaping on suffering, abuse, and injustice, these individuals and groups show kindness, compassion, and unconditional love.

Volunteers begin helping with a migrant ministry for a variety of reasons. I started volunteering in 2014. In August of that year, I brought members of my congregation on a service trip to the Humanitarian Respite Center, located at Sacred Heart Catholic Church in McAllen, Texas, to help in various capacities with the arriving refugee families. We were a mission- and service-focused congregation, and this border trip gave us easy access to do "global mission" stateside, five hours south. I really didn't know anything about immigration and the southern border until I was asked in October 2014 to chair the Mission Outreach and Justice Committee for my region in the Presbyterian Church (USA). I systematically began participating in the various ministry opportunities that this connectional entity oversees for some 140 churches in South Texas, including its very active involvement with refugees through its immigration task force. In November 2014, I attended a training session to be a visitor volunteer for families who are detained, and I immediately began visiting families inside Karnes several times a month. The art ministry emerged from there.

I quickly fell in love with the families. After I was kicked out of Karnes, I continued my connection with the families by volunteering at the Greyhound bus station in San Antonio. As I've had the privilege of spending time with thousands of families, they've become part of my heart and soul. Another volunteer said, "These families have become my life friends."

An Arizona resident started a nonprofit home for children in Honduras because she felt so overwhelmed at the magnitude of all the suffering that she wanted to make a tangible difference in the lives of children on an individual basis. The ministry is home to twelve girls who all come from sexual abuse in their homes, and generally the father has been the abuser. The American in Honduras said, "If I can make a difference in the lives of these twelve, I will feel like I've done what I can." She added, "I'm teaching these girls that they have control over their bodies, that they have the right and the authority to say no."

A volunteer in San Antonio explained that her weekly assistance at the bus station was in direct response to the 2016 presidential election. She said, "There was so much angry rhetoric in the world that I wanted to do something positive." After her initial encounters, she continued to volunteer because she felt like she was making a difference by being present with the families, one-on-one. She added, "I think of all the love and compassion that we're able to give in these moments. I cannot imagine how much more chaotic, how much more stressful, it would be for the families if we weren't here to welcome them and help them through the process." She said that the sense of fulfillment she receives from her weekly encounters with the families exceeds description. Another volunteer summarized her motivation for choosing to assist the families, saying, "This work breaks my heart, but it also heals it."

NOGALES OFFERS AID TO MIGRANTS COMING AND GOING

There are a myriad of nongovernmental agencies that assist migrants coming and going on both sides of the U.S.-Mexico border.[1] For example, in Nogales, Sonora, Mexico, a faith-based organization, the Network of Migrants Rights, offers food, clothing, and overnight lodging at various locations. A U.S. resident who regularly helps in migrant shelters on the Mexico side of the border explained, "They have all the same laws in Mexico as we do. The migrants aren't supposed to be in churches, schools, etc., but they're full of migrants." The Catholic church in Nogales houses 160 migrants every day in men's and women's dorms. A small Pentecostal church houses fifteen people every night. The shelter volunteer said, "I wonder why churches in the U.S. have so much trouble hosting migrants. They have the same laws in Mexico as we do in the U.S., but still they take risks."

Shelter for Migrants in Nogales, Sonora, Mexico

An independent shelter in Nogales was opened in 1982 by a husband and wife who decided to help immigrants because, at the time, no one else was offering any assistance for migrants. Instead, migrants were forced to stay on the street, in the plaza, or at the train station, which of course was very dangerous. The couple found the current building when it was broken down and abandoned. They named it after San Juan Bosco, a patron saint of children. Initially, people slept on the floor, but through the donations of friends and family the structure was refurbished and a security system was installed to keep predators at bay. This shelter hosted 20,000 migrants in 2017, and 70 percent who stayed there already had been deported from the United States.

The shelter offers assistance to men, women, and children who come accompanied by an adult, either a parent or an aunt or uncle. The owner explained, "We have helped people who have broken their arms, legs, or back from being pushed off the trains by the *maras* [gangs]. Many migrants fall off the trains, either on this side or on that side, and then they are deported. We took care of one man for two months when he was deported with a spine fracture." Guests can stay for three days, depending on the case of each person. The shelter provides breakfast and supper and a bed with a shared bathroom. Guests can use the phone to call family and receive help with legal issues. The owner added that some of the migrants are protected by Mexican law, but for others it's just as difficult to get asylum in Mexico as it is in the United States.

El Comedor

El Comedor (the Dining Room) is a small but mighty mission run by the Missionary Sisters of the Eucharist and by Catholic Jesuits, who provide two meals a day, seven days a week, at 9 a.m. and 4 p.m. Located barely inside the Mexico border crossing gate to Nogales, Arizona, El Comedor hosts migrants when they're coming or going. Guests include Central Americans about to cross to the United States and Mexicans who have been picked up and sent back to Mexico. An American who regularly volunteers at El Comedor explained, "First-timers are asked to raise their hands and then everyone applauds. It's a way to humanize them after their experience in the desert and the detention centers. We give them a lesson on human rights as outlined by the United Nations so they know they have the right to seek asylum and the right to be a family. Then we lead them in a prayer." The meal is typically beans, rice, tortilla, eggs, and maybe soup. After they eat, they're asked to leave, because the space is small. A U.S. resident who volunteers weekly at El Comedor said, "We've seen 35–120 people in this small room. I feel like we have saved the lives of so many people. I always give a short speech to say, 'Do not cross alone.'"

The small facility also offers clothing for migrants. Three or four migrants at a time enter the small building to make their clothing selections. A volunteer explained, "The light blue shirts and jeans mark them as recently released from detention, so they become a target on the street." It's a bitter irony that the same clothing that the families are so grateful to receive when they're discharged and deported, which often is much sturdier than what they arrived in the United States wearing (particularly the women, whose clothing may have been ripped off during a sexual assault), makes them targets for more violence on the southern side of the U.S.-Mexico border.

El Comedor offers free phone calls home. Most migrants don't carry phones, because if the phone got into the hands of the cartel, it could be used to extort money from the family. They also are offered medical attention on-site, and a dentist in Mexico does dental work for free for the migrants. They call him "Vinny" because this dentist loves Vincent van Gogh. Volunteers at El Comedor also offer spiritual and emotional support. A volunteer relayed, "One mother was silent, and she finally said that the day before she had watched her husband die of dehydration in the desert." El Comedor bridges another kink in the international injustice system by cashing checks for deported migrants. A volunteer explained, "People are deported with a check which can't be cashed because it's in U.S. funds. So we developed a system where someone here takes these checks back to the U.S. and records the money, then brings back the cash."

A first-time volunteer at El Comedor reflected on a teenager she saw there, age thirteen or fourteen. The volunteer said, "He looked so young. The look in his eyes was one of emptiness, with no hope. I'll never know what happened to this young boy with the vacant look in his eyes." Another volunteer who helps weekly said that people ask her why she goes so often to Mexico to help serve breakfast. She said, "I think it comes down to this. We have eye contact and often share a hug. We look at each other. We physically and emotionally touch each other. We shake hands and share a laugh. We don't look away when we talk about life experiences. I feel connected with these people at this crossroad to their journey."[2] She said it is her privilege to serve these sojourners.

NO MORE DEATHS/NO MÁS MUERTES

No More Deaths/No Más Muertes began in southern Arizona in 2004 as a coalition of community and faith groups dedicated to helping to prevent migrant deaths in the desert, and it became the official ministry of the Unitarian Church of Tucson in 2008. This organization works on immigration reform, provides humanitarian assistance, and seeks to raise the consciousness of this nation about our inhumane policies and practices against migrants. In a December 2018 article in the *New York Times*, No More Deaths staff member Justine Orlovsky-Schnitzler explained that during the past ten years, attempted crossings decreased but migrant deaths increased, both factors as a result of policies and practices implemented in Washington to deter migration. The militarization of the border forces migrants to go farther out, into more remote sections of the desert, which means migrants spend much more time in the desert. Orlovsky-Schnitzler explained, "It is impossible to carry enough water to survive even a two- or three-day trek through the barren reaches of the Sonoran. Without help, migrants die painful, cruel deaths—often alone, delirious with fatigue, hunger and thirst." She added, "Policymakers didn't bother outfitting the entire length of the border with a wall because they knew that parts of the terrain were so harsh that people would die trying to cross them. The desert became a weapon—a formidable expanse that swallowed crossers whole."[3]

A network of volunteers for No More Deaths provides basic humanitarian assistance, like putting out water in remote sections of the Arizona desert. The federal government has become so obsessed with the "illegality" of undocumented immigrants, whether asylum seekers or otherwise, that it is "trying to make our humanitarian aid criminal," says Orlovsky-Schnitzler.[4] Eight humanitarian volunteers were arrested in January 2018 and charged with a variety of offenses related to leaving water, food, and blankets on the paths through remote sections of the desert that migrants use. Scott Warren was prosecuted for one count of harboring and one count of "conspiracy to harbor" undocumented human beings who were suffering in the desert, but a federal jury couldn't reach a verdict. If convicted, he would have faced up to twenty years in prison. It is uncertain if the government will attempt another trial. No More Deaths presses on with its mantra, "Humanitarian aid is *never* a crime." The lives of human beings walking through the desert are at risk.

THE GOOD SAMARITANS IN THE SOUTHERN ARIZONA DESERT

The Green Valley-Sahuarita Samaritans describes itself as "an organization comprising people of conscience who offer humanitarian aid to migrants in the Arizona-Sonora borderlands." It was founded in 2005 to provide humanitarian assistance to migrants, working independently, but also as a complement to the Tucson Samaritans. Located about twenty miles south of Tucson and forty-five miles north of the Arizona-Mexico border, the group has a stated mission: "To offer humanitarian assistance to migrants in the Arizona-Sonora borderlands. Samaritans believe in respect for human rights, the rendering of humanitarian aid, and one's ethical responsibility to assist those who are suffering." A volunteer who helps with searches in remote sections of the desert asked, "What do you do when somebody dies in your neighborhood? For us, we have decided we want to be present."

The Samaritans provide humanitarian assistance in the desert in a variety of ways. The point of every aspect of their assistance is to save lives. A critical component includes searches in remote areas of the desert. They have six vehicles doing search and rescues with a team of three hundred volunteers. One of the drivers explained, "We have to stop the deaths because our politicians on both sides have chosen very differently. We've found thousands and thousands of people over the years. Last week, we encountered two migrants. They'd tried to flag down a helicopter that hovered over them and two other unmarked cars, but they couldn't get them to stop. This man threw his arms around us and said in Spanish, 'You saved my life.' He was trembling. He thought we were going to pass him by." The Samaritans were restocking a water station about a half mile down the road from where they encountered these two men.

Figure 12.1. **The Green Valley-Sahuarita Samaritans conduct daily searches to cover the remote sections of the vast Sonoran Desert in southern Arizona, where it's easy for migrants to become dehydrated, disoriented, and lost.**

The searchers never travel alone. There are at least two, preferably four, so they are prepared in case an emergency arises and the group needs to split up. A volunteer said, "It's quite stunning to go out for three, four, or five hours on a search this time of year [August]. We do try to stop and talk to anyone we see, including the border patrol and the militia people, because part of our mission is to be out there and to be bold. We also try to be in the remote areas to look for people who are lost." Another search volunteer described pulling onto a remote winding road where they found a dead body. He said, "There was no sign of foul play. He had been dead three or four hours." Two stayed with the body and two went to find help. They met with a border patrol agent. The volunteer explained, "The family couldn't afford to have his body sent back, so we had him cremated. His son sent a lovely note thanking us. His son is a cab driver in L.A." He added, "I wrote back to him that if he ever came here, I'll show him where we found his father."

The relationship with the border patrol depends on the agent and which Samaritan is doing the search. A volunteer said, "Me? I get out of the car and greet them; it helps if you don't treat them as the enemy. When we come across an agent, we ask if they have any migrants with them. Then we say, 'I'm sure you don't mind if we give them food and water.' We don't ask." Another volunteer shared her experience of the border patrol asking her for help. She relayed, "He had an older man with diabetes and he needed help, as his feet were in horrible shape, and the agent said he couldn't help him. I washed his feet and put salve on them." The volunteer added, "Another time, seventeen young kids and four adults were lost and the border patrol asked if we could work together to find them. We responded, 'Yes, of course we can help.' We looked together for them, but the kids had scattered. All we can hope for is that they died together."

The Samaritans stock water stations in remote sections of the desert, about which a volunteer explained, "We named them Matthew, Mark, Luke, and John so if someone destroyed them then they would be destroying the Gospel." They once had a station underneath a bridge that's lined with American flags on each post. A volunteer explained, "There are about thirty-five to forty flags on this bridge, so it's very patriotic. We used to have a water source underneath it, but sometime after 9/11 it kept being destroyed. We replaced it four or five times, but it was always destroyed, so we switched locations to private property." A first-time volunteer who went with the Samaritans to restock the water supply said, "It really impressed me that the Samaritans can put three water jugs in a backpack and hold one in each hand to hike in to refill water tanks located in remote sections away from the road." The volunteer added, "It also was heartbreaking to see water containers riddled with bullet holes and signs warning that the water has been poisoned."

The Samaritans have an ongoing collection for clothing, shoes, and blankets, which they bring to El Comedor in Nogales, Mexico, where they volunteer on Tuesdays.[5] The Samaritans also purchased 1,100 water filtration straws at $12 each, which they distributed at El Comedor for migrants who are traveling north across the border. A Samaritan volunteer explained, "They can stick the straw in rancid water like a cattle trough or a stagnant pond, and it filters it so they can drink the water and stay healthy. They're expensive, so we wonder if they're worth it. Then we heard of two people whose lives were saved. They were deported, but they returned to Mexico alive."

Operation Streamline Courtroom Presence

Someone from the Samaritans is present to witness and document Operation Streamline proceedings Monday through Thursday at the United States District Court in Tucson. The specifics of each witness session are posted on the Green Valley-Sahuarita Samaritan website. These updates include details that bear an ongoing witness to this mass-production injustice and to the individuals who are harmed by this farce of "due process."[6] This Samaritan group also maintains a phenomenal cache of resources on their website, including links to reports for CBP apprehensions of undocumented migrants from 1960 to 2017, maps that show the location of recovered human remains, articles and publications, and special maps related to migration and migration assistance. This wealth of information is available for individuals who want to do their own research and reading on the vast factors that impact migration.[7]

AID STATION IN SOUTH TEXAS WELCOMES MIGRANTS

Catholic Charities of the Rio Grande Valley (CCRGV), with the help of Sacred Heart Church, the city of McAllen, Texas, as well as volunteers and donations, opened the Humanitarian Respite Center, originally located at Sacred Heart Catholic Church in McAllen, during the summer of 2014 when unaccompanied minors began arriving by the thousands to request asylum in the United States. Located at the heart of the migration portal at the Texas-Mexico border, the center assisted more than 23,000 individuals during its first twelve months of operation. People come from across the United States to volunteer at this center, which provides tangible assistance for men, women, and children seeking asylum. Sister Norma Pimentel, executive director there, once compared the experience of the South Texas migration crisis to that of people who have jumped from a burning building. She asked, "They're already here. Do we put them back into that burning building, or do we respond with humanitarian assistance?"[8] The respite center offers individuals and families a place to rest, have a warm meal and a shower, and change into clean clothing, as well as receive medicine and other supplies, before continuing on their journey. They arrive exhausted and they leave restored, encouraged, inspired, and loved.

One of the most poignant moments for hospitality between volunteers and the travelers is the traditional greeting migrants receive upon arrival to the center. Everyone stops whatever they're doing, stands, and applauds the travelers as they make their way in the front door to the registration tables. It's a moving moment that brings tears to the faces as humanitarian aid volunteers cheer the families for their victory in arriving safely to the United States. The applause also offers a magnanimous welcome that says, "We are so very glad you are here. *Bienvenidos*. Welcome!"

DETENTION CENTER VISITOR VOLUNTEERS

Volunteers across the United States participate in visitation programs for migrants who are detained and waiting for the interminably slow legal due process. There are more than two hundred detention centers in the United States and only fifty-five visitation programs. The primary role of the visitor volunteer is to be present, fully present, with and for the detained migrant for the simple reason that, as one volunteer explained, "People deserve the dignity of being heard." Isolation is one of the biggest challenges for incarceration, and it is magnified tenfold at an immigrant detention facility, because the inmates are literally strangers in America and far from the support system of family and friends in their homelands. By being physically present, the visitors encourage the migrants and remind them that they are children of God. Visitors also are channels of compassion, portals for family and friends who are located too far away to make a personal visit. Visitors bring news in and take more news out. They listen to what needs to be said during the visit, and they follow up however they are able to afterward.

After release from sixteen months of incarceration, an undocumented mother of three children compared her experience of immigrant detention to that of being on death row. She said, "Waiting. Appeal. Waiting. No information. Nothing but silence. You are a nobody. A nothing. Just a number." A visitor volunteer explained, "Visitors provide solidarity. We believe in them. We respond with pastoral care and advocacy and public witness. We listen. We sit with them in the ashes."

OVERNIGHT HOSPITALITY FOR RELEASED FAMILIES

The Interfaith Welcome Coalition (IWC) of San Antonio began organizing overnight hospitality for migrant families in 2014 in response to the irresponsible manner in which ICE released the families from detention. When a family met the qualifications to be released, which includes passing the credible fear interviews, posting the bond set by an immigration judge, and obtaining approval of the U.S. family member designated as the responsible party for the family (not unlike a U.S. citizen being released on bond to a family member), ICE shuttled the families to the bus station in downtown San Antonio. The families were dumped without food, clothing, or shelter. Their bus might not leave until the next day, but they were stranded with small children in an inner-city section known for its overflow of homelessness. It was, and is, unsafe for the women and children to be stranded overnight.

IWC rallied to offer overnight lodging in private homes. An interfaith volunteer checked the bus station during the early evening hours to see if any of the families needed overnight hospitality. My congregation happily participated in the "Welcome Home Host" program, and I hosted our first family on December 14, 2014: a mother and her two daughters, one age six and the other nine months. Members of Community Fellowship Presbyterian Church gathered helpful travel items for the trio's long journey, which would include seven buses over the three-day trip to the mother's mother and aunts and uncles, who live outside of New York City. The congregation was inspired by this initial blessing of hosting families, and they continued to offer overnight hospitality and transportation to the airport or bus station for several months until IWC shifted to hosting the families at a house located a short distance from the bus station.

Mennonite Hospitality House in San Antonio

It made it much easier for everyone to have nearby lodging provided by the San Antonio Mennonite Church in their "hospitality house." A member of the congregation coordinates all of the volunteers. Some people focus on material support, transportation, and/or opening their own home for overnight lodging as needed, whereas others volunteer to be assistants at the hospitality house. Pastor John Garland said, "I see this as we are bearing witness to a sacred, sacrificial journey. We are far, far from the center of this story. Just like in the Gospel of Matthew (2:13-18) when Joseph and Mary took Jesus and fled to Egypt from Herod, it doesn't mention anything about the families that housed them or those who helped them along the journey. It's a story about sacred love; it's about the future of the child, Jesus." He said that while readers don't get to see all of the details of any sacred story, the story is there to teach us about sacred ancestors. He added, "This story today isn't about us, or about the United States. It's about the families and their journey to safety."[9]

Overnight hosting made another transition in 2016 when a nonprofit group began overseeing the hospitality house, and again in 2017 when the facility wasn't needed as often because the advocacy finally bore fruit. ICE shifted to "normal" release times, dropping the families off at the bus station several hours prior to departure. Overnight lodging became the exception, rather than the rule.

SANCTUARY CHURCHES AND OPPORTUNITIES FOR ACCOMPANIMENT

There are many opportunities for accompaniment that support migrants long before deportation looms large on the horizon. It's a common, but false, perspective that "sanctuary church" describes the most extreme scenario of offering physical sanctuary for undocumented migrants who are about to be deported. Jennie Belle, a community organizer with Church World Service, explained, "Sanctuary church works on a spectrum of concerns. You don't necessarily have to physically shelter an immigrant. The immediate, local goal is to fight individual deportation, but on a national scale, the goal is to say that current immigration policies are against our faith values." The spectrum of sanctuary support includes hosting "know your rights" seminars; leading with values and dealing with the moral element of immigration and deportation and not the political point, which politicians have created; remembering that family is sacred and speaking out on the importance of respecting this sacred value; sharing personal stories about people who have been directly impacted by unjust immigration policies and practices; focusing on the moral aspect; calling out inaccuracies; and staying hopeful. Physical sanctuary is the last resort, and these other options help to prevent that from becoming necessary. It's also a form of nonviolent disobedience. ICE has its own policy not to go into churches, schools, or health centers. It's a memo and not a law, so it could change. Belle explained, "With private sanctuary you're harboring privately. I don't know about it, and I shouldn't know about it. It is illegal! Public sanctuary is done in a church, and you tell ICE, the media, everyone. It's something you're proud of."

Sanctuary Church Assists with Family Separation and Reunification

Covenant Baptist, a small church in San Antonio, which has only about thirty-five adult members and twenty-five to thirty children, became a sanctuary church during the spring of 2017. Pastor Natalie Webb explained that as the church board discerned whether or not to take this step, a member of the board asked, "If we don't do this, then who are we? We're a small church that's all about justice, and this clearly is a justice issue." They hosted several families during the reunification process to reconnect parents with the children who had been taken from them at the border. Pastor Natalie said, "After hosting the first two families, it makes it so much more real. Now we're friends with these mothers. We know them. We care about them." She summarized their experiences in hosting families by noting that, for the congregation, it was "an altogether positive experience. I think it's really rallied them together. They all jumped in and became connected. We know these families. We love them, and we got to be a part of their journey in a positive way during a really horrible situation." She added, "It gave us a real claim on our Christianity." Soon after Pastor Natalie took a new call in Massachusetts, the church leadership quickly responded to another plea for hospitality. They remain poised and ready to do likewise again and again.

BACKPACK MINISTRY FOR TRAVELING FAMILIES

Early into the hospitality response, IWC began providing backpacks filled with travel supplies to make the journey easier for the families.[10] Each Monday morning a group of volunteers gathers to stuff 250 backpacks with travel toiletries, snacks, and water, plus coloring books, crayons, and small toys for the children. During 2017, IWC distributed 4,185 backpacks, and during 2018 the group distributed almost 13,000 backpacks to traveling refugee families. The contents are paid for by donations. ICW distributed over 14,000 stuffed backpacks at the bus station and almost 5,000 at the airport during the first six months of 2019.

IWC OFFERS BUS STATION AND
AIRPORT HOSPITALITY FOR ASYLUM SEEKERS

When asylum seekers pass the credible fear interview and are released from detention, Homeland Security delivers the families daily to the San Antonio airport and Greyhound bus station. IWC has volunteers at the bus station and airport seven days a week, including high holy days, to ensure that the newly released families receive unconditional welcome, tangible assistance, encouragement, and prayers for the journey. On any given day, the bus station hospitality team welcomes anywhere from a handful of families to an overwhelming 140 families. The low end allows the volunteers to spend more one-on-one time visiting with the families. The high side resembles controlled chaos! The families generally have two to four hours prior to departure.

Sister Denise LaRock coordinates this all-volunteer ministry. She shared one of what she calls her "classic" stories from her daily presence at the bus station: "A father from El Salvador who was going to be traveling on a Greyhound bus with his young

Figure 12.2. Fathers and sons line up to get their tickets at the bus station in San Antonio.

son, age three or four, asked me if the buses in the U.S. were safe. I asked him if the buses were safe in El Salvador. He said, 'Where I live, they board the bus and kill people, or they take people off the bus and then kill them.' I assured him that the buses are very safe. He looked relieved. I wouldn't go as far as a smile, but he looked relieved." She added, "Can you imagine the courage it took for him to be willing to board a bus with that risk of his homeland in his mind? Yet, the only way to safety and his family in the U.S. was to board that bus."

Figure 12.3. A volunteer helps a traveler understand the complicated bus ticket.

Bus Station Hospitality Flow of Events Journal Entry

The following entry from my journal is from Valentine's Day 2018, which also was Ash Wednesday. It shows the ebb and flow of hospitality at the bus station. I brought art supplies to make Valentine cards with children, my liturgical stole, and a bowl of ashes for anyone who wanted to mark the forty-day Lent journey to Easter with imposition of ashes on the forehead.

The white bus the families travel in from Dilley is parked across the street from the bus station at 10:40 a.m. It takes 10–15 minutes from arrival until the families actually off-load the bus. The families line up in a single line with an ICE agent in front and another ICE agent in back. The mini parade of mothers and children, each carrying one tote bag which holds all of their belongings, crosses the street at the traffic light and then turns into the front entrance of the Greyhound bus station.

The ICE agent directs the families to get in line for the ticket counter. I walked up and down the long line that wound its way through the bus station and greeted each family. I explained that people from local churches are here to help them while they wait for the bus. I invited them to the section of the interior of the bus station, located at the far opposite side, across from the ticket counter. I explained, "Volunteers from churches in San Antonio are here to help you." After the families have confirmed their tickets, an IWC volunteer puts a white sticker on their T-shirt, which indicates the time of departure and city. The stickers make it visibly easier for volunteers to help the families get in line to board their bus at the appropriate time.

As the families make their way to the hospitality section, which has rows of wire chairs and seats about 30 people, the IWC volunteers begin their assistance. Each family arrives with a blue and white cardboard lunch box from Dilley or a brown paper bag lunch from Karnes. IWC also distributes an additional lunch for travel, one bag per family. They also give one backpack per family which contains helpful items for the journey. Several of the IWC volunteers scatter about to explain the travel logistics with the mothers and fathers. They have clipboards which contain a grid/chart on the front side which volunteers use to copy the details of the travel schedule from the otherwise very small type and difficult to read bus ticket. The volunteer notes their departure and arrival times at the cities where the families will change buses. Many of the families change buses four to seven times over the duration of a cross-country trip to, for example, North Carolina or Washington State. The reverse side has a map of the USA. The volunteer draws a rough sketch on the map of the route and notes the cities where the family will change buses.

After all the bus tickets have been explained, someone from IWC gives a general overview in Spanish of what to expect traveling on a bus across the U.S. Sister Denise asks if there are any questions, but there rarely are as most of the parents prefer to ask their questions one-on-one rather than with the entire group. One asked if there would be people helping them at all of the bus stations like they were being helped in San Antonio. (Unfortunately, no!) Depending on the number of families and the number of volunteers, it takes about 45 minutes to get all the bus tickets individually explained and the speech given. The response of volunteers is impressively consistent with their faithfulness to volunteer at the bus station.

There's also a cell phone which is available for calls in the U.S., and IWC has a tote bag of basic medical supplies, feminine hygiene products, and diapers. After all of the official helping is done, then IWC breaks out the gifts for the kids. There may be a few teenagers, but most of the children are age eight or younger. The kids can choose one small toy, either a Matchbox-type mini car or a stuffed animal. Different churches and individuals donate funds for the toys. A volunteer also brings different treats to give the children: lollipops or cookies. Today there were bags of tangerines to pass around.

If time permits, a volunteer will take a group to a nearby bank to exchange currency. Once when Sister Denise was about to walk a group to the bank, she asked a mother where her child was. The mother pointed to her daughter, who was happily doing art on the floor of the bus station with a visiting volunteer. Denise said, no, the child must go with the mother as the errand could take as long as an hour. While Denise was a bit flabbergasted that the mother would leave her six-year-old daughter with a stranger doing art at the bus station, it also speaks to the immediate sense of safety and trust that the mother felt with the warm reception from the various volunteers.

When it's about time for the first bus to depart, there's a flurry of goodbyes and "Vaya con Dios!" (Go with God!), as families say goodbye to new friends. A volunteer waits with them in the boarding area designated for persons who need special assistance. Today we gathered in a group hug as one of the fluent Spanish speakers prayed for their safe journey. We concluded with a big prayer hug with three volunteers, two mothers, and three children. As the families departed to board the bus, we offered encouraging words one last time.

Then back to the rest of the group to see what might be done to help.

During this interim time, some of the mothers simply stare off into space, holding their small child and clearly anxious about what lies before them. Some of the smaller children are fussy by now. As the call to board each bus is given, the group gets smaller and smaller. Before the last of the Dilley families are gone, the bus arrives from Karnes City, and the process begins all over again. The few who remain from the first bus become consumed into the second group, often the volunteers forgetting that they already have been helped. The mother inevitably says, "Ya" [Already].

Throughout all of this, the ICE agents are "off camera" or "stage right" so to speak, just on the edge of the view and not playing any active role. I'm slowly getting over my discomfort of there being two ICE agents who stand guard at the bus station. Often they're playing with their cell phones, scrolling emails or texts, but never actually talking to anyone on their phone. Their silent watching can be a bit unnerving when I consciously think about their presence. They typically stand against the wall and do not interact in any way with the families. The IWC volunteers intentionally meet and greet the ICE officers, and I do likewise. Today was a first for me. An ICE agent asked me to give him imposition of ashes for Ash Wednesday. I did my usual short spiel about having one short life to live on earth and to live it for the honor and glory of Jesus Christ. Amen!

A sweet little girl ran over to me, threw her arms around my waist, and spoke in rapid Spanish. I asked her to repeat it slowly. Then she said, "I want you to play with me." I was touched and humbled by her trust and unconditional love after so short a time together at the bus station. I sat with her on the floor of the bus station and together we made a Valentine card.

Near my time to leave, I helped the mothers practice saying their U.S. city destination in English. One knew that she was going to Florida, but she didn't know the city. I looked at her ticket and saw that it was Ft. Meyers. We joked about coming all this long ways and then getting off at the wrong city! She came to realize the importance of knowing and saying the city name.

The unsettling part of the day for me was the single men at the bus station who arrived from Pearsall [South Texas Detention Complex]. *Three single men were there before the Dilley families, and another three men arrived a short time later with small children. None of the men released from Pearsall had anything: no lunch, no travel supplies, nothing. Sister Denise asked the single men if they would please move to make more room for the mothers. In doing so, she discovered that they also are refugees seeking asylum. She said to me, "Look at those men. That is everything they own." They had absolutely nothing. Yet, they graciously gave up their seats to make more space for the mothers and children.*

The three fathers with small children who arrived later on the Greyhound bus from McAllen were a bit better prepared. The father with an eight-month-old had a diaper bag for the infant, but no lunch box was given for the fathers or for the two children ages eight and nine. All of the men were clearly hungry. It was 1:30 p.m. and they'd already had a long travel day up from McAllen in South Texas, as they'd been released for a journey of unknown length without anything, not even a brown paper bag lunch for the journey. The fathers exemplify the disparity between how residents of for-profit prisons are treated, including something as basic as offering a lunch for the long journey. Instead, the volunteer organizations offer their assistance for hospitality and welcome. It doesn't take a lot of effort to be kind. Kind. What a basic concept. What would it look like to move toward kindness, not even generosity? Simple, basic kindness.

A day at the bus station is exhausting, but it's totally and completely worthwhile.

After this particularly hectic day, I asked Sister Denise how she kept from being overwhelmed. She said, "I have to focus on the present moment here and now, offering comfort and tangible assistance to the families at the bus station. If I start thinking ahead, to what might happen to any of these families, it's too overwhelming. So many will most likely be deported eventually. I can't go there. I stay centered in my time here, with them now, helping however I am able to." I responded that I didn't how she could do this every day, serving at the bus station with the families. I said, "I'm exhausted, physically and spiritually, from this one day." She replied, "It doesn't take as much energy once it becomes ordinary in a sense." Another volunteer said, "Of all the things I could've been doing today, I can't imagine anything being more worthwhile than spending these hours being fully present with the families." During these various expressions of hospitality, kindness, compassion, and love are given and received unconditionally, fully, freely, generously, and with joy. We welcome *you*, and the "I-Thou" indelibly is formed between strangers who become friends. This friendship makes the political personal and provides irrefutable personal testimony for public witness and civic engagement.

13

Public Witness and Civic Engagement

The purpose of public witness and civic engagement is to identify and then challenge the evil that is lurking within the good. Not all evil is blatant. It also can be very subtle, what's been called the "double character" of evil, "its existence and its hidden-ness."[1] Evil changes how it manifests itself and hides in unexpected and unassuming contexts. Its changeability and hiddenness also make it difficult to confront or thwart evil because, as theologian James Newton Poling warns, "Evil is a chameleon that maintains itself by remaining intertwined with the good and masking itself as good."[2] For example, the rule of law sounds like it's a good thing, and clearly it could and should be a good thing, but it becomes evil when the laws have been manipulated to further an unjust agenda. Silence will not make the evil magically disappear. It requires dedication to goodness, truth, and justice. It bears repeating that, in a democratic nation, all of the citizens are part of our broken immigration matrix. We voted for the legislators who make these unjust laws, and we fund this injustice with our taxes. We're also culpable when we disbelieve, ignore, or disregard the cries of these families pleading for safe asylum.

SILENCE IS NOT AN OPTION

An editorial in the *San Antonio Express-News* lamented the silence of individuals and groups who aren't doing anything to challenge or change the injustice of children being locked inside detention facilities. "Where Are the Voices Defending Detained Children?" specified disappointment in

> local churches, newspapers, civic leaders and on-the-air media personalities. All of those in a position to take a stand against wrong and then use their public voice to create a

communitywide discussion and search for a positive way to affect a change. Or maybe it's my disbelief in parents, grandparents, uncles, aunts and stepparents, anyone who cares about children. I could throw in coaches, teachers, Scout leaders, anyone and everyone, because we all have a role in bringing this injustice back to the front of the newspaper, in the voice of the minister in the church and into a discussion over the airwaves.

The editorial concluded with the plea: "I ask for nothing from the government; my family will cover everything. These are just kids. Let's all help. Please, someone with a more effective voice, stand up."[3] I agree wholeheartedly with this editorial on all but one point. I do ask something from our government: justice. *We the people* must hold our elected officials, our lawmakers, accountable to be compassionate, honest, and forthright with genuine and selfless justice. Now is the time for voters to be vocal. Silence is not an option. U.S. citizens and registered voters have the civic and moral responsibility to call our elected officials to answerability. They're supposed to be public servants who work for the greater good. It's our job, as voters, to hold them to it.

CIVIC DUTY ACTIONS FOR RESPONSIBLE RESPONSE

When you're considering how to engage in public witness and/or political engagement, contemplate what I once heard a professor say during a public workshop on immigration: "People protect democracy, not the other way around."[4] There are tangible civic duty actions accessible to every citizen to help protect our democracy:

- Vote in every election (not just the big ones).
- Go door-to-door and encourage people to vote.
- Contact your elected officials and hold them accountable (have an action item and be specific).
- Learn about upcoming legislation.
- File legislation.
- File specific complaints to slow down legislation, such as requiring childcare licensing for the for-profit immigrant family detention facilities.
- Write an opinion editorial (op-ed) that can be tweaked to address a current issue and then send it to a local or national newspaper.

Professional advocates identify what they term a "hierarchy of effects" for communicating with elected officials regarding any given issue. The baseline or lowest level would be a "click here" to forward something to your congressperson. Next up would be emails and phone calls. Meeting your elected officials in person clearly has more influence than phone calls, emails, and letters, and it's most impactful to meet in D.C. rather than the easier option of meeting in-district. A disappointing, but important, note to self is that constituency drives everything when it comes to phone calls and letters. If you don't live in an elected official's district, your phone call won't get logged, and your mail will be thrown right in the trash. The process is completely constituent focused. Even if your elected officials are the most anti-immigration persons in D.C., they are "yours," and that's where you must attempt to engender change.

For in-person advocacy, find out if your member has a town hall. Rehearse and be prepared. You want to know what you're going to say, but you don't want to sound like you're reading it. Tell personal stories. Describe some of the moments you've experienced. Have a specific actional ask, such as the examples below. When you make the expectation specific, then you can follow up and ask for particular points. For example, "So, how are you doing on this? What specifically are you doing? What's your boss doing?" When you follow up and the office worker doesn't have a response to your questions, then ask for a specific timeframe when you can follow up again. It takes the visit to another level when you then write a letter to the editor and mention that you met with your official. You also could get a group together to send multiple tweets to one person; that person will wonder why they're getting so many tweets. An easy option is to regularly write postcards, which are short and sweet and on target, to remind your official that you are paying attention to what they are, or are not, doing. You also could pick up the phone and call the White House comments line at 202-456-1111 and the switchboard at 202-456-1414; leave a short message that specifies your concerns about a current issue. Always specify that you are a registered voter.

When you visit, write, or call your elected officials, your job is not to be an authority. Your job is to tell stories about what you care about. Use language that reflects who you are. Feel free to include whatever personal experience shapes your viewpoint. For example, at a refugee advocacy event at the Texas statehouse, one participant shared from her experience as a grandmother. She said, "If the detention centers aren't acceptable for my grandchildren, then they're not acceptable for the refugee kids either."

Don't be afraid to claim your civic power beyond your personal circle of influence. If you're a member of a denomination, church, or particular organization, include the numbers of the voices you are speaking for. For example, when I wrote my state senator, I included a postscript that said I'm a member of the local ministerial alliance this senator regularly visits on the National Day of Prayer. Whatever you have to empower your personal insights and authority regarding why you're contacting your elected officials, don't hold back. Let them know the platform that empowers your voice. When "my" Texas state senator headed the committee recommending that Karnes and Dilley be designated licensed childcare facilities, I challenged the justice of this recommendation. I specified my longtime experience inside Karnes as a volunteer chaplain. I also threw in the weight of my ordination in the Presbyterian Church (USA), my doctorate in practical theology with an emphasis on social justice, and all the research and reading I do specifically on immigration and refugees seeking asylum. Essentially, through my letters and personal visit, I said to my state senator, "I know what I'm talking about and this is why . . ." The United Church of Christ has an excellent free resource available that includes basic tips for how to engage in public policy advocacy.[5]

HOLDING ELECTED OFFICIALS
ACCOUNTABLE FOR CHILDREN

Bearing in mind the point made in chapter 3, that how a nation treats refugees in camps and detention centers is indicative of the nation's DNA, advocacy for justice for children is a foundational place to begin. If we can't become more compassionate for children, *children*, what does that indicate about the moral compass of the United States of America? Attorney Hope Frye said, "When you speak to your representative in Congress, you talk about what you know. You talk about the evil. It's a matter of basic human rights. We want there to be legislative changes which will prevent this treatment. Children should never be detained in a CBP facility. Congress needs to legislate, literally create laws which prevent this injustice to children. The basic tenet is that children have human rights. Go to the government and say, 'Stop childhood detention. Stop the taxpayers from paying for this.'" As noted earlier, it's important to make a tangible request. Frye specified the following:

Specific "Asks" to Bring to Your Elected Officials on Behalf of Detained Children

- Establish a law to ensure that children should never be detained in a CBP facility (i.e, dog kennels and refrigerators); they must go right to ORR.
- Establish short detention periods with a mechanism for quickly vetting the sponsor for release. These terms should be set as law and specified as required by the law. The *Flores* limit for detention is twenty days, but timelines for detainment should be short; twenty days is too long. Shorten it; tighten it; create accountability. Because detention further traumatizes children, they should be released promptly.
- Mandate that no child shall ever be separated from the parent/adult they travel with without the permission of that responsible adult; establish a law to enforce this principle. Children stay with their parent or legal guardian. Always.
- Establish specific parameters for a "least restrictive" detention setting. Take detained children to church, to the library, to the park like you would any other child. If children know that they can leave, it is psychologically better. If they're getting the help and care they need, they won't want to run away.
- Mandate independent oversight to ensure that specifications for care in a "least restrictive" setting are met.
- Require an independent audit of everything related to the oversight and care of unaccompanied children. Mandate that the government cannot audit itself. Outsiders must be allowed inside to hold ORR accountable.
- Children must have real access to lawyers. They should have the right to a lawyer paid for by the government. They have the right to due process, which means being represented by a lawyer at every turn. Release should not be delayed while the lawyer is being procured.

- Children have the right to communicate with anyone they want to, without restriction or charge, in any mode including, but not limited to, telephone, video, email, written correspondence, and in-person visitations.
- Make a law that no child can be drugged without parental consent; if there is not a parent, then have a mechanism in place for assigning independent guardianship.
- Establish a law that requires independent licensing oversight with criteria and enforcement mechanisms that are outside of the agencies, such that the oversight is not supervised by the federal government. Again, outsiders must have full disclosure of what's happening inside. Establish a law that if there are X number of violations, then the facility is closed.
- Establish parameters for independent licensing oversight with a six-month report to Congress. Stakeholders testify, too. Develop a specific enforcement mechanism that's outside of the agencies— in other words, not supervised by the federal government. For example, state licensure is ideal because it's completely independent of the feds.
- Require public access whereby local people can come inside detention centers and run programs so that the children aren't isolated from the community. Find ways to allow people to come inside, such as programs for pastoral care, art, and music.
- Offer religious services.
- Set down a basic standard of care that includes a full medical exam upon arrival.
- Tie the rules to standards that already exist in the public domain, like the standards for the American Academy of Pediatrics. Hold these facilities accountable to the same standards that everyone else is held to.
- Disallow confinement at a remote center.
- If a child cannot be released as defined by *Flores*, then establish a law that they have the right to an immediate bond hearing before an immigration judge.
- Ensure that children have the rights granted under *Flores* for clean, safe, humanitarian care, which we understand to include . . . (specify those basic parameters).

Ask, follow up, and ask again. Frye emphasized, "Sanctity of life means that no child should ever be detained in a dog kennel or ice box. Period. Ever. End of story."

Examples from Texas

Lobbyists for the two for-profit family detention centers in Texas pushed legislators to change the limitation for how long children could be detained in "family detention." They argued that these two level-one prison facilities (Karnes and Dilley) qualify as childcare facilities, despite the fact that they had not passed requirements to become officially licensed as childcare facilities by the state of Texas.[6] When the Texas legislature was playing games, making it possible for children to be detained

long-term so that privatized detention facilities could profit while the families suffered, I moved from my ignorance and inertia to advocate for the families with
lawmakers and in the public square. I'd never contacted any elected official. In fact,
I had to look up who my officials were. But I knew that I couldn't live with myself
if the Texas legislators passed laws that would harm the families and I hadn't done
everything within my power to be a voice for the families.

In solidarity with these mothers and fathers and sons and daughters fleeing from
violence and seeking safe asylum in our country, I embraced the authority of my
experience and background and went to Austin to bear witness on their behalf. My
advocacy embodied Emmanuel Levinas's edict that "The forgetting of self moves
justice."[7] With the image of the thousands of beautiful faces I've directly interacted
with in my mind's eye, I, like many other volunteers who have become advocates,
forgot my fears and insecurities. I embraced vulnerability and acted to help move
justice. I also joined a letter-writing campaign and wrote multiple letters to my state
and national elected officials.

Public witness, civic action, and solidarity with refugees seeking asylum will always be needed. The challenge to hold legislators accountable to justice resembles
Homer's story about Sisyphus, whom the ancient Greek gods had condemned to
ceaselessly push a massive stone up a hill in Hades. Every time Sisyphus got the boulder to the top, it rolled right back down to the bottom, and he had to push it up to
the top again. One action for justice might be rolled to the top of Capitol Hill, but
the ball inevitably comes crashing back to the bottom of the steep slope of justice,
where another issue needs to be pushed back to the top. Reiterating theologian Reinhold Niebuhr's words, "The fight for [refugee] justice will always be a fight."[8] Congress could stop this gross injustice at our southern border by creating laws. They're
lawmakers. It's their job to create immigration laws that keep this democracy safe,
honorable, and just. With the massive and daunting intricacies of anything and everything related to immigration reform, Congress needs to develop legal mechanisms
that protect the most vulnerable of the vulnerable. An immigration attorney turned
advocate for children who are detained said, "People of conscience don't incarcerate
children in cages like they're animals. Congress can stop this." Again, silence on our
part isn't an option. As the family separation policy escalated, I wrote the following
to my elected officials:

June 15, 2018
Dear Senator:

*I am a registered voter in Comal County, Texas. I called your office earlier today, but
this matter is so critical it requires following up with a letter.*

*I have provided pastoral care for refugee families seeking asylum since 2014, including
two years as a volunteer chaplain inside the immigrant family detention center at Karnes
City. The families are pursuing the internationally respected right to flee when their
lives are threatened. The treatment of families at the border is a blatant disregard to the
foundational principal of nonrefoulement imbedded within the 1951 UN Convention*

on Refugees and the 1967 Protocol, of which the U.S. is a signatory nation. Signatory states of the UNHCR are "supposed to" follow up with asylum policy which offers an option for safety and security for people like the families from the Northern Triangle whose lives are in danger.

Ripping children from their parents at the border is unjust, inhumane, and has too many similarities to Nazi Germany. (Have you read Elie Wiesel's Night*? It bears a striking resemblance to what is now happening at our border!) It also reeks of dictatorship rather than the democratic nation which the U.S. is supposed to be. The mothers and children are victims of horrific violence in their homelands. They have the right to flee and the right to seek asylum in the U.S. We have a moral and legal responsibility to offer the families fair treatment and reasonable opportunity to follow due process to seek asylum. The current treatment of the families is intolerable.*

Is this really what/who you want the U.S. to be, a xenophobic nation that locks up children in an abandoned Walmart? Is there no shame? No embarrassment? Where is the moral outrage? How did this become even remotely (A) allowable; (B) implemented so unilaterally and dictatorially; and (C) tolerated for even a single moment?

I'm writing to ask you to do your part to stop this inhumane, unjust, and blatantly immoral and illegal treatment of the families.

Regards,
Rev. Dr. Helen Boursier, Ph.D.

I wrote another letter to my elected officials in Washington when the Trump administration was rallying the troops to "defend" the border against the migrant caravan slowly creeping its way to the Mexico-U.S. border in October 2018:

October 30, 2018
Dear Senator:

I have been a volunteer chaplain with refugee families seeking asylum since 2014, and I object to the pending plan to deploy U.S. troops to "defend" the Southwestern border against the "invasion" of refugee families seeking asylum. It is ridiculous. It is unjust. It lacks any remote sense of humanitarian response to the issues behind the mass migration from the Northern Triangle to the U.S. It also disregards U.S. contributions to the problems contributing to their necessary flight to safety (importing narcotics, paying for the drugs with stolen arms, and exporting the gangs which prey upon the families).

Many of these families are vulnerable victims seeking necessary asylum, and Trump's plan blatantly disregards the UNHCR's Convention and Protocol regarding asylum, of which the U.S. is a signatory state. It is unjust, immoral, racist, disturbing, and appalling that the U.S. would even contemplate such an action. Where are the checks and balances of this American democracy? Where is Congress? Regardless of any "Commander-in-Chief" authority, Congress must have a voice and a vote for a responsible response which takes into consideration our international connections to neighbors seeking asylum.

I appeal to you, as my elected official, to find the appropriate democratic measures to stop Trump's "counter invasion" ploy and instead to find ways for a humanitarian response

to receive refugees seeking asylum. Otherwise, the most vulnerable will suffer exorbitantly.
I appeal to your human decency on behalf of these mothers and children, fathers and sons,
boys and girls.
Regards,
Rev. Dr. Helen Boursier, Ph.D.

I also posted this letter on social media and asked the public to call and email their respective elected officials in Washington, D.C. The following Sunday, a ministry colleague used my letter as an example for her congregation as she set aside time during the worship service for everyone to write letters to their elected officials. The pastor recalled, "I wasn't sure how it would be received to write letters during worship, but everyone got totally into writing their own letters, which we mailed off the next day." In a democracy, change requires advocacy with elected officials and witness in the public square.

WITNESS IN THE PUBLIC SQUARE

When the authorities force the families into silence about their degrading treatment at the border, the voices of people of conscience, religious and secular, must create a visible, vocal, and very public outcry against this systemic injustice. For example, the interfaith community in greater San Antonio staged the first public rally in the country (#RallyForOurChildren), speaking, praying, and lobbying against the cruel and unjust Trump administration policy of separating children from their parents, which callously disregarded their moral and legal right to seek asylum.[9] Similar rallies were held across the United States as "we the people" gathered to protest unjust policies and practices by the current administration.

In his public witness for justice, a professor at Boston College explains, "I'm trying to plead with the world, but people are locked in with hardheartedness. I'm resisting by saying, 'Please don't be cruel. Please don't do that.'"[10] Speaking at a Project Lifeline education event on migration, Dr. Fernando Stein, past president of the American Academy of Pediatrics and a native Guatemalan whose father fled there to escape Nazi Germany, said, "Cruelty has never been a good policy. It's never been who or what we're about. It's not a political issue; it's a moral question about being cruel." He added, "We are hardwired for compassion. That's why we are here. We're compassionate people."[11] An immigration advocate explained, "There is a globalization of indifference with the international refugee crisis. Consciousness needs to be raised spiritually and morally."

I appreciate that immigration is a complex problem. I've heard the common objections for participation: lack of resources, lack of time, lack of motivation. In an effort to help move my circle of influence from indifference and inaction to public witness, I focus my preaching, teaching, and education to help people become disturbed about the injustice that our nation is heaping upon families and children seeking asylum. My hope and prayer is that my circle of influence will be disturbed enough to move from apathy, inertia, and inaction to find ways to offer compassion, kindness, and love. Together, we can make a transformative difference.

VARIATIONS OF PUBLIC WITNESS

All public witness doesn't look or feel the same. There are several variations—such as education, peaceful witness, prayer, activism, and celebration—and you might be more comfortable or uncomfortable with one version than another (that is certainly true for me). Give yourself permission to experiment with the options, some of which are illustrated in the following examples. You'll never know your comfort zone until you experiment to see where and how your voice and presence are most suited for your witness and advocacy in the public square.

Witness Operation Streamline Proceedings in a Federal Courtroom

Attending the proceedings in an Operation Streamline courtroom is a form of witness and solidarity. Federal courts are located across the United States. For example, if you live in the Tucson area, Operation Streamline court is held most weekdays at 1:30 p.m. on the second floor of the Evo A. DeConcini U.S. Courthouse, 405 West Congress Street. Members of the public may attend. Bring a government-issued ID and expect to go through security screening. No photos or recordings are permitted. Before you go, visit the court website (http://www.azd.uscourts.gov/calendars) and download the Streamline calendar to confirm that court will be in session and to see the list of defendants by name. It will make it easier to follow what's happening in the courtroom if you print the list and bring it to court. If you'd like to be an End Streamline volunteer and document the prosecutions of asylum seekers in the Tucson Streamline court proceedings, contact endstreamline@gmail.com. You can contact an immigration advocacy or support agency in your area to learn about the Operation Streamline courtroom nearest you.

ACLU Rally in Brownsville, Texas

Vocal participation in the public square for an ethical-moral response raises awareness and helps to keep the government honest about the current unjust treatment for refugees seeking asylum and the necessity for urgent and immediate immigration reform. Approximately 1,100 refugee advocates traveled in buses from major cities across Texas to attend the Families Belong Together rally in Brownsville, Texas, sponsored by the ACLU to protest family separation and the unjust treatment of refugees and migrants. Family separation had just been repealed, but the rally proceeded as scheduled to raise public education and advocacy about the many injustices against refugees and migrants. My journal entry for June 28, 2018, includes the following:

I left the house at 3:20 a.m. to drive to San Antonio to catch the ACLU chartered bus to Brownsville. As a visual witness and a deliberate expression of my faith and the theological connection of love of God including love of refugees, I wore a black liturgical shirt and a white "dog collar" with my brightly colored stole that I'd purchased in Guatemala. Upon arrival to Brownsville, there were media peeps everywhere, including print, radio, and TV. Some had a sound/boom person and others had a separate journalist to deal with the notes and details. Some were self-contained: notebook, camera, digital recorder. I floated around and observed. I intentionally sought out media to share a bit of my story with the families. I also brought one of my poetic reflection journals, and I read a different one to each of the four media persons who interviewed me.

Intentional witness: I made it a point to bring up the aspects of the families which consistently are not addressed in the media. I affirmed that Family Separation is wrong, but I noted that other big issues also need to be addressed. The #1 issue is deportation and particularly the stats for those arriving from Guatemala, El Salvador, Honduras, and Mexico. #2 is the issue of credible fear and that these families have legitimate asylum claims which they are eligible for under the UNHCR. I also brought up that when the U.S. interferes with their credible fear claims by delimiting the parameters, i.e., Jeff Sessions and our Department of "Justice" saying gang violence and domestic violence do not "count" as valid credible fear, the U.S. becomes culpable to feminicide. When the media rep was unfamiliar with the term, I carefully specified what it means and how we become culpable when we send the mothers back to the violence they are fleeing.

The speeches were rah-rah upbeat about justice for the families and there were also shared experiences of those who have been detained. They also read letters and statements, not unlike what I've collected from the families.

As the speeches wound down, everyone gathered on the back side of the stage, right across the street from the courthouse. They asked clergy-dressed people to be up front so we would be the most visible in the pictures the press took. I was about four people back from the front line. There were 30-40 cameras in the press core—right in the faces of the front row of the crowd, which gradually started pressing closer and closer to the courthouse, literally filling the middle of the street and blocking the road.

Someone with a bullhorn got the crown shouting, "Justicia! Justicia!" and then "Shut it down! Shut it down!" Fists were raised with the chanting and the crowd was becoming more and more intense.

The point of the gathering at this time was to get inside the courthouse to watch the court proceedings for Operation Streamline. The bullhorn had the people so wound up that it didn't seem like a reasonable or possible option to be allowed inside with this crowd chanting. I was uncomfortable with the increasingly aggressive mood of the crowd, so I opted for my default position to be an observer of the events. I slid out of the crowd to the right and photographed the event from the rear.

There were only a handful of police officers in front of the courthouse, and they did not present a hostile or menacing presence. It was actually impressive how calm and friendly they looked given this loud crowd of about 1,000 people bearing down on them. Soon after I had slid out of the throng, someone called the crowd to back up, to get out of the

Figure 13.1.   Media coverage at the ACLU rally in Brownsville, Texas, on June 28, 2018.

*middle of the street and back onto the sidewalk on the opposite side/across the street from
the courthouse. Everyone moved back! The crowd remained loud, but they did move back
as directed. Again, very impressive.*

*As the crowd prepared to line up to go inside, all of the media people collected every-
one's cell phones from the people up front, and put them in a leather backpack which
was literally overflowing with cell phones. No cell phones allowed inside. I didn't have
anyone to give my phone to, nor a car to put it in, so I found a quiet place to sit in the
shade on this hot, 100-degree afternoon. The rest of our group gradually joined me to
wait for the 3 p.m. bus rendezvous. One woman was so overheated that someone called
911; she declined to be transported to the hospital because she didn't want to be stuck in
Brownsville with no way home.*

*People were allowed inside the courtroom. The line was long and slow. One person who
had waited in the line was upset because of the dress code: no shorts or skimpy summer
tops allowed inside. I think I would've expected this rule, but I also suspect that for many,
it would flat not occur to them that there would be a dress code inside a courtroom.*

*The bus left Brownsville at 3 p.m., making the mandatory stop at the border check-
point located approximately 100 miles north of Brownsville, near Sarita, Texas. Several*

CPB officials boarded the bus and checked each passenger to confirm that everyone had a government-issued ID to confirm (legal) citizenship status. The bus arrived back to San Antonio at 7:30 p.m., and I arrived home at 8:15 p.m. It was a super-long day, but profoundly worthwhile.

Similar Families Belong Together rallies were organized across the United States two days later, on June 30, 2018.

Ecumenical Witness at CBP Facility in Nogales, Arizona

I attended an ecumenical witness event outside of the CBP facility in Nogales, Arizona, on August 28, 2018, as part of the United Church of Christ's "Faithful Witness at the Border" action. The interdenominational gathering showcased ecumenical commonality around the issue of immigration and the current treatment of migrants at our southern border. We crossed the borders of our ecumenical differences and expressed solidarity in love of God for all God's people. My journal entry includes the following:

While we were at a nearby church and preparing for this witness event, an organizer explained, "This will be seen as confrontational. The only people who go through the gate are detainees and elected officials. It's a site of injustice, a site of disappearance. Our presence out there is going to be confrontational enough; we aren't going to escalate beyond that." He described the scene so participants could anticipate what to expect. The federal property line is across the street from where the group would gather, and there would be a lot of traffic, including lots of semi-trucks going in and out, including cartel traffic. The organizer warned, "The last thing we want to do is block or disrupt the cartel. The message is specifically targeted to ICE; tie it to Family Separation and dismantling ICE." We were advised to watch out for one another, and participants were given designated roles. An organizer said, "You are there to be grounded in the witness. Hold signs and join the chants."

Part of witness is discerning where you fit and then, perhaps, pushing yourself a wee bit further beyond your current comfort zone to whatever might be next steps. Some of the group opted not to attend the CBP action event. Others, like myself, attended but with hesitancy because of the adversarial nature we'd been forewarned about.

It was shift change time at the CBP facility when our group of approximately 50 people arrived, so there was lots of traffic going in and out through the security guard entrance. We waved at everyone. ICE came out with a video camera and a still camera and took pictures and videos of us. Soon after our group assembled opposite the main gate to the CBP compound, three police cars arrived and parked in the side driveway of CBP, outside of the enclosed fence. Several police officers stood outside of their cars and observed. A busload of recently picked up migrants rolled through the front gate while we were there. We couldn't see much through the heavily tinted windows, but hopefully the migrants could see us and be encouraged by our presence.

Figure 13.2. An ecumenical group gathers for an action event outside of the CBP facility in Nogales, Arizona, where migrants are detained in an *hielera* (cooler).

Participants held white crosses and homemade signs which said, "No More Blood," "Deport Racist Politicians Now," "We Can Be Compassionate," "No More Separating Families," "Reunite All Families Now," "Familias Juntas Ahora," "End Border Militarization," "Kids Belong with Their Parents," and "End ICE." Some people put their signs over their faces, partly to shade them from the harsh afternoon sun, but perhaps also a little from the intimidation of the experience. I documented the event through photographing and notetaking as I observed the people coming and going. I stood in the shade, slightly around the corner and behind the main group.

We sang one song, then there were several short speeches or declarations directed toward ICE and CBP. The most poignant words were spoken from the heart by one of the leaders at this ecumenical witness event. She directed her remarks to CBP and ICE personnel:

Have we exercised our rights? Many of us have been photographed. Some will be matched with names. If the same attention would have been paid to document—to photograph and record the names of the children and their parents—now these children would not still be separated from their parents. I ask you, ICE and border patrol enforcement, as you guard our borders, I ask you to also guard your hearts. You must also guard your souls from the evil that is being permeated by our nation. You must guard your souls. Guard your ears that you will always be able to hear the cries of the suffering. This suffering will pass. It passed with the indigenous people, against slavery, against the Jews, and this too will pass. Guard your hearts and guard your souls for you will be held accountable when this evil passes.[12]

After the shout-outs, we were led in several chants. For example:

> *Say it loud. Say it clear.*
> *Refugees are welcome here!*
> *Say it loud. Say it clear.*
> *Immigrants are welcome here!*
>
> *Don't give in to racist fears!*
> *Refugees are welcome here!*
>
> *Refugees are here to stay.*
> *Welcome them in every way!*

After the speeches and chants were over, we offered prayers that this evil time will pass and the names of deceased migrants wouldn't be forgotten. Someone read a litany of names of migrants who had died in the borderland. A short chant followed each name: "Presente!" (Present!) to signify that they're not forgotten, that their spirit is very much here. During this litany one of the police cars left; two still remained across the street on CBP property.

Witness of and Humanitarian Aid to the *Perrera* in McAllen, Texas

Project Lifeline organized an interfaith witness and humanitarian aid event outside of the CPB facility in McAllen, Texas, the one known as Ursula that houses the infamous "dog kennel." One of the organizers, Hope Frye, said, "Witness events are pure activism. It's the ultimate action." She asked, "What do we do in the face of a policy that strips people of their human dignity? We bear witness." She continued, "Old-fashioned action is called for. I want to see us outside of these places. Let's have actions on issues of detaining children. When you do that, the media comes and your voice then becomes stronger, more public." She cited the examples of Gandhi's walk across India, Martin Luther King Jr.'s march across the bridge at Selma, and Jesus witnessing in solidarity with the poor and marginalized of his day. She added, "When you get enough people to stand in witness—it is powerful."

The following statements are from people who rode buses to McAllen, explaining why they dedicated a day to this public witness.

- A homeless member of Travis Park UMC: "I came in solidarity."
- A Sisters of Charity member: "It seems like all I've done is talk about it, so I wanted to come and be and do."

- A Trinity University student: "I'm really tired of human rights violations."
- A parent: "I am a mother. My heart breaks for these children."
- A college professor: "This makes me so upset and sad; I don't think it's who we are. It has to change."
- A volunteer with refugees: "We see the children after they've been released from detention, and we know how hurt they are."
- A grandson: "My grandparents fled Mexico when my mother was three years old. I am here in their memory."
- A minister: "I am appalled by how we are treating these children, and I am here to hope to make a statement of solidarity."
- A nurse: "This is an emotional holocaust for these children."
- A musician: "The pastor had just preached on this topic last Sunday. When she asked me to lead the music for the witness event, there was no question or doubt that I would go to McAllen instead of to our friend's wedding."

Caravans of cars and buses converged from San Antonio and Houston outside of the CBP facility in McAllen on September 29, 2018, to protest what an immigration and human rights attorney of forty years called "one of the most inhumane facilities of its kind in the U.S." Despite the public denial of its presence, the reality of its existence is verified in each testimony of the families who've been separated from their children inside this supposedly nonexistent facility.

This interfaith witness event, nicknamed "White Coats and White Collars" because of the contingent of clergy and medical doctors, gathered outside of the *perrera* and sang as Reeder Hoke led a call-and-response song, "Everybody Oughta Know" (. . . what justice is, what love is, etc.). Then we sang "This Land Is Your Land" as we slowly walked across the street to the edge of the CBP property line. Mennonite pastor John Garland passed through the barricades and approached the front door of CBP. He asked the CBP official who met him at the door if we could donate a tractor-trailer filled with supplies for the children who were detained inside the facility. The CBP official said that they don't accept donations, and he ordered the minister to leave the property immediately. CBP escorted this pastor to the other side of the barricade located curbside in front of this massive, nondescript warehouse where thousands of migrants are detained within chain-link cages each year.

Whatever the to-be-determined ripple effect will be, witness events immediately impact participants. During the bus ride back to San Antonio, the music leader reflected on his experience. He said, "I saw over one hundred mostly strangers who came together to sing and to witness for these children. We all came to be in solidarity with people whom we couldn't even see inside those locked walls with no windows." He said that it was a "powerfully moving experience" and something that he could share with his middle school students. Another participant said, "The reality of the experience in person is very profound. I've seen this dog kennel facility on TV, but to experience this in person was very impactful. I saw the preacher get ejected and told they weren't going to take the humanitarian supplies we brought. I saw that

Figure 13.3. Project Lifeline interfaith witness event outside of Ursula, the CBP facility in McAllen, Texas, which houses a *perrera* (dog kennel). Nicknamed "White Coats and White Collars," this event featured Jewish, Islamic, and Christian faith-based leaders joining medical personnel to protest the detention of children.

there are no windows anywhere. I saw this harsh reality." He added, "I cannot believe this is happening in America. It's not who we are." He shared his experiences on social media throughout the day and continued to challenge his network of family, friends, and colleagues about the injustice he witnessed firsthand in McAllen. This witness event was an interfaith and ecumenical worship with solidarity and love for and with the families locked away. We couldn't see each other, but kindness, compassion, and love were clearly present.

Witness Includes Celebration

Celebration is another form of witness because it affirms and uplifts compassion, mercy, and love. Covenant Baptist Church in San Antonio hosted a fiesta the evening after some children were reunited with their mothers (see chapter 12). This impromptu party honored the reunion of the families and the transformation of the congregation members who journeyed through the pain and uncertainty with the families to a place of unprecedented joy. Pastor Natalie Webb said, "We went out and got buckets of food and fired up the grill that we hadn't used in ages. People played guitars and there was a dog running around the sanctuary, which became a fiestaship hall. The kids were falling asleep at the table. We feasted and laughed and talked and celebrated." She said she kept apologizing on behalf of our country, and the mothers kept telling her not to worry. The pastor explained, "They told me again and again that after going through all that they've been through, they were even more surprised by the love and welcome that they received in San Antonio, and especially here by this congregation." She added, "It was the hardest and the holiest week in the life of this church, but transformed people transform systems."

Public Worship as Witness

Public worship is a powerful witness to express solidarity with migrants. It was profoundly moving to participate in an ecumenical prayer vigil and communion service alongside the border wall in Nogales, Mexico. Saying the words of the confession of sin with a delegation of some seventy Americans who gathered in Mexico was a poignant experience. Participants felt our culpability in this systemic migration mess as we said a UCC prayer of confession:

> Leader: Standing in the shadows of this wall, it is obvious that something has gone horribly wrong. It is a symbol of greed and fear. It stops people but perpetuates tragedies.
>
> People: As people of faith, we are called to struggle against everything that separates us from the love of God and Neighbor.
>
> Leader: Pridefully we have torn apart our Neighbors' forests, farms, and families, and then blamed and criminalized them for fleeing for safety.
>
> People: We have betrayed our Neighbors by considering our interests more important than theirs.
>
> Leader: Dividing walls, private prisons, family separation, mass deportations, and the bullet holes in these walls are painful reminders that we have a lot of repenting to do.
>
> People: We acknowledge our sin and the sin of our nation's leaders. We ask, Spirit, that you recreate us and we pledge our cooperation in Your effort. We seek Your courage and Your blessing, O God, in the struggle for human rights. Enliven and impassion us so that we can bring about change and usher in justice—help us to build bigger tables even as we tear down these walls.

The artwork on and alongside the wall speaks to the suffering that this dividing wall between nations inflicts upon our sisters and brothers in Mexico. The iron artwork was especially moving because it made the witness the families have shared with me one-on-one visceral and very real, particularly the three-dimensional depiction of a shrouded body being returned to Mexico for burial after a migrant's failed attempt to cross the harsh Arizona desert.

Figure 13.4. Iron artwork at the wall in Nogales, Sonora, Mexico, depicts the gruesome reality of the risks migrants face when crossing the Mexico-U.S. border.

Presente! Celebrating the Memory of Deceased Migrants

Another form of worship as witness is keeping the memories alive of migrants who died on U.S. soil. I went with a group of about fifty people on a morning hike in the southern Arizona desert to the site where the remains of a migrant had been recovered in May 2001. Miguel Vasquez Lara had been dead a day or two when his body was found.

A resident who lives nearby explained Miguel's story: "The group he'd traveled with had tried to revive him. They put water on him; the guide said to put garlic under his nose, and they'd done that." One of his fellow travelers went to find help; the others stayed with Miguel. When he died, they left his identification but took the rest of his things back to his family. The local continued, "The police report says he died of a heart attack, but the coroner said he died from dehydration. The Samaritans had a ceremony for him, and someone goes there occasionally to tend the site. It's not a grave; it's the site where his body was found." The Samaritans put a white cross there, and the site is marked by a second cross made by artist Alvaro Enciso, a Colombian migrant who lives locally and has planted more than eight hundred crosses at locations where human remains have been found (see chapter 2, figure 2.2).[13] After our straggling group arrived at the remote site, we placed silk flowers and small crosses as memorial tributes to Miguel. The service included songs and a reading honoring migrants. Several in the group offered impromptu prayers:

- "We repent from looking away."
- "Help us to be the church that you called us to be."
- "Miguel, I'm sorry for your family. You live through your witness to us in this moment."
- "You left with great hope, and we experience you as a teacher. You help us to understand the hopelessness of the laws of this nation."
- "I'm mindful of the mother who wrote her advice to other mothers: 'No, no, no! It was a very bad trip. It is better to die with your family than alone to be eaten by wild animals.' I pray for the ones who died along the journey and for the families making this journey at this moment."
- "We resist. We refuse to let hatred win. We refuse to give up. We are here to the end."

After the short memorial service we slowly and silently made our way back through the desert to the cars.

FINDING YOUR PLACE AND ENTERING IN

There's something each one of us can do, some way each person can help. Hospitality and advocacy for refugees seeking asylum is not limited to states located along the southern border. There's something to do wherever you live! The families begin at the southern border, but they scatter throughout the United States. They need help to be enculturated and supported emotionally and spiritually during the very slow process to asylum. They have to wait six to twelve months to get a work permit, so they also need physical support.

Changing the policies and practices that harm refugee families seeking asylum means that we need to be involved with institutions. A longtime volunteer advised, "If you want to change how things are, you have to become involved in the system. Otherwise, you have limited access to effect change." Another volunteer explained, "If we look historically, when ugliness has been exposed, when we've been forced to deal with it, then we can have a sense of what needs to be done with the new ugly." With the witness of the families and the testimonies of the volunteers in view, how will you begin to make your responsible response to help these families who are desperately seeking asylum? Will you be the one who is going to make the world better?

14

Resources for Education and Action

The humanitarian crisis is real. The threat to life for mothers and fathers and sons and daughters desperately seeking asylum is not a farce. Real people are suffering; real people are asking for our help.

PARTING WITNESS: JORGE "FARRUKO"

Here's a final testimony, penned by the director of the Children's Home Project, an Arizona nonprofit with deep ties to Honduras. It's the story of Jorge, a boy from a children's home (Proniño) in Honduras that was founded by an American. He joined the migrant caravan from Honduras to seek asylum in the United States. His journey is a parting witness to the reality of the suffering in the Northern Triangle, the dangerous journey through Mexico, and the urgent need to reinvent the broken immigration matrix to make a way clear for mothers and fathers and boys and girls who are desperately seeking asylum.

This is a tough post. But I also don't want time to continue going by without acknowledgment of loss. I've had lots of people asking me about the caravan the last few months. My quick response until I know that someone wants to dive deeper is always "It's a complex issue. One of my kids is currently part of it."

His name is Jorge, but his nickname was Farruko after the popular reggaeton singer. At some point he started calling me Farruka. He left Proniño because he wanted to be with his family. We knew that nothing good awaited him there, but try telling that to a 13-year-old who just wants to belong.

In September, the now 16-year-old Jorge sent me [two] pictures [of the two of us when he was a boy] and said, "I wish I could be a child again." You know, back when the world *was full of possibilities and he still thought he was invincible. I asked him about work. He was helping at a wood shop, making $10 a week. (Minimum wage in Honduras is around $350 a month.) He said he was thinking about coming to the U.S. He had no money to study and not enough education to get a job that would enable him to survive. As I always do, I talked to him about the dangers of the journey and stressed that the States isn't the Promised Land.*

By mid-October he had started his journey and had found his mom in Mexico. He hadn't seen her in over a decade. "Ok," I thought, "He's with his mom. He will stay there and create a life in Mexico." Nope. Within days he was on the road again.

This is when he started talking about turning himself in at the border and seeking asylum. "I've been told that since I'm a minor and my family is in a gang and very dangerous that I'll be accepted. I have my ID and my school tag that shows I'm 16."

I asked if he had any sort of proof that his family was dangerous. Police reports? Testimony from neighbors?

He said that his uncles threatened him. "I don't want to become one of those people who kill."

This is real. A real decision he had to make. When I was 16 my biggest decision was to decide if I was going to be 'one of those people' who took four years of French or settled for only three. He had to decide if he had it in himself to kill if commanded in order to stay with his family.

There is zero doubt in my mind that he was telling the truth. But his word and my confidence hold not one ounce of weight in our judicial system.

Mid-November he was in Mexico City and joining the caravan.

November 25th, he arrives in Tijuana. The day tear gas was fired on women and children at the border.

November 28th he asks me to send him money for food (I didn't do it) and says that things are terrible there. There are a lot of people "golpeado"—beaten.

December 7th he tells me that he's going to cross and turn himself in.

December 18th is when we find out that he is gone. It sounds more or less like a mugging. He or one of his two friends made it sound like they had money. Word spread. When it was discovered that that was a lie, he and one of the friends were killed. (By people from Tijuana, not by fellow migrants.)

We could blame him for this. Say that if he had just stayed in Proniño he would be studying, enjoying his childhood . . . and alive.

I cannot stress enough that 13-year-olds do not make good decisions. There is not one decision at 13 that justifies death at 16.

I started writing this weeks ago. I couldn't figure out how to end it. What's my point? Who is to blame? How can this be fixed? I have lots of ideas and opinions, but mainly I don't know.

But I know I loved Farruko a lot and we lost a bright light on December 18th [2018].

I used to recommend that everyone read Enrique's Journey *[by Sonia Nozario]. Not because I want it to make you pro-immigrant or anti, but because it gives a deeper understanding of why this is happening and who is coming. It humanizes the numbers. You may not have time to read* Enrique's Journey, *but you have read this. This is a migrant. A sweet and silly 16-year-old who wanted to make a living wage when he worked hard, who wanted to study, who chose the excitement and dangers of a new world as opposed to becoming part of the problem and a victim of violence in his own country.*

I'm going to miss your random messages my friend. The confused look in your eye when I try to convince you that something preposterous is true. Your faithfulness to your friends. You deserved so much more than this.[1]

Presente! *Farruko, may we hear and heed your witness.*

FIND YOUR POINT OF ENTRY AND BEGIN

There's something for everyone to do. It can be as easy or as dramatic as you're comfortable with. It's up to you to take the initiative to begin. What are you interested in, and willing and able to do? You don't have to reinvent the wheel and figure things out totally on your own. There already are thousands of nongovernmental agencies, religious and secular, that offer direct assistance to migrants. The resources below offer a bare sampling of the options to get started in education and advocacy. You don't have to live in a border state. You can find something near where you live by using your favorite search engine and typing in "immigration advocacy (add the name of your state)." What is yours to do? Find your point of entry . . . and begin. It will take all of us to make a dent and a difference so that the current harsh reality of injustice at our southern border can be transformed into a fair and warm welcome for future generations of mothers and fathers, boys and girls, who are desperately seeking asylum.

RESOURCES TO GET STARTED
WITH EDUCATION AND ADVOCACY

- Al Otro Lado: https://alotrolado.org
  Provides direct legal services to indigent deportees, migrants, and refugees in Tijuana, Mexico.
- American Civil Liberties Union, "Know Your Rights": https://www.aclu.org/know-your-rights
  Publicizes rights in a variety of categories, including immigration.
- Border Angels (Angeles de la Frontera): https://www.borderangels.org
  Promotes education and advocacy for human rights, humane immigration reform, and social justice concerns along the U.S.-Mexico border. Also offers services for the immigrant population in San Diego County.
- Border Community Alliance: https://bordercommunityalliance.org
  Supports the education of Americans about Mexico with trips, seminars, etc.

- Borderlinks: www.borderlinks.org
  Offers education on migration through immersion experiences in Arizona.

- Catholic Charities Archdiocese of San Antonio: https://ccaosa.org
  Assists refugee and immigrant families as part of its mission to emphasize social justice, social teaching, and community service. See the Volunteer Opportunities page.

- Catholic Charities of the Rio Grande Valley, Humanitarian Crisis Response: http://www.catholiccharitiesrgv.org/HumanitarianRespiteCenter.shtml
  Offers direct assistance to immigrants and refugees. See the Volunteer page.

- Catholic Legal Immigration Network: https://cliniclegal.org
  Offers training on immigration law and works with volunteers to provide legal services for migrants.

- Central American Resource Center (CARECEN): http://www.carecen-la.org
  Provides immigrant integration programs and legal services.

- Children's Home Project, Arizona and Honduras: http://www.tchproject.org
  Provides safe housing and education for at-risk children in Honduras.

- Church World Service: https://cwsglobal.org
  Provides information on how to become involved in broad aspects of immigration.

- Colibrí Center for Human Rights: http://www.colibricenter.org
  Reunites families with the remains of their loved ones through the Missing Migrant Project.

- End Streamline Coalition: https://derechoshumanosaz.net/coalition-work/end -streamline-coalition
  Offers education and advocacy to stop Operation Streamline.

- Florence Immigrant and Refugee Rights Project: https://firrp.org
  Provides free legal services to men, women, and unaccompanied children in immigration custody in Arizona.

- Freedom for Immigrants: https://www.freedomforimmigrants.org
  Uses community organizing, coalition building, and legislative advocacy to try to end immigration detention.

- Grassroots International: www.grassrootsonline.org
  Offers education, advocacy, and support to foster social change locally and globally. Very active in immigration.

- Green Valley-Sahuarita Samaritans: https://www.gvs-samaritans.org
  Prevents death at the border with water drops and searches, observes Operation Streamline, and volunteers at a soup kitchen in Nogales, Sonora, Mexico.

- HEPAC—Home of Hope and Peace (Hogar de Esperanza y Paz): https://www
.hepacnogales.org
Assists migrants in Nogales, Mexico, to become sustainable so they do not feel
like their only hope for survival is to make the dangerous desert crossing to the
United States.

- Hope Border Institute: https://www.hopeborder.org
Works for justice through research, reflection, leadership development, and
education in the El Paso–Ciudad Juárez–Las Cruces area of the border.

- Immigrants' Rights: https://sites.google.com/view/immigrantsrights
Promotes education and advocacy for immigrants' rights. Also offers legal assistance, working primarily in greater San Antonio, Texas.

- Interfaith Welcome Coalition of San Antonio: http://www.interfaithwelcome
coalition.org
Provides a variety of hospitality assistance for refugee families.

- Kino Border Initiative: https://www.kinoborderinitiative.org
Supports "removed" Mexicans at Nogales, manages El Comedor soup kitchen,
conducts research about deportees, and does advocacy about CBP. For a video
overview, see https://vimeo.com/206180020.

- La Familia Latina Unida: http://www.lafamiliaunida.org
From Chicago, Illinois, offers counseling services and intervention programs for
domestic violence and anger management.

- Lutheran Immigration and Refugee Services (LIRS), Visitation Ministries:
https://www.lirs.org/detention-visitation
Empowers congregations, community groups, and individual volunteers to
launch and grow detention visitation ministries.

- Mariposas Sin Fronteras: https://mariposassinfronteras.org
From Tucson, Arizona, advocates to end violence and abuse of LGBTQ people
held in prison and immigration detention.

- No More Deaths/No Más Muertes: http://forms.nomoredeaths.org
Provides humanitarian aid in the desert.

- Project Lifeline Toolkit for Children and Parents: https://projectlifeline.us/wp
-content/uploads/2018/10/ChildrensToolkit_ProjectLifeline.pdf
Catalogues age-appropriate books and online resources for children to learn
about immigrants and refugees.

- Pueblo Sin Fronteras: https://www.pueblosinfronteras.org
Monitors and challenges human rights abuses against migrants and refugees on
both sides of the U.S.-Mexico border. Provides accompaniment services during
and after migration; runs two shelters in Sonora, Mexico.

- Refugee and Immigrant Center for Education and Legal Services (RAICES): https://www.raicestexas.org
  Largest immigration legal services provider in Texas. Promotes justice by providing free and low-cost legal services to underserved refugees and immigrant children and families.

- Report checkpoints and raids: Call 800-717-8121; text 210-920-6612.

- SA Stands: https://www.sastands.org
  Monitors and addresses concerns in San Antonio, Texas, on several key issues, including immigration.

- Sanctuary Movement: https://www.sanctuarynotdeportation.org
  Offers the *Rapid Response Toolkit for Faith Allies*, which prepares people to stop immigration raids and deportations and support impacted communities.

- School of the Americas Watch: http://www.soaw.org
  Largest Latin American solidarity organization in the United States. Monitors and calls attention to militarized U.S. foreign policy, which contributes to forced migration.

- Southern Border Communities Coalition: https://sites.google.com/site/border stakeholderforum/home
  Educates and advocates for necessary policy changes along the southern border.

- Trans-Border Institute at University of San Diego: https://www.sandiego.edu/peace/institutes/tbi
  Creates paths for peacebuilding on both sides of the U.S.-Mexico border. Sees itself as a think tank that provides direction for policymakers.

- United Church of Christ, *Take Action: Public Policy Advocacy Guide*: https://www.uccresources.com/products/take-action-public-policy-advocacy-guide-pdf-download
  Provides tips, tools, and theological insights for understanding the call to work for justice through public policy advocacy.

- United States Conference of Catholic Bishops, Migration and Refugee Services: http://www.usccb.org/about/migration-and-refugee-services/index.cfm
  Advocates for refugees, asylees, migrants, unaccompanied children, and victims of human trafficking.

- United States House of Representatives, find your representative: https://www.house.gov/representatives/find-your-representative

- United States Senate, contact your senators: https://www.senate.gov/general/contact_information/senators_cfm.cfm

Notes

INTRODUCTION

1. For personal stories of refugees in a broader context, see, e.g., Malala Yousafzai, *We Are Displaced: My Journey and Stories from Refugee Girls around the World* (New York: Little, Brown, 2019).

CHAPTER ONE: DESPERATELY SEEKING ASYLUM

1. Jürgen Moltmann, *The Livingness of God and the Fullness of Life*, trans. Margaret Kohl (Louisville, KY: Westminster John Knox Press, 2016), 23.

2. Marcelo M. Suárez-Orozco, "Speaking of the Unspeakable: Toward a Psychosocial Understanding of Responses to Terror," *Ethos* 18, no. 3 (1990), 361.

3. "You Have Only One Life to Live," *Refugee Art: Testimonies of Immigrant Families Seeking Asylum* (blog edited by Helen T. Boursier), posted February 18, 2019, https://refugeeart blog.com/2019/02/18/you-have-only-one-life-to-live.

4. Octavio Paz, *The Labyrinth of Solitude and Other Writings* (New York: Grove Press, 1985), 198.

5. Juan Forero, "Latin America Turns Deadly for Women: Violence by Domestic Partners and Gangs Has Driven 'Femicide' Rates to Crisis Levels," *Wall Street Journal*, December 20, 2018, A1.

6. Julian Borger, "Fleeing a Hell the U.S. Helped Create: Why Central Americans Journey North," *The Guardian*, December 19, 2018, https://www.theguardian.com/us-news/2018/dec/19/central-america-migrants-us-foreign-policy.

7. Oscar Romero, "Letter to President Carter, February 17, 1980," in *Voice of the Voiceless: The Four Pastoral Letters and Other Statements* (Maryknoll, NY: Orbis Books, 1985), 188–89.

8. Michael Deibert, "What Is Forcing Thousands of Migrants to Flee Their Home Countries?" *The Guardian*, December 5, 2018, https://www.theguardian.com/commentis free/2018/dec/05/why-migrants-flee-home-countries.

9. For a detailed example of the economic connection between NAFTA, the U.S. economic invasion of Central America, and the subsequent desperate exodus of migrants from Central American countries to the United States because of their inability to earn a basic living, see *Trails of Hope and Terror, The Movie*, directed by Vincent De La Torre (Centennial, CO: V1 Educational Media, 2018), available at https://www.trailsofhopeandterrorthemovie .com; see also Miguel A. De La Torre, *Trails of Hope and Terror: Testimonies of Immigration* (Maryknoll, NY: Orbis Books, 2009).

10. For an excellent detailed report, see Cristina Eguizábal et al., "The Central America Regional Security Initiative: A Key Piece of U.S. Security Assistance to El Salvador, But Not the Only One," in *Crime and Violence in Central America's Northern Triangle: How U.S. Policy Responses Are Helping, Hurting, and Can Be Improved*, ed. Eric L. Olson (Washington, D.C.: Woodrow Wilson International Center for Scholars, Latin American Program, 2015), https://www.wilsoncenter.org/sites/default/files/FINAL%20PDF_CARSI%20REPORT_0.pdf .

11. See, e.g., United States Government Accountability Office, *Firearms Trafficking: U.S. Efforts to Combat Arms Trafficking to Mexico Face Planning and Coordination Challenges*, Report GAO-09-709 to Congressional Requesters, June 2009, https://www.gao.gov/new.items/d09709.pdf.

12. For a chart comparing criminal versus noncriminal removals, see figure 15, page 13, and for a list of deportees by nationality, see appendix B in United States Immigration and Customs Enforcement, *Fiscal Year 2017 ICE Enforcement and Removal Operations Report*, https://www.ice.gov/sites/default/files/documents/Report/2017/iceEndOfYearFY2017.pdf.

13. See, e.g., United States Department of State, Bureau for International Narcotics and Law Enforcement Affairs, "Honduras," in *International Narcotics Control Strategy Report*, March 2017, 181–85, https://www.state.gov/documents/organization/268025.pdf.

14. Peg Bowden, "Bach and 45," *La Frontera: The Border. Migrant Journeys in the Desert* (blog), February 19, 2017, http://www.arroya.org/?p=1644. See also her book, *A Land of Hard Edges: Serving the Front Lines of the Border* (Tucson, AZ: Peer Publishing, 2014).

15. "The Laws Do Not Help People," *Refugee Art* (blog edited by Boursier), posted February 2, 2019, https://refugeeartblog.com/2019/02/25/the-laws-do-not-help-people/.

16. Guatemala Human Rights Commission, *Guatemala's Feminicide Law: Progress against Impunity?* May 2009, http://www.ghrc-usa.org/wp-content/uploads/2012/01/Guatemalas-Femicide-Law-Progress-Against-Impunity.pdf.

CHAPTER TWO: FLEEING FOR THEIR LIVES

1. See, e.g., Helen T. Boursier, *The Ethics of Hospitality: An Interfaith Response to U.S. Immigration Policy* (Lanham, MD: Lexington Books, 2019), 33–46.

2. Thomas A. Tweed, *Crossing and Dwelling: A Theory of Religion* (Cambridge, MA: Harvard University Press, 2006), 123.

3. Monica Maher, "The Truth Will Set Us Free: Religion, Violence, and Women's Empowerment in Latin America," in *Global Empowerment of Women: Responses to Globalization and Politicized Religions*, ed. Carolyn M. Elliott (New York: Routledge, 2008), 273.

4. "Things I Miss from Home," *Refugee Art: Testimonies of Immigrant Families Seeking Asylum* (blog edited by Helen T. Boursier), posted March 18, 2019, https://refugeeartblog .com/2019/03/18/things-i-miss-from-home/.

5. "The Children Suffered," *Refugee Art* (blog edited by Boursier), posted February 11, 2019, https://refugeeartblog.com/2019/02/11/the-children-suffered/.

6. Madeleine Penman, "Mexico, a Death-Trap for Migrants: 'It Was the Worst Day of My Life,'" Amnesty International, June 19, 2015, https://www.amnesty.org/en/latest/news/2015/06/mexico-a-death-trap-for-migrants-it-was-the-worst-day-of-my-life/.

7. J. J. Messner, "Factionalization and Group Grievance Fuel Rise in Instability," Fragile States Index 2017, Fund for Peace, May 10, 2017, https://reliefweb.int/report/world/fragile -states-index-2017; and George Lehner, "'So Far from God, So Close to the United States.' Mexico Most Worsened in 2017," Fragile States Index, Fund for Peace, May 14, 2017, https://fragilestatesindex.org/2017/05/14/so-far-from-god-so-close-to-the-united-states-mex ico-most-worsened-in-2017.

8. "A Very Difficult Trip," *Refugee Art* (blog edited by Boursier), posted January 14, 2019, https://refugeeartblog.com/2019/01/14/a-very-difficult-trip/.

9. Pueblo Sin Fronteras, "Central American Exodus Statement," accessed December 27, 2018, https://www.pueblosinfronteras.org/.

10. Doctors Without Borders, "The Facts about the Humanitarian Crisis in Mexico and Central America," February 5, 2019, https://www.doctorswithoutborders.org/what-we-do/news-stories/news/facts-about-humanitarian-crisis-mexico-and-central-america.

11. Peg Bowden, "The Children," *La Frontera: The Border. Migrant Journeys in the Desert* (blog), June 19, 2014, http://www.arroya.org/?p=1421.

12. Travis Fedschun, "San Antonio Trailer Deaths: Driver Charged after Ten Die in Sweltering Truck," Fox News, July 24, 2017, http://www.foxnews.com/us/2017/07/24/san -antonio-trailer-deaths-suspect-due-in-court-after-10-die-in-sweltering-truck.html.

13. Conversation with Gavin Rogers, Pub Theology ministry of Travis Park UMC, Friendly Spot Ice House, San Antonio, TX, December 10, 2018. Excerpt of the verbatim transcript shared by permission.

14. Green Valley-Sahuarita Samaritans, weekly email update, November 28, 2018.

15. Arizona OpenGIS Initiative for Deceased Migrants, accessed September 19, 2018, http://humaneborders.info/app/map.asp.

16. Personal email correspondence, November 27, 2018. She concluded her update with this: "If you want to repost, please use copy/paste and do not attribute it to me. I do not wish to be harassed."

CHAPTER THREE: THE HARSH REALITY

1. "Five Horrible Days in the *Hielera*," *Refugee Art: Testimonies of Immigrant Families Seeking Asylum* (blog edited by Helen T. Boursier), posted March 25, 2019, https://refugeeartblog.com/2019/03/25/five-horrible-days-in-the-hielera/.

2. Elie Wiesel, *Night*, trans. Stella Rodway (New York: Bantam Books, 1960, 1986), 20–21.

3. "The *Hielera* Was Horrible," *Refugee Art* (blog edited by Boursier), posted October 27, 2018, https://refugeeartblog.com/2018/10/27/the-hielera-was-horrible/.

4. For more examples, see Helen T. Boursier, "Faithful Doxology—Allyship with Immigrants Seeking Asylum as the Church's Missional Hermeneutic," *International Bulletin of Mission Journal* 41, no. 2 (April 2017): 170–77.

5. Elizabeth Cassidy and Tiffany Lynch, *Barriers to Protection: The Treatment of Asylum Seekers in Expedited Removal* (Washington, D.C.: U.S. Commission on International Religious Freedom, August 8, 2016), 58, https://www.uscirf.gov/sites/default/files/Barriers%20To%20 Protection.pdf.

6. Cassidy and Lynch, *Barriers to Protection*, 40.

7. *New York Times* Editorial Board, "Deported from the Middle of Nowhere," August 25, 2014, https://www.nytimes.com/2014/08/26/opinion/at-an-immigrant-detention-center -due-process-denied.html.

8. Cassidy and Lynch, *Barriers to Protection*, 60–62.

9. "Apprehension, Processing, Care, and Custody of Alien Minors and Unaccompanied Alien Children," *Federal Register* 83, no. 174 (September 7, 2018), https://www.aila.org/File/ DownloadEmbeddedFile/77287. The executive summary states, "In Fiscal Year (FY) 2017, CBP apprehended 113,920 juveniles. Generally, ICE encounters minors either upon transfer from CBP to a family residential center (FRC), or during interior enforcement actions. In FY 2017, 37,825 family members were booked into ICE's three FRCs, 20,606 of whom were minors." Adding 113,920 juveniles to 20,606 juveniles from family units totals 134,526.

10. Rafael Bernal and Brett Samuels, "Border Apprehensions Up Nearly 100,000 in Fiscal 2018," The Hill, October 23, 2018, https://thehill.com/latino/412781-border-apprehen sions-up-nearly-100000-in-fiscal-year-2018.

11. United States Immigration and Customs Enforcement, Operations and Support. *Fiscal Year 2019 Congressional Justification*, O&S 13, https://www.dhs.gov/sites/default/files/ publications/U.S.%20Immigration%20and%20Customs%20Enforcement.pdf. For the 2019 budget supporting documents, see https://www.dhs.gov/publication/congressional-budget -justification-fy-2019.

12. Julia Ainsley, "Trump Admin's 'Tent Cities' Cost More Than Keeping Migrant Kids with Parents," NBC News, June 20, 2018, https://www.nbcnews.com/storyline/immigration -border-crisis/trump-admin-s-tent-cities-cost-more-keeping-migrant-kids-n884871. A speaker at a refugee rally cited the foster care cost. According to one center in Texas, foster parents receive approximately $675 per child per month, or $22.50 per day (see https://www.depelchin .org/relative-kinship-faq).

13. Reinhold Niebuhr, *Moral Man and Immoral Society: A Study in Ethics and Politics* (Louisville, KY: Westminster John Knox, 1932, 2001), 117.

14. Giorgio Agamben, *Homo Sacer: Sovereign Power and Bare Life*, trans. Daniel Heller-Roazen (Stanford, CA: Stanford University Press, 1998), 181.

CHAPTER FOUR: THE MESSY IMMIGRATION MATRIX

1. United Nations High Commissioner for Refugees, "Universal Declaration of Human Rights," accessed January 8, 2019, www.un.org/en/universal-declaration-human-rights/index .html.

2. Alexander Betts, *Survival Migration: Failed Governance and the Crisis of Displacement* (Ithaca, NY: Cornell University Press, 2013), 5.

3. Silas Allard, "Interreligious Reflections on Immigration," American Academy of Religion Annual Meetings, Denver, CO, November 17, 2018.

4. Joshua Jamerson and Juan Montes, "US Shifts Border Policy," *Wall Street Journal*, December 21, 2018, A3.

5. William A. Kandel, *U.S. Family-Based Immigration Policy* (Washington, D.C.: Congressional Research Service, February 9, 2018), https://fas.org/sgp/crs/homesec/R43145.pdf.

6. Ted Hesson, "Trump Officials Pressing to Slash Refugee Admissions to Zero Next Year," *Politico*, July 18, 2019, https://www.politico.com/story/2019/07/18/trump-officials-refugee-zero-1603503.

7. Hope M. Frye, JD, interview with the author, November 5, 2018; used by permission. Frye is the executive director of Project Lifeline (https://projectlifeline.us/).

8. *Flores v. Meese* Stipulated Settlement Agreement, January 17, 1997, https://www.aclu.org/files/pdfs/immigrants/flores_v_meese_agreement.pdf.

9. Project Lifeline, "Comment on the Proposed Regulations: Apprehension, Processing, Care, and Custody of Alien Minors and Unaccompanied Alien Children," November 6, 2018, https://projectlifeline.us/wp-content/uploads/2018/11/Project-Lifeline-Comment-on-Proposed-RegulationsFlores.pdf.

10. Hope Frye, JD, "Hope Frye Testifies [Before Congress]," *Families Belong Together*, July 10, 2019, https://www.facebook.com/fams2gether/videos/464808130986800/UzpfSTEw MDAwMzYyNzU5ODU0MjozMDYwNjExMjk0OTk0OMTQ6MTA6MDoxNTY0NjQy Nzk5OjMxNzk1MjE1ODU1YjE1ODA2MjM2MTgyOTc/.

11. KTAR News, "Southwest Key Employee Sentenced for Sexually Abusing Migrants," February 1, 2019, http://ktar.com/story/2420982/southwest-key-employee-sentenced-for-sexually-abusing-migrants/.

12. Michael Cohen, "How For-Profit Prisons Have Become the Biggest Lobby Nobody Notices," *Washington Post*, April 28, 2015, https://www.washingtonpost.com/?utm_term=.8678d99a78f8.

13. Tal Kopan, "More Than 14,000 Immigrant Children Are in U.S. Custody, an All-Time High," *San Francisco Chronicle*, November 16, 2018, https://www.sfchronicle.com/nation/article/More-than-14-000-immigrant-children-are-in-U-S-13399510.php.

14. Kopan, "More Than 14,000 Immigrant Children."

15. Garance Burke and Martha Mendoza, "'A Moral Disaster': AP Reveals Scope of Migrant Kids Program," Associated Press News, December 20, 2018, https://apnews.com/a857e04de9bc4871995b65784ed7ccd8.

16. Ron Nixon, "$10 Million from FEMA Diverted to Pay for Immigration Detention Centers, Document Shows," *New York Times*, September 12, 2018, https://www.nytimes.com/2018/09/12/us/politics/fema-ice-immigration-detention.html.

17. Emily Green, "Head of Controversial Tent City Says the Trump Administration Pressured Him to Detain More Young Migrants," Vice News, January 11, 2019, https://news.vice.com/en_us/article/kzvmg3/head-of-controversial-tent-city-says-the-trump-administration-pressured-him-to-detain-more-young-migrants.

18. Hope Frye, January 29, 2019; personal correspondence used by permission. See also Senate Amendment 5 to H.R. 268. Per the American Immigration Lawyers Association (Doc 19012238, January 21, 2019, https://www.aila.org/advo-media/whats-happening-in-congress/pending-legislation/senate-bill-end-the-shutdown-and-secure-the-border), "The bill aims to end the partial government shutdown by funding the Wall, more detention beds, and additional border patrol and ICE agents, while providing limited protection for Dreamers and TPS-holders, and banning Central American minors from seeking asylum at the border." It failed the Senate, 50–47.

CHAPTER FIVE: NATIONAL LEADERSHIP SHAPES
U.S. IMMIGRATION POLICIES AND PRACTICES

1. Hope M. Frye on *The Source*, Texas Public Radio live call-in show, noon, November 1, 2018.

2. See, e.g., Stephen Dinan, "Catch-and-Release of Illegals Restarted in Texas, Border Patrol Agents Say," *Washington Times*, November 15, 2017, https://www.washingtontimes.com/news/2017/nov/15/catch-and-release-illegal-immigrant-restarted-texa/.

3. American Immigration Council, "How the United States Immigration System Works," accessed January 7, 2019, https://www.americanimmigrationcouncil.org/research/how-united-states-immigration-system-works.

4. Donald J. Trump, "Presidential Memorandum for the Secretary of State," Presidential Determination no. 2017-13, September 29, 2017, http://myattorneyusa.com/storage/upload/files/matters/presidential-memorandum-secretary-of-state.pdf.

5. BBC News, "'Drug Dealers, Criminals, Rapists': What Trump Thinks of Mexicans," August 31, 2016, https://www.bbc.com/news/av/world-us-canada-37230916/drug-dealers-criminals-rapists-what-trump-thinks-of-mexicans; and Carolina Moreno, "Nine Outrageous Things Donald Trump Has Said about Latinos," *Huffington Post*, November 9, 2016, https://www.huffingtonpost.com/entry/9-outrageous-things-donald-trump-has-said-about-latinos_us_55e483a1e4b0c818f618904b.

6. Elizabeth Cassidy and Tiffany Lynch, *Barriers to Protection: The Treatment of Asylum Seekers in Expedited Removal* (Washington, D.C.: U.S. Commission on International Religious Freedom, August 8, 2016), 11–14, https://www.uscirf.gov/sites/default/files/Barriers%20To%20Protection.pdf. DHS reports are available at https://www.dhs.gov/publications-library/collections/immigration-data-and-statistics. Annual statistics are available through CBP (https://www.cbp.gov/newsroom/stats/ofo-sw-border-inadmissibles) and TRAC Immigration (https://trac.syr.edu/immigration/).

7. Sara Compos and Joan Friedland, "Mexican and Central American Asylum and Credible Fear Claims: Background and Context," American Immigration Council, May 2014, https://www.americanimmigrationcouncil.org/research/mexican-and-central-american-asylum-and-credible-fear-claims-background-and-context.

8. For the profitability factor of family detention see, e.g., Jeff Sommer, "Trump Immigration Crackdown Is Great for Private Prison Stocks," *New York Times*, March 12, 2017, https://www.nytimes.com/2017/03/10/your-money/immigrants-prison-stocks.html.

9. John Fife, "From the Sanctuary Movement to No More Deaths: The Challenge to Communities of Faith," in *Religious and Ethical Perspectives on Global Migration*, eds. Elizabeth W. Collier and Charles R. Strain (Lanham, MD: Lexington Books, 2014), 257–71.

10. Green Valley-Sahuarita Samaritans, "Operation Streamline–August, 27, 2018," Resources–Samaritan News, updated September 3, 2018, https://www.gvs-samaritans.org/samaritan-news/previous/8.

11. Alistair Graham Robertson, Rachel Beaty, Jane Atkinson, and Bob Libal, *Operation Streamline: Costs and Consequences*, Grassroots Leadership, September 2012, 23–24, http://grassrootsleadership.org/sites/default/files/uploads/GRL_Sept2012_Report%20final.pdf; End Streamline Coalition, "What Is Operation Streamline?" (particularly the section titled "How Much Does This Cost the U.S. Taxpayers?"), accessed May 21, 2019, https://www.endstreamline.org/what-is-operation-streamline/; and ACLU, "Fact Sheet: Criminal Prosecu-

tions for Unauthorized Border Crossing," accessed May 21, 2019, https://www.aclu.org/sites/default/files/field_document/15_12_14_aclu_1325_1326_recommendations_final2.pdf.

12. Judith A. Green, Bethany Carson, and Andrea Black, *Indefensible: A Decade of Mass Incarceration of Migrants Prosecuted for Crossing the Border*, Grassroots Leadership, July 2016, https://grassrootsleadership.org/sites/default/files/reports/indefensible_book_web.pdf.

13. American Immigration Council, "The Cost of Immigration Enforcement and Border Security," January 25, 2017, https://www.americanimmigrationcouncil.org/research/the-cost-of-immigration-enforcement-and-border-security.

14. Miriam Jordan and Ron Nixon, "Trump Administration Threatens Jail and Separating Children from Parents for Those Who Illegally Cross Southwest Border," *New York Times*, May 7, 2018, https://www.nytimes.com/2018/05/07/us/politics/homeland-security-prosecute-undocumented-immigrants.html; and Jeff Sessions, "If You Are Smuggling a Child, We Will Prosecute You," NBC News, YouTube, May 7, 2018, https://www.youtube.com/watch?v=MCSeeAB7g3A.

15. See, e.g., United States Holocaust Memorial Museum, "Life in the Shadows: Hidden Children and the Holocaust," August 28, 2003, https://www.ushmm.org/exhibition/hidden-children/insideX/. For a chilling dramatization of separating children from their parents, see *Schindler's List*, directed and produced by Steven Spielberg (Hollywood, CA: Universal Studios, 1993) and based on the 1982 novel *Schindler's Ark* by Thomas Kenneally.

16. Elie Wiesel, *Night*, trans. Stella Rodway (New York: Bantam Books, 1960, 1986), 27.

17. Masha Gessen, "Taking Children from Their Parents Is a Form of State Terror," *New Yorker*, May 9, 2018, https://www.newyorker.com/news/our-columnists/taking-children-from-their-parents-is-a-form-of-state-terror.

18. Louise Radnofsky, "Many More Children Separated at Border," *Wall Street Journal*, January 18, 2019, A3.

19. Patrick Greenfield, "Family Separation: Hundreds of Migrant Children Still Not Reunited with Families in U.S.," *The Guardian*, U.S. ed., July 16, 2018, https://www.theguardian.com/us-news/2018/jul/26/trump-administration-family-separations-children-reunited; Jay Root and Elsa Cavazos, "Trump's Family Separation Policy Split This Family Apart. They're Still Not Back Together," *Time* and *Texas Tribune*, September 12, 2018, https://www.yahoo.com/news/trump-apos-family-separation-policy-154454376.html.

CHAPTER SIX: REALITY CHECK

1. United States Senate, Appropriations Committee, 115th Congressional Meeting, second session, "End the Shutdown and Secure the Border Act," January 22, 2019, https://www.appropriations.senate.gov/imo/media/doc/End%20the%20Shutdown%20and%20Secure%20the%20Border%20Act.pdf.

2. Joseph H. Carens, *The Ethics of Immigration* (Oxford: Oxford University Press, 2013), 209.

3. Personal correspondence, June 15, 2018; shared by permission. The fact-finding trip took place June 12–13, 2018.

4. Human Rights First, *Crossing the Line: U.S. Border Agents Illegally Reject Asylum Seekers*, May 2017, http://www.humanrightsfirst.org/sites/default/files/hrf-crossing-the-line-report.pdf.

5. *Cojones* (balls) is slang for testicles and is used to describe men who show guts and gumption. The feminine ending, *cojonas*, emphasizes the mother's bravery and boldness.

6. To view the statistics available as of February 6, 2019, see, United States Immigration and Customs Enforcement, "Credible Fear Cases Completed and Referrals for Credible Fear Interview," January 8, 2017, https://www.dhs.gov/immigration-statistics/readingroom/RFA/credible-fear-cases-interview.

7. For government statistics on inadmissibles, see United States Customs and Border Protection, "Southwest Border Inadmissibles by Field Office FY2017," December 15, 2017, https://www.cbp.gov/newsroom/stats/ofo-sw-border-inadmissibles-fy2017; and "Southwest Border Migration FY2017," December 15, 2017, https://www.cbp.gov/newsroom/stats/sw-border-migration-fy2017.

8. United States Department of Homeland Security, Office of Inspector General, *Special Review: Initial Observations Regarding Family Separation Issues Under the Zero Tolerance Policy*, OIG-18-84, September 27, 2018, https://www.oig.dhs.gov/sites/default/files/assets/2018-10/OIG-18-84-Sep18.pdf.

9. Immigration and Nationality Act (INA) of 1952, No. 8 U.S. Code § 1158.

10. "Order Granting Temporary Restraining Order; Order to Show Cause re Preliminary Injunction–East Bay Sanctuary Covenant vs. Donald J. Trump," November 19, 2018, cited by Stephanie Leutert et al., *Asylum Processing and Waitlists at the U.S.-Mexico Border*, December 2018, 1–2, https://www.strausscenter.org/images/MSI/AsylumReport_MSI.pdf.

11. Human Rights First, *Crossing the Line*, 1.

12. Ana Adlerstein, "Asylum Seekers Routinely Turned Away from Ports of Entry, Advocates Say," *The Guardian*, December 19, 2018, https://www.theguardian.com/us-news/2018/dec/19/us-mexico-border-migrants-claim-asylum-difficulties.

13. William M. Lyons, email correspondence, October 24, 2018; used by permission.

14. Trump, Donald J., "Presidential Proclamation Addressing Mass Migration Through the Southern Border of the United States," November 9, 2018, https://www.whitehouse.gov/presidential-actions/presidential-proclamation-addressing-mass-migration-southern-border-united-states/; and "Order Granting Temporary Restraining Order; Order to Show Cause re Preliminary Injunction–East Bay Sanctuary Covenant vs. Donald J. Trump," November 19, 2018, https://assets.documentcloud.org/documents/5198146/Order-granting-temporary-restraining-order.pdf.

15. Leutert, et al., *Asylum Processing and Waitlists*, 2.

16. Al Otro Lado, Inc. et al v. Kirstjen Nielsen, et al, No. 3:2017cv02366–Document 138 (S.D. Cal. 2017), December 20, 2017, https://law.justia.com/cases/federal/district-courts/california/casdce/3:2017cv02366/553300/138/.

17. Molly Hennessy-Fiske, "Asylum Seekers Blocked at Texas Border Bridges Say Mexican Officials Are Demanding Money to Let Them Pass," *Los Angeles Times*, November 22, 2018, https://www.latimes.com/nation/la-fg-asylum-list-border-2018-story.html.

18. U.S. Department of Homeland Security, *Initial Observations Regarding Family Separation*, 5.

19. United States Commission on International Religious Freedom, "Who We Are/What We Do," https://www.uscirf.gov/about-uscirf/who-we-arewhat-we-do.

20. Elizabeth Cassidy and Tiffany Lynch, *Barriers to Protection: The Treatment of Asylum Seekers in Expedited Removal* (Washington, DC: U.S. Commission on International Religious Freedom, August 8, 2016), 7, https://www.uscirf.gov/sites/default/files/Barriers%20To%20Protection.pdf.

21. Cassidy and Lynch, *Barriers to Protection*, 2–3.

22. Justin Rohrlich and Adam Rawnsley, "A Native American Tribe Has an $800 Million Contract to Run ICE Detention Centers," *Daily Beast*, July 6, 2018, https://www.thedaily beast.com/a-native-american-tribe-has-a-dollar800-million-contract-to-run-ice-detention -centers.

23. Jenny Perkins Kiser, Facebook post, July 13, 2018; shared by permission.

24. U.S. Department of Homeland Security, *Initial Observations Regarding Family Separation*, 5.

25. Katelyn Caralle, "Supreme Court Rules Immigrants Can Be Held Indefinitely with No Bond Hearings," *Washington Examiner*, February 27, 2018, https://www.washingtonexam iner.com/supreme-court-rules-immigrants-can-be-held-indefinitely-with-no-bond-hearings/ article/2650154.

26. Maya Rhodan, "The Trump Administration Dropped Asylum Protection for Survivors of Domestic Violence," *Time*, June 11, 2018, www.time.com/5308781/the-trump-adminis tration-dropped-asylum-protection-for-survivors-of-domestic-violence/; and Madison Pauly and Noah Lanard, "Sessions Makes It Vastly Harder for Victims of Domestic Abuse and Gang Violence to Receive Asylum," *Mother Jones*, June 11, 2018, https://www.motherjones.com/ politics/2018/06/sessions-rules-that-victims-of-domestic-abuse-and-gang-violence-arent -grounds-for-asylum/.

27. Matt Zapotosky, "Judge Strikes Down Trump Administration Effort to Deny Asylum for Migrants Fleeing Gang Violence, Domestic Abuse," *Washington Post*, December 19, 2018, https://www.washingtonpost.com/world/national-security/judge-strikes-down-trump -administration-effort-to-deny-asylum-for-migrants-fleeing-gang-violence-domestic-abuse/20 18/12/19/61687d00-03b1-11e9-b6a9-0aa5c2fcc9e4_story.html.

28. Katie Benner and Caitlin Dickerson, "Sessions Says Domestic and Gang Violence Are Not Grounds for Asylum," *New York Times*, June 11, 2018, https://www.nytimes.com/ 2018/06/11/us/politics/sessions-domestic-violence-asylum.html.

CHAPTER SEVEN: CREDIBLE FEAR FOR ASYLUM

1. United States Citizenship and Immigration Services, "Questions and Answers: Credible Fear Screening," July 15, 2015, https://www.uscis.gov/humanitarian/refugees-asylum/ asylum/questions-answers-credible-fear-screening.

2. Sara Compos and Joan Friedland, "Mexican and Central American Asylum and Credible Fear Claims: Background and Context," American Immigration Council, May 2014, https:// www.americanimmigrationcouncil.org/research/mexican-and-central-american-asylum-and -credible-fear-claims-background-and-context.

3. Maria Sacchetti, "Trump Administration Cancels English Classes, Soccer, Legal Aid for Unaccompanied Child Migrants in U.S. Shelters," *Washington Post*, June 5, 2019, https:// www.washingtonpost.com/immigration/trump-administration-cancels-english-classes-soccer -legal-aid-for-unaccompanied-child-migrants-in-us-shelters/2019/06/05/df2a0008-8712 -11e9-a491-25df61c78dc4_story.html?utm_term=.5d0810161f1e.

4. For pending cases and length of wait by nationality, state, and court, see Syracuse University, "Immigration Court Backlog Tool," TRAC Immigration Backlog, FY2018 through July 2018, http://trac.syr.edu/phptools/immigration/court_backlog/.

5. Elizabeth Cassidy and Tiffany Lynch, *Barriers to Protection: The Treatment of Asylum Seekers in Expedited Removal* (Washington, D.C.: U.S. Commission on International Religious Freedom, August 8, 2016), 30, https://www.uscirf.gov/sites/default/files/Barriers%20To%20Protection.pdf.

6. "I Seek Safety," *Refugee Art: Testimonies of Immigrant Families Seeking Asylum* (blog edited by Helen T. Boursier), posted January 21, 2019, https://refugeeartblog.com/2019/01/21/i-seek-safety/.

7. Cassidy and Lynch, *Barriers to Protection*, 21–22.

8. Cassidy and Lynch, *Barriers to Protection*, 31.

9. Victoria Rossi, "Seeking Asylum in Karnes City: An Up-Close-and-Personal View of Family Detention in a For-Profit Lock-Up in South Texas," *Texas Observer*, February 2, 2015, https://www.texasobserver.org/seeking-asylum-karnes-city/.

10. Compos and Friedland, "Mexican and Central American Asylum."

CHAPTER EIGHT: THE SCARCITY MENTALITY AND THE LANGUAGE OF INJUSTICE AT THE BORDER

1. Brené Brown, *Daring Greatly: How the Courage to Be Vulnerable Transforms the Way We Live, Love, Parent, and Lead* (New York: Avery, Random House, 2012), 24–25.

2. Philip Bump, "Trump Retweeted a False Claim about Government Benefits Received by Undocumented Immigrants," *Washington Post*, November 28, 2018, https://www.washingtonpost.com/politics/2018/11/28/trump-retweeted-false-claim-about-government-benefits-received-by-undocumented-immigrants/.

3. Andrew Prevot, "Against Cruelty," Political Theology Seminar, American Academy of Religion Annual Meetings, Boston, MA, November 18, 2017.

4. Brené Brown, *Braving the Wilderness: The Quest for True Belonging and the Courage to Stand Alone* (New York: Random House, 2017), 75.

5. Edward Farley, *Deep Symbols: Their Postmodern Effacement and Reclamation* (Harrisburg, PA: Trinity Press International, 1996), 3.

6. Martin Luther King Jr., "Letter from a Birmingham Jail" (1963), in *I Have a Dream: Writings and Speeches That Changed the World*, ed. James M. Washington (New York: Harper Collins, 1992), 89–93.

7. Doug Dalglish, Pre-Presbytery Workshop, Mission Presbytery, McAllen, TX, October 28, 2016.

8. Eli Rosenberg, "Trump's Troop Deployment Strung 'Lethal' Razor Wire on the Border. This City Has Had Enough," *Washington Post*, February 7, 2019, https://www.washingtonpost.com/nation/2019/02/07/trumps-troop-deployment-strung-lethal-razor-wire-border-this-city-has-had-enough.

9. Martin Luther King Jr., *Where Do We Go from Here—Chaos or Community?* (Boston: Beacon Press, 1967, 2016), 196–97.

10. James Newton Poling, *The Abuse of Power: A Theological Problem* (Nashville, TN: Abington Press, 1991), 31.

11. Rob Buford, pastor of the Congregation Community Church in Sunnyvale, California, started a twelve-step program he calls Racists Anonymous to help people become more aware of their own racist thinking, feelings, and behaviors and to provide a pathway to recovery from racism. For a list of the twelve steps, see http://rainternational.org/the-12-steps/.

12. James McBride, "From the American Protective Association to Trump's America First: American Xenophobia in Historical Perspective," in *The Meaning of My Neighbor's Faith: Interreligious Reflections on Immigration*, eds. Alexander Y. Hwang and Laura E. Alexander (Lanham, MD: Lexington Books/Fortress Academic, 2019), 31–61.

13. Justin Ashworth, "Creation, Christ, Church: Three Approaches to Christian Ethics of Borders," Interreligious Reflections on Immigration Seminar, American Academy of Religion Annual Meetings, Denver, CO, November, 17, 2018.

CHAPTER NINE: THE BIGGER PICTURE

1. Iris Murdoch, *The Sovereignty of Good* (New York: Routledge, 1970).

2. Joseph H. Carens, *The Ethics of Immigration* (Oxford: Oxford University Press, 2013), 195.

3. Carens, *Ethics of Immigration*, 196.

4. Søren Kierkegaard, *Fear and Trembling*, eds. C. Stephen Evans and Sylvia Walsh (Cambridge, UK: Cambridge University Press, 2006), cited in John D. Caputo, *Radical Hermeneutics: Repetition, Deconstruction, and the Hermeneutic Project* (Indianapolis, IN: Indiana University Press, 1987), 239.

5. Martin Luther King Jr., *Where Do We Go from Here—Chaos or Community?* (Boston: Beacon Press, 1967, 2016), 200.

6. King Jr., *Where Do We Go from Here*, 202.

7. Jacques Derrida, *Of Hospitality: Ann Dufourmantelle Invites Jacques Derrida to Respond*, trans. Rachel Bowlby (Stanford, CA: Stanford University Press, 2000), and *The Politics of Friendship*, trans. George Collins (London: Verso, 2005).

8. John D. Caputo, ed., *Deconstruction in a Nutshell: A Conversation with Jacques Derrida* (New York: Fordham University Press, 1997), 110.

9. Derrida is following the etymology of Émile Benveniste, in *Le vocabulare dés institutions indo-européennes* 1 (Paris: Minuit, 1969), chapter 7, "*L'hospitalité*"; referenced by Caputo, *Deconstruction in a Nutshell*, 110.

10. Caputo, *Deconstruction in a Nutshell*, 111, emphasis his.

11. Emmanuel Levinas, *Existence and Existents*, trans. Alphonso Lingis (Dordrecht, Netherlands: Kluwer Academic, 1978, 1988), 13–14.

12. Jacques Derrida, *Positions*, trans. and annotated by Alan Bass (Chicago, IL: University of Chicago Press, 1981), xvi.

13. John D. Caputo, *The Weakness of God: A Theology of the Event* (Bloomington, IN: Indiana University Press, 2006), 24–25.

14. For a detailed argument on love of God embodied through love of neighbor in the Abrahamic traditions (Islam, Judaism, and Christianity), see Helen T. Boursier, *The Ethics of Hospitality: An Interfaith Response to U.S. Immigration Policies* (Lanham, MD: Lexington Books, 2019).

15. Helen T. Boursier, "Watercolor Sketch," *Art as Spiritual Care* (blog), posted October 27, 2018, https://artasspiritualcare.com/2018/10/27/watercolor-sketch/.

16. John D. Caputo, *The Insistence of God: A Theology of Perhaps*, Indiana Series in the Philosophy of Religion, ed. Merold Westphal (Bloomington and Indianapolis, IN: Indiana University Press, 2013), 39.

17. Søren Kierkegaard, *Works of Love*, ed. and trans. Howard V. Hong and Edna H. Hong (Princeton, NJ: Princeton University Press, 1995), 53, emphasis his; see also Matthew 5:46–47.

18. Kierkegaard, *Works of Love*, 53–54.

19. Caputo, *Insistence of God*, 82.

20. Helen T. Boursier, "The Great Exchange: An Interfaith Praxis of Absolute Hospitality for Asylum Seekers," in *The Meaning of My Neighbor's Faith: Interreligious Reflections on Immigration*, eds. Alexander Y. Hwang and Laura E. Alexander (Lanham, MD: Lexington Books/ Fortress Academic, 2019), 133–47.

21. Martin Buber, *I and Thou*, trans. Walter Kaufmann (New York: Simon and Schuster, 1970), 62.

22. Søren Kierkegaard, *Purity of Heart Is to Will One Thing: Spiritual Preparation for the Office of Confession*, trans. Douglas V. Steere (New York: Harper and Row, 1956), 55.

23. Jacques Derrida, *Given Time: I. Counterfeit Money*, trans. Peggy Kamuf (Chicago: University of Chicago Press, 1983), 7.

24. Buber, *I and Thou*, 62.

25. Caputo, *Deconstruction in a Nutshell*, 19.

26. Michael D. Shear and Zolan Kanno-Youngs, "Most Migrants at Border with Mexico Would Be Denied Asylum Protections under New Trump Rule." *New York Times*, July 15, 2019, https://www.nytimes.com/2019/07/15/us/politics/trump-asylum-rule.html.

27. American Civil Liberties Union (ACLU). "Complaint for Declaratory and Injunctive Relief: Immigration Action." July 16, 2019, https://www.aclu.org/legal-document/complaint-5.

28. Derrida, *Of Hospitality*, 25.

CHAPTER TEN: MOVING TOWARD RESPONSIBLE RESPONSE

1. Dorothee Söelle, *Against the Wind: Memoir of a Radical Christian*, trans. Barbara and Martin Rumscheidt (Minneapolis, MN: Fortress Press, 1999), 16.

2. Norma Pimentel, "Children in Crisis: Dehumanization and Immigration Detention, a Conversation between Doctors and Faith Leaders," University of the Incarnate Word, San Antonio, TX, September 28, 2018.

3. Miguel A. de la Torre, film screening for *Trails of Hope and Terror: The Movie*, Society of Arts in Theological and Religious Studies, American Academy of Religion Annual Meetings, Denver, CO, November 16, 2018.

4. Andrew Davis, *Blessing* (Norwich, UK: Canterbury Press, 2014), 103.

5. Jim Armstrong, "There Are Problems—But No Crisis at the Southern Border," *Indy Star*, January 10, 2019.

6. Susan Sanders, "Letter to the Editor," *Green Valley News* (AZ), January 9, 2019.

7. JR, *Giant Picnic*, 2017 art installation photographed in *Plough Quarterly: Breaking Ground for a Renewed World* 18 (August 2018): inside cover.

CHAPTER ELEVEN: MAKING THE POLITICAL PERSONAL

1. Megan Elliott, interview with the author, December 12, 2018; shared by permission.

2. Gavin Rogers with Rey Saldaña, Pub Theology ministry of Travis Park UMC, December 10, 2018. Excerpt of the verbatim transcript shared by permission.

3. Personal email correspondence, November 27, 2018. She concluded her update with this: "If you want to repost, please use copy/paste and do not attribute it to me. I do not wish to be harassed."

CHAPTER TWELVE: HELP AND HOPE FOR MIGRANTS

1. For more information about the response assistance for migrants in Arizona, see Lane Van Ham, *A Common Humanity: Ritual, Religion, and Immigrant Advocacy in Tucson, Arizona* (Tucson: University of Arizona Press, 2011).

2. Peg Bowden, "The Children," *La Frontera* (blog), June 19, 2014, http://www.arroya.org/?p=1421.

3. Justine Orlovsky-Schnitzler, "The Desert Should Not Be a Death Sentence," *New York Times*, December 18, 2018, https://www.nytimes.com/2018/12/18/opinion/migrants-border-death.html.

4. Orlovsky-Schnitzler, "The Desert Should Not Be a Death Sentence."

5. Green Valley-Sahuarita Samaritans, "How to Help," accessed February 6, 2019, https://www.gvs-samaritans.org/how-to-help.html.

6. Green Valley-Sahuarita Samaritans, "Resources-Samaritan News," accessed February 6, 2019, https://www.gvs-samaritans.org/samaritan-news.

7. Green Valley-Sahuarita Samaritans, "Reports and Publications," accessed February 6, 2019, https://www.gvs-samaritans.org/reports-articles—publications.html.

8. Norma Pimentel, presentation to the Immigration Task Force of Mission Presbytery, Corpus Christi, TX, March 6, 2015.

9. John Garland, interview with the author, October 16, 2016; shared by permission.

10. Interfaith Welcome Coalition, "Get Involved: Backpack Ministry," accessed February 6, 2019, http://interfaithwelcomecoalition.org/get-involved/.

CHAPTER THIRTEEN: PUBLIC WITNESS
AND CIVIC ENGAGEMENT

1. James Newton Poling, *Deliver Us from Evil: Resisting Racial and Gender Oppression* (Minneapolis, MN: Fortress Press, 1996), 119.

2. Poling, *Deliver Us*, 119.

3. Greg Bosk, "Where Are the Voices Defending Detained Children?" *San Antonio Express-News*, September 10, 2018, https://www.mysanantonio.com/opinion/commentary/article/Where-are-the-voices-defending-detained-children-13218934.php.

4. Paul Wise, "Children in Crisis: Dehumanization and Immigration Detention, a Conversation between Doctors and Faith Leaders," Project Lifeline, University of the Incarnate Word, San Antonio, TX, September 28, 2018.

5. United Church of Christ, Justice and Witness Ministries, Wider Church Ministries, *Take Action: Public Policy Advocacy Guide*, 2018, https://www.uccresources.com/products/take-action-public-policy-advocacy-guide-pdf-download.

6. Teo Armus, "A Court Ruling May Allow Migrant Families to Be Held Indefinitely. These Families Know What That Could Be Like," *Texas Tribune*, December 10, 2018, https://www.texastribune.org/2018/12/10/migrant-families-indefinite-detention-in-dilley/.

7. Emmanuel Levinas, *Otherwise Than Being or Beyond Essence*, trans. Alphonso Lingis (Pittsburgh, PA: Duquesne University Press, 1981, 1997), 159.

8. Original quote: "The fight for justice in society will always be a fight." Reinhold Niebuhr, *Love and Justice: Selections from the Shorter Writings of Reinhold Niebuhr*, ed. D. B. Robertson (Louisville, KY: Westminster John Knox Press, 1957), 38.

9. #RallyForOurChildren was sponsored by Congressman Joaquin Castro and the Mexican American Legislative Caucus of the Texas House of Representatives. See NowCastSA, "Three Hundred Rally in San Antonio to Protest Family Separation," YouTube, June 4, 2018, https://www.youtube.com/watch?v=9kv5Kw1ih4s&feature=youtu.be.

10. Andrew Prevot, "Against Cruelty," Political Theology Seminar, American Academy of Religion Annual Meetings, Boston, MA, November 18, 2017.

11. Fernando Stein, "Children in Crisis: Dehumanization and Immigration Detention, a Conversation between Doctors and Faith Leaders," Project Lifeline, University of the Incarnate Word, San Antonio, TX, September 28, 2018.

12. The speaker was Reverend Traci Blackmon, executive director of the United Church of Christ Justice and Witness Ministries.

13. Stefan Falke, "La Frontera: Artists along the U.S.-Mexico Border, Alvaro Enciso," September 27, 2019, https://borderartists.com/2018/09/27/alvaro-enciso/.

CHAPTER FOURTEEN: RESOURCES FOR EDUCATION AND ACTION

1. Jenny Owens Kast, Facebook post, January 16, 2018; shared by permission.

Works Cited

Adlerstein, Ana. "Asylum Seekers Routinely Turned Away from Ports of Entry, Advocates Say." *The Guardian*, December 19, 2018. https://www.theguardian.com/us-news/2018/dec/19/us-mexico-border-migrants-claim-asylum-difficulties.

Agamben, Giorgio. *Homo Sacer: Sovereign Power and Bare Life.* Translated by Daniel Heller-Roazen. Stanford, CA: Stanford University Press, 1998.

Ainsley, Julia. "Trump Admin's 'Tent Cities' Cost More Than Keeping Migrant Kids with Parents." NBC News, June 20, 2018. https://www.nbcnews.com/storyline/immigration-border-crisis/trump-admin-s-tent-cities-cost-more-keeping-migrant-kids-n884871.

Allard, Silas. "Interreligious Reflections on Immigration." American Academy of Religion Annual Meetings, Denver, CO, November 17, 2018.

American Civil Liberties Union. American Civil Liberties Union (ACLU). "Complaint for Declaratory and Injunctive Relief: Immigration Action." July 16, 2019. https://www.aclu.org/legal-document/complaint-5.

———. "Fact Sheet: Criminal Prosecutions for Unauthorized Border Crossing." Accessed May 21, 2019. https://www.aclu.org/sites/default/files/field_document/15_12_14_aclu_1325_1326_recommendations_final2.pdf.

American Immigration Council. "The Cost of Immigration Enforcement and Border Security." January 25, 2017. https://www.americanimmigrationcouncil.org/research/the-cost-of-immigration-enforcement-and-border-security.

———. "How the United States Immigration System Works." Accessed January 8, 2019. https://www.americanimmigrationcouncil.org/research/how-united-states-immigration-system-works.

Arizona OpenGIS Initiative for Deceased Migrants. Accessed September 19, 2018. http://humaneborders.info/app/map.asp.

Armus, Teo. "A Court Ruling May Allow Migrant Families to Be Held Indefinitely. These Families Know What That Could Be Like." *Texas Tribune*, December 10, 2018. https://www.texastribune.org/2018/12/10/migrant-families-indefinite-detention-in-dilley/.

BBC News. "'Drug Dealers, Criminals, Rapists': What Trump Thinks of Mexicans." August 31, 2016. https://www.bbc.com/news/av/world-us-canada-37230916/drug-dealers-crimi nals-rapists-what-trump-thinks-of-mexicans.

Benner, Katie, and Caitlin Dickerson. "Sessions Says Domestic and Gang Violence Are Not Grounds for Asylum." *New York Times*, June 11, 2018. https://www.nytimes .com/2018/06/11/us/politics/sessions-domestic-violence-asylum.html.

Bernal, Rafael, and Brett Samuels. "Border Apprehensions Up Nearly 100,000 in Fiscal 2018." The Hill, October 23, 2018. https://thehill.com/latino/412781-border-apprehensions-up -nearly-100000-in-fiscal-year-2018.

Betts, Alexander. *Survival Migration: Failed Governance and the Crisis of Displacement.* Ithaca, NY: Cornell University Press, 2013.

Borger, Julian. "Fleeing a Hell the U.S. Helped Create: Why Central Americans Journey North." *The Guardian*, December 19, 2018. https://www.theguardian.com/us-news/2018/ dec/19/central-america-migrants-us-foreign-policy.

Bosk, Greg. "Where Are the Voices Defending Detained Children?" *San Antonio Express-News*, September 10, 2018. https://www.mysanantonio.com/opinion/commentary/article/ Where-are-the-voices-defending-detained-children-13218934.php.

Boursier, Helen T. *Art as Spiritual Care* (blog). https://artasspiritualcare.com/.

———. *The Ethics of Hospitality: An Interfaith Response to U.S. Immigration Policies.* Lanham, MD: Lexington Books, 2019.

———. "Faithful Doxology—Allyship with Immigrants Seeking Asylum as the Church's Missional Hermeneutic." *International Bulletin of Mission Journal* 41, no. 2 (April 2017): 170–77.

———. *Refugee Art: Testimonies of Immigrant Families Seeking Asylum* (blog). https://refugee artblog.com/.

Bowden, Peg. *La Frontera: The Border. Migrant Journeys in the Desert* (blog). http://www .arroya.org/.

———. *A Land of Hard Edges: Serving the Front Lines of the Border.* Tucson, AZ: Peer Publishing, 2014.

Brown, Brené. *Braving the Wilderness: The Quest for True Belonging and the Courage to Stand Alone.* New York: Random House, 2017.

———. *Daring Greatly: How the Courage to Be Vulnerable Transforms the Way We Live, Love, Parent, and Lead.* New York: Avery, Random House, 2012.

Buber, Martin. *I and Thou.* Translated by Walter Kaufmann. New York: Simon and Schuster, 1970.

Bump, Philip. "Trump Retweeted a False Claim about Government Benefits Received by Undocumented Immigrants." *Washington Post*, November 28, 2018. https://www.washing tonpost.com/politics/2018/11/28/trump-retweeted-false-claim-about-government-bene fits-received-by-undocumented-immigrants/.

Burke, Garance, and Martha Mendoza. "'A Moral Disaster': AP Reveals Scope of Migrant Kids Program." Associated Press News, December 20, 2018. https://apnews.com/a857e04de9bc 4871995b65784ed7ccd8.

Caputo, John D., ed. *Deconstruction in a Nutshell: A Conversation with Jacques Derrida.* New York: Fordham University Press, 1997.

Caputo, John D. *The Insistence of God: A Theology of Perhaps.* Indiana Series in the Philosophy of Religion. Edited by Merold Westphal. Bloomington and Indianapolis: Indiana University Press, 2013.

———. *Radical Hermeneutics: Repetition, Deconstruction, and the Hermeneutic Project.* Indianapolis: Indiana University Press, 1987.

———. *The Weakness of God: A Theology of the Event.* Bloomington: Indiana University Press, 2006.

Caralle, Katelyn. "Supreme Court Rules Immigrants Can Be Held Indefinitely with No Bond Hearings." *Washington Examiner,* February 27, 2018. https://www.washingtonexaminer.com/supreme-court-rules-immigrants-can-be-held-indefinitely-with-no-bond-hearings/article/2650154.

Carens, Joseph H. *The Ethics of Immigration.* Oxford: Oxford University Press, 2013.

Cassidy, Elizabeth, and Tiffany Lynch. *Barriers to Protection: The Treatment of Asylum Seekers in Expedited Removal.* Washington, D.C.: U.S. Commission on International Religious Freedom, August 8, 2016. https://www.uscirf.gov/sites/default/files/Barriers%20To%20Protection.pdf. Spanish translation of the executive summary available at https://www.uscirf.gov/sites/default/files/Obstáculos%20a%20la%20protección.Español.pdf.

Cohen, Michael. "How For-Profit Prisons Have Become the Biggest Lobby Nobody Notices." *Washington Post,* April 28, 2015. https://www.washingtonpost.com/?utm_term=.8678d99a78f8.

Compos, Sara, and Joan Friedland. "Mexican and Central American Asylum and Credible Fear Claims: Background and Context." American Immigration Council, May 2014. https://www.americanimmigrationcouncil.org/research/mexican-and-central-american-asylum-and-credible-fear-claims-background-and-context.

Davis, Andrew. *Blessing.* Norwich, UK: Canterbury Press, 2014.

Deibert, Michael. "What Is Forcing Thousands of Migrants to Flee Their Home Countries?" *The Guardian,* December 5, 2018. https://www.theguardian.com/commentisfree/2018/dec/05/why-migrants-flee-home-countries.

De La Torre, Miguel A. *Trails of Hope and Terror: Testimonies of Immigration.* Maryknoll, NY: Orbis Books, 2009.

De La Torre, Vincent. *Trails of Hope and Terror, The Movie.* Centennial, CO: V1 Educational Media, 2018. https://www.trailsofhopeandterrorthemovie.com.

Derrida, Jacques. *Given Time: I. Counterfeit Money.* Translated by Peggy Kamuf. Chicago: University of Chicago Press, 1983.

———. *Of Hospitality: Ann Dufourmantelle Invites Jacques Derrida to Respond.* Translated by Rachel Bowlby. Stanford, CA: Stanford University Press, 2000.

———. *The Politics of Friendship.* Translated by George Collins. London: Verso, 2005.

———. *Positions.* Translated and annotated by Alan Bass. Chicago: University of Chicago Press, 1981.

Doctors Without Borders. "The Facts about the Humanitarian Crisis in Mexico and Central America." February 5, 2019. https://www.doctorswithoutborders.org/what-we-do/news-stories/news/facts-about-humanitarian-crisis-mexico-and-central-america.

Dinan, Stephen. "Catch-and-Release of Illegals Restarted in Texas, Border Patrol Agents Say." *Washington Times,* November 15, 2017. https://www.washingtontimes.com/news/2017/nov/15/catch-and-release-illegal-immigrant-restarted-texa/.

Eguizábal, Cristina, Matthew C. Ingram, Karise M. Curtis, Aaron Korthuis, Eric L. Olson, and Nicholas Phillips. *Crime and Violence in Central America's Northern Triangle: How U.S. Policy Responses Are Helping, Hurting, and Can Be Improved.* Edited by Eric L. Olson. Washington, D.C.: Woodrow Wilson International Center for Scholars, Latin

American Program, 2015. https://www.wilsoncenter.org/sites/default/files/FINAL%20 PDF_CARSI%20REPORT_0.pdf.

Falke, Stefan. "La Frontera: Artists along the U.S.-Mexico Border, Alvaro Enciso," September 27, 2019. https://borderartists.com/2018/09/27/alvaro-enciso/.

Farley, Edward. *Deep Symbols: Their Postmodern Effacement and Reclamation.* Harrisburg, PA: Trinity Press International, 1996.

Fedschun, Travis. "San Antonio Trailer Deaths: Driver Charged after Ten Die in Sweltering Truck." Fox News, July 24, 2017. http://www.foxnews.com/us/2017/07/24/san-antonio -trailer-deaths-suspect-due-in-court-after-10-die-in-sweltering-truck.html.

Fife, John. "From the Sanctuary Movement to No More Deaths: The Challenge to Communities of Faith." In *Religious and Ethical Perspectives on Global Migration,* edited by Elizabeth W. Collier and Charles R. Strain, 257–71. Lanham, MD: Lexington Books, 2014.

Forero, Juan. "Latin America Turns Deadly for Women: Violence by Domestic Partners and Gangs Has Driven 'Femicide' Rates to Crisis Levels." *Wall Street Journal,* December 20, 2018, A1.

Frye, Hope, JD. "Hope Frye Testifies [Before Congress]." Families Belong Together, July 10, 2019. https://www.facebook.com/fams2gether/videos/464808130986800/UzpfSTEw MDAwMzYyNzU5ODU0MjozMDYwNjExMjk0OTk0MTQ6MTQ6MDoxNTY0 NjQyNzk5OjMxNzk1MjE1ODA2NjM2MTgyOTc/.

Gessen, Masha. "Taking Children from Their Parents Is a Form of State Terror." *New Yorker,* May 9, 2018. https://www.newyorker.com/news/our-columnists/taking-children-from -their-parents-is-a-form-of-state-terror.

Green, Emily. "Head of Controversial Tent City Says the Trump Administration Pressured Him to Detain More Young Migrants." Vice News, January 11, 2019. https://news.vice .com/en_us/article/kzvmg3/head-of-controversial-tent-city-says-the-trump-administration -pressured-him-to-detain-more-young-migrants.

Green, Judith A., Bethany Carson, and Andrea Black. *Indefensible: A Decade of Mass Incarceration of Migrants Prosecuted for Crossing the Border.* Grassroots Leadership, July 2016. https:// grassrootsleadership.org/sites/default/files/reports/indefensible_book_web.pdf.

Green Valley-Sahuarita Samaritans. "Operation Streamline–August, 27, 2018." Resources– Samaritan News, updated September 3, 2018. https://www.gvs-samaritans.org/samaritan -news/previous/8.

Greenfield, Patrick. "Family Separation: Hundreds of Migrant Children Still Not Reunited with Families in U.S." *The Guardian,* U.S. edition, July 16, 2018. https://www.theguard ian.com/us-news/2018/jul/26/trump-administration-family-separations-children-reunited.

Guatemala Human Rights Commission. *Guatemala's Feminicide Law: Progress against Impunity?* May 2009. Washington, D.C. http://www.ghrc-usa.org/wp-content/uploads/2012/01/ Guatemalas-Feminicide-Law-Progress-Against-Impunity.pdf.

Hennessy-Fiske, Molly. "Asylum Seekers Blocked at Texas Border Bridges Say Mexican Officials Are Demanding Money to Let Them Pass." *Los Angeles Times,* November 22, 2018. https://www.latimes.com/nation/la-fg-asylum-list-border-2018-story.html.

Hesson, Ted. "Trump Officials Pressing to Slash Refugee Admissions to Zero Next Year." *Politico,* July 18, 2019. https://www.politico.com/story/2019/07/18/trump-officials-refugee -zero-1603503.

Human Rights First. *Crossing the Line: U.S. Border Agents Illegally Reject Asylum Seekers.* May 2017. http://www.humanrightsfirst.org/sites/default/files/hrf-crossing-the-line-report.pdf.

Hwang, Alexander Y., and Laura E. Alexander, eds. *The Meaning of My Neighbor's Faith: Interreligious Reflections on Immigration*. Lanham, MD: Lexington Books/Fortress Academic, 2019.

Jamerson, Joshua, and Juan Montes. "U.S. Shifts Border Policy." *Wall Street Journal*, December 21, 2018, A3.

Jordan, Miriam, and Ron Nixon. "Trump Administration Threatens Jail and Separating Children from Parents for Those Who Illegally Cross Southwest Border." *New York Times*, May 7, 2018. https://www.nytimes.com/2018/05/07/us/politics/homeland-security-prosecute-undocumented-immigrants.html.

JR. *Giant Picnic*. 2017. Art installation photographed in *Plough Quarterly: Breaking Ground for a Renewed World*, 18 (August 2018).

Kandel, William A. *U.S. Family-Based Immigration Policy*. Washington, D.C.: Congressional Research Service (R43145), February 9, 2018. https://fas.org/sgp/crs/homesec/R43145.pdf.

Kierkegaard, Søren. *Fear and Trembling*. Cambridge Texts in the History of Philosophy. Edited by C. Stephen Evans and Sylvia Walsh. Translated by Sylvia Walsh. Cambridge, UK: Cambridge University Press, 2006.

———. *Purity of Heart Is to Will One Thing: Spiritual Preparation for the Office of Confession*. Translated by Douglas V. Steere. New York: Harper and Row, 1956.

———. *Works of Love*. Edited and translated by Howard V. Hong and Edna H. Hong. Princeton, NJ: Princeton University Press, 1995.

King, Martin Luther, Jr. *I Have a Dream: Writings and Speeches That Changed the World*. Edited by James M. Washington. New York: Harper Collins, 1992.

———. *Where Do We Go from Here—Chaos or Community?* Boston: Beacon Press, 1967, 2016.

Kopan, Tal. "More Than 14,000 Immigrant Children Are in U.S. Custody, an All-Time High." *San Francisco Chronicle*, November 16, 2018. https://www.sfchronicle.com/nation/article/More-than-14-000-immigrant-children-are-in-U-S-13399510.php.

KTAR News. "Southwest Key Employee Sentenced for Sexually Abusing Migrants." February 1, 2019. http://ktar.com/story/2420982/southwest-key-employee-sentenced-for-sexually-abusing-migrants/.

Lehner, George. "'So Far from God, So Close to the United States.' Mexico Most Worsened in 2017." Fragile States Index, Fund for Peace, May 14, 2017. https://fragilestatesindex.org/2017/05/14/so-far-from-god-so-close-to-the-united-states-mexico-most-worsened-in-2017.

Leutert, Stephanie, Ellie Eizzell, Savitri Arvey, Gabriella Sanchez, Caitlyn Yates, and Paul Kuhne. *Asylum Processing and Waitlists at the U.S.-Mexico Border*. December 2018. https://www.strausscenter.org/images/MSI/AsylumReport_MSI.pdf.

Levinas, Emmanuel. *Existence and Existents*. Translated by Alphonso Lingis. Dordrecht, Netherlands: Kluwer Academic, 1978, 1988.

———. *Otherwise Than Being or Beyond Essence*. Translated by Alphonso Lingis. Pittsburgh, PA: Duquesne University Press, 1981, 1997.

Maher, Monica. "The Truth Will Set Us Free: Religion, Violence, and Women's Empowerment in Latin America." In *Global Empowerment of Women: Responses to Globalization and Politicized Religions*, edited by Carolyn M. Elliott, 265–84. New York: Routledge, 2008.

Messner, J. J. "Factionalization and Group Grievance Fuel Rise in Instability." Fragile States Index 2017, Fund for Peace, May 10, 2017. https://reliefweb.int/report/world/fragile-states-index-2017.

Moltmann, Jürgen. *The Livingness of God and the Fullness of Life.* Translated by Margaret Kohl. Louisville, KY: Westminster John Knox Press, 2016.

Moreno, Carolina. "Nine Outrageous Things Donald Trump Has Said about Latinos." *Huffington Post,* November 9, 2016. https://www.huffingtonpost.com/entry/9-outrageous -things-donald-trump-has-said-about-latinos_us_55e483a1e4b0c818f618904b.

Murdoch, Iris. *The Sovereignty of Good.* New York: Routledge, 1970.

New York Times Editorial Board. "Deported from the Middle of Nowhere." August 25, 2014. https://www.nytimes.com/2014/08/26/opinion/at-an-immigrant-detention-center-due -process-denied.html.

Niebuhr, Reinhold. *Love and Justice: Selections from the Shorter Writings of Reinhold Niebuhr.* Edited by D. B. Robertson. Louisville, KY: Westminster John Knox Press, 1957.

———. *Moral Man and Immoral Society: A Study in Ethics and Politics.* Louisville, KY: Westminster John Knox, 1932, 2001.

Nixon, Ron. "$10 Million from FEMA Diverted to Pay for Immigration Detention Centers, Document Shows." *New York Times,* September 12, 2018. https://www.nytimes .com/2018/09/12/us/politics/fema-ice-immigration-detention.html.

NOWCastSA. "Three Hundred Rally in San Antonio to Protest Family Separation." YouTube, June 4, 2018. https://www.youtube.com/watch?v=9kv5Kw1ih4s&feature=youtu.be.

Orlovsky-Schnitzler, Justine. "The Desert Should Not Be a Death Sentence." *New York Times,* December 18, 2018. https://www.nytimes.com/2018/12/18/opinion/migrants-border -death.html.

Pauly, Madison, and Noah Lanard. "Sessions Makes It Vastly Harder for Victims of Domestic Abuse and Gang Violence to Receive Asylum." *Mother Jones,* June 11, 2018. https://www .motherjones.com/politics/2018/06/sessions-rules-that-victims-of-domestic-abuse-and -gang-violence-arent-grounds-for-asylum/.

Paz, Octavio. *The Labyrinth of Solitude and Other Writings.* New York: Grove Press, 1985.

Penman, Madeleine. "Mexico, a Death-Trap for Migrants: 'It Was the Worst Day of My Life.'" Amnesty International, June 19, 2015. https://www.amnesty.org/en/latest/news/2015/06/ mexico-a-death-trap-for-migrants-it-was-the-worst-day-of-my-life/.

Poling, James Newton. *The Abuse of Power: A Theological Problem.* Nashville, TN: Abington Press, 1991.

———. *Deliver Us from Evil: Resisting Racial and Gender Oppression.* Minneapolis, MN: Fortress Press, 1996.

Prevot, Andrew. "Against Cruelty," Political Theology Seminar, American Academy of Religion Annual Meetings, Boston, MA, November 18, 2017.

Project Lifeline. "Comment on the Proposed Regulations: Apprehension Processing, Care, and Custody of Alien Minors and Unaccompanied Alien Children." November 6, 2018. https://projectlifeline.us/wp-content/uploads/2018/11/Project-Lifeline-Comment-on-Pro posed-RegulationsFlores.pdf.

Pueblo Sin Fronteras. "Central American Exodus Statement." Accessed December 27, 2018. https://www.pueblosinfronteras.org/.

Radnofsky, Louise. "Many More Children Separated at Border." *Wall Street Journal,* January 18, 2019, A3.

Rhodan, Maya. "The Trump Administration Dropped Asylum Protection for Survivors of Domestic Violence." *Time,* June 11, 2018. www.time.com/5308781/the-trump-adminis tration-dropped-asylum-protection-for-survivors-of-domestic-violence/.

Robertson, Alistair Graham, Rachel Beaty, Jane Atkinson, and Bob Libal. *Operation Stream-line: Costs and Consequences.* Grassroots Leadership, September 2012. http://grassrootslead ership.org/sites/defau8lt/files/uploads/GRL_Sept2012_Report%20final.pdf.

Rohrlich, Justin, and Adam Rawnsley. "A Native American Tribe Has an $800 Million Contract to Run ICE Detention Centers." *Daily Beast,* July 6, 2018. https://www.thedailybeast.com/ a-native-american-tribe-has-a-dollar800-million-contract-to-run-ice-detention-centers.

Romero, Oscar. "Letter to President Carter, February 17, 1980." In *Voice of the Voiceless: The Four Pastoral Letters and Other Statements.* Maryknoll, NY: Orbis Books, 1985.

Root, Jay, and Elsa Cavazos. "Trump's Family Separation Policy Split This Family Apart. They're Still Not Back Together." *Time* and *Texas Tribune,* September 12, 2018. https:// www.yahoo.com/news/trump-apos-family-separation-policy-154454376.html.

Rosenberg, Eli. "Trump's Troop Deployment Strung 'Lethal' Razor Wire on the Border. This City Has Had Enough." *Washington Post,* February 7, 2019. https://www.washingtonpost .com/nation/2019/02/07/trumps-troop-deployment-strung-lethal-razor-wire-border-this -city-has-had-enough/.

Rossi, Victoria. "Seeking Asylum in Karnes City: An Up-Close-and-Personal View of Fam-ily Detention in a For-Profit Lock-Up in South Texas." *Texas Observer,* February 2, 2015. https://www.texasobserver.org/seeking-asylum-karnes-city/.

Sacchetti, Maria. "Trump Administration Cancels English Classes, Soccer, Legal Aid for Unaccompanied Child Migrants in U.S. Shelters." *Washington Post,* June 5, 2019. https:// www.washingtonpost.com/immigration/trump-administration-cancels-english-classes -soccer-legal-aid-for-unaccompanied-child-migrants-in-us-shelters/2019/06/05/df2a0008 -8712-11e9-a491-25df61c78dc4_story.html.

Sessions, Jeff. "If You Are Smuggling a Child, We Will Prosecute You." NBC News, YouTube, May 7, 2018. https://www.youtube.com/watch?v=MCSeeAB7g3A.

Shear, Michael D. and Zolan Kanno-Youngs. "Most Migrants at Border with Mexico Would be Denied Asylum Protections Under New Trump Rule." *New York Times,* July 15, 2019. https://www.nytimes.com/2019/07/15/us/politics/trump-asylum-rule.html.

Söelle, Dorothee. *Against the Wind: Memoir of a Radical Christian.* Translated by Barbara and Martin Rumscheidt. Minneapolis, MN: Fortress Press, 1999.

Sommer, Jeff. "Trump Immigration Crackdown Is Great for Private Prison Stocks." *New York Times,* March 12, 2017. https://www.nytimes.com/2017/03/10/your-money/immigrants -prison-stocks.html.

Suárez-Orozco, Marcelo M. "Speaking of the Unspeakable: Toward a Psychosocial Under-standing of Responses to Terror." *Ethos* 18, no. 3 (1990): 353–83.

Trump, Donald J. "Presidential Memorandum for the Secretary of State." Presidential Deter-mination no. 2017-13, September 29, 2017. http://myattorneyusa.com/storage/upload/ files/matters/presidential-memorandum-secretary-of-state.pdf.

———. "Presidential Proclamation Addressing Mass Migration Through the Southern Bor-der of the United States." The White House, November 9, 2018. https://www.whitehouse .gov/presidential-actions/presidential-proclamation-addressing-mass-migration-southern -border-united-states/.

Tweed, Thomas. *Crossing and Dwelling: A Theory of Religion.* Cambridge, MA: Harvard Uni-versity Press, 2006.

United Church of Christ, Justice and Witness Ministries, Wider Church Ministries. *Take Action: Public Policy Advocacy Guide.* 2018. https://www.uccresources.com/products/take -action-public-policy-advocacy-guide-pdf-download.

United Nations High Commissioner for Refugees. "Universal Declaration of Human Rights." Accessed January 8, 2019. www.un.org/en/universal-declaration-human-rights/index.html.

United States Citizenship and Immigration Services. "Questions and Answers: Credible Fear Screening." July 15, 2015. https://www.uscis.gov/humanitarian/refugees-asylum/asylum/questions-answers-credible-fear-screening.

United States Customs and Border Protection. "Southwest Border Inadmissibles by Field Office FY2017." December 15, 2017. https://www.cbp.gov/newsroom/stats/ofo-sw-border-inadmissibles-fy2017.

———. "Southwest Border Migration FY2017." December 15, 2017. https://www.cbp.gov/newsroom/stats/sw-border-migration-fy2017.

United States Department of Homeland Security. *FY2017 Agency Financial Report.* https://www.dhs.gov/sites/default/files/publications/dhs_agency_financial_report_fy2017_1.pdf.

United States Department of Homeland Security, Office of Inspector General. *Special Review: Initial Observations Regarding Family Separation Issues Under the Zero Tolerance Policy.* OIG-18-84. September 27, 2018. https://www.oig.dhs.gov/sites/default/files/assets/2018-10/OIG-18-84-Sep18.pdf.

United States Department of State, Bureau for International Narcotics and Law Enforcement Affairs. *International Narcotics Control Strategy Report. Volume 1: Drug and Chemical Control.* March 2017. https://www.state.gov/documents/organization/268025.pdf.

United States Government Accountability Office. *Firearms Trafficking: U.S. Efforts to Combat Arms Trafficking to Mexico Face Planning and Coordination Challenges.* Report GAO-09-709 to Congressional Requesters. June 2009. https://www.gao.gov/new.items/d09709.pdf.

United States Holocaust Memorial Museum. "Life in the Shadows: Hidden Children and the Holocaust." Exhibition script, August 28, 2003–September 6, 2004. https://www.ushmm.org/exhibition/hidden-children/insideX/.

United States Immigration and Customs Enforcement. "Credible Fear Cases Completed and Referrals for Credible Fear Interview." January 8, 2017. https://www.dhs.gov/immigration-statistics/readingroom/RFA/credible-fear-cases-interview.

———. *Fiscal Year 2017 ICE Enforcement and Removal Operations Report.* https://www.ice.gov/sites/default/files/documents/Report/2017/iceEndOfYearFY2017.pdf.

United States Immigration and Customs Enforcement, Operations and Support. *Fiscal Year 2019 Congressional Justification.* https://www.dhs.gov/sites/default/files/publications/U.S.%20Immigration%20and%20Customs%20Enforcement.pdf.

United States Senate, Appropriations Committee. End the Shutdown and Secure the Border Act. 115th Congressional Meeting, Second Session, January 22, 2019. https://www.appropriations.senate.gov/imo/media/doc/End%20the%20Shutdown%20and%20Secure%20the%20Border%20Act.pdf.

Van Ham, Lane. *A Common Humanity: Ritual, Religion, and Immigrant Advocacy in Tucson, Arizona.* Tucson: University of Arizona Press, 2001.

Wiesel, Elie. *Night.* Translated by Stella Rodway. New York: Bantam Books, 1960, 1986.

Yousafzai, Malala. *We Are Displaced: My Journey and Stories from Refugee Girls around the World.* New York: Little, Brown, 2019.

Zapotosky, Matt. "Judge Strikes Down Trump Administration Effort to Deny Asylum for Migrants Fleeing Gang Violence, Domestic Abuse." *Washington Post,* December 19, 2018. https://www.washingtonpost.com/world/national-security/judge-strikes-down-trump-administration-effort-to-deny-asylum-for-migrants-fleeing-gang-violence-domestic-abuse/2018/12/19/61687d00-03b1-11e9-b6a9-0aa5c2fcc9e4_story.html.

Index